China's Financial Markets

This book provides an overview of China's financial markets and their latest developments. The book explores and discusses the difficulties in building modern financial markets that are compatible with an increasingly complicated market economy and examines the various strategies to reform China's financial system. It covers a range of topics: China's financial structure, financial regulation, financial repression and liberalization, monetary policy and the People's Bank of China, banking reforms, exchange rate policy, capital control and capital-account liberalization and development of the stock markets.

The book provides a basic understanding of the current issues related to the development of China's financial markets. It enhances knowledge of China's regulatory framework which has helped to shape China's financial landscape. It provides specific, useful knowledge about investment in China, such as market sense, to identify the investment opportunities in various asset classes.

Ming Wang is currently Assistant Professor of Tung Wah College, Hong Kong. Dr Wang received his two PhDs at City University of Hong Kong and University of Science and Technology of China. He has been Postdoctoral Fellow at Center for Transport, Trade and Financial Studies, City University before joining Tung Wah College.

Jerome Yen is currently a Professor of the College of Business at Tung Wah College, Hong Kong, and also a visiting professor in the Department of Finance at Hong Kong University of Science and Technology. He is also the director of HKUST's Quantitative Finance program where over 70 percent of graduates went to investment banks like Goldman Sachs and Morgan Stanley. He received his PhD in 1992 in Systems Engineering and Management Information Systems from the University of Arizona. His PhD research was conducted in the Economic Science Lab at the University of Arizona, led by Professor Vernon Smith – a Nobel Laureate.

Kin Keung Lai received his PhD at Michigan State University, USA. He is currently the Chair Professor of Management Science at the City University of Hong Kong. He is also the Director of the Invesco-Great Wall Research Unit on Risk Analysis and Business Intelligence (RABI) at the College of Business. He is the editor-in-chief of the *International Journal of Computational Science, International Journal of Optimization: Theory, Methods and Applications* and *International Journal of Operations Research.*

Routledge Advances in Risk Management
Edited by Kin Keung Lai and Shouyang Wang

1. **Volatility Surface and Term Structure**
   High-profit options trading strategies
   Kin Keung Lai, Jerome Yen, Shifei Zhou and Hao Wang

2. **China's Financial Markets**
   Issues and opportunities
   Ming Wang, Jerome Yen and Kin Keung Lai

China's Financial Markets
Issues and opportunities

Ming Wang, Jerome Yen
and Kin Keung Lai

Routledge
Taylor & Francis Group
LONDON AND NEW YORK

First published 2014
by Routledge
2 Park Square, Milton Park, Abingdon, Oxon OX14 4RN

and by Routledge
711 Third Avenue, New York, NY 10017

Routledge is an imprint of the Taylor & Francis Group, an informa business

British Library Cataloguing-in-Publication Data
A catalogue record for this book is available from the British Library

Library of Congress Cataloging-in-Publication Data

Wang, Ming, 1981–
China's financial markets : issues and opportunities / Ming Wang, Jerome Yen and Kin Keung Lai.
pages cm. — (Routledge advances in risk management ; 2)
1. Finance—China. 2. Banks and banking—China. 3. Financial services industry—China. I. Title.
HG187.C6W386 2014
332.0951—dc23 2013042185

ISBN: 978-0-415-83087-4 (hbk)
ISBN: 978-1-315-77892-1 (ebk)

Typeset in TimesNewRoman
by Apex CoVantage, LLC

Contents

Preface

Since it embraced economic reforms and the free-market principle, China's economic boom has spawned burgeoning financial markets and driven them up into unprecedented levels. China's government has succeeded in creating a financial sector that has served as an engine for this massive economic growth in spite of global problems elsewhere in the world. But alone with the consumption of reforms bonuses, new challenges emerge in China's financial markets.

This book will deep-dive into the study of the different factors or issues that will make or break the future of China's financial markets, and will take a close look at the various measures that the government could take to prevent heavy headwind from threatening the health of the financial markets, and by channel effect, the overall Chinese economy. Besides, opportunities should be explored in some sectors.

This book is intended as a manual for investors, researchers and professionals. Recent practices were collected in major financial markets in China. Analyses of hot topics were emphasized in some markets. Some chapters present a brief description of the developing history of the market during the past 30 years.

As China and Chinese markets are still undergoing reformation, some of the discussion in this book will become obsolete soon. Most of our data is updated to annual data for 2012, some earlier. After publication we will continue revising data used in this book. Important reforms and regulatory changes will also be followed closely. We hope to revise the data and publish new editions every two years.

Ming Wang
School of Business
Yung Wah College
Kowloon, Hong Kong
Email: Vincentwang@twc.edu.hk

Jerome Yen
School of Business
Yung Wah College
Kowloon, Hong Kong
Email: risksolution@gmail.com

Kin Keung Lai
Department of Management Sciences
City University of Hong Kong
Kowloon, Hong Kong
Email: mskklai@cityu.edu.hk
October 10, 2013

1 Development of China's banking industry and new direction

China's banking industry has experienced rapid growth in recent years in terms of both profitability and outstanding credit. Despite the sluggish global economy and declining growth of China's own economy due to reduction in external trade volume, the banking industry has reported great performance in its financial statements. It is intriguing that the performance of banks was largely contrary to the macro-environment, when it is viewed as the primary vehicle of the local economy.

The two main reasons for the rapid growth are the comparable fast growth of the Chinese economy and the high net interest margin earned by China's banks. Although the growth of China started weakening, infrastructure development was still growing at a higher pace compared to US and Europe, resulting in continued and large expansion of credit. Besides, interest rates payables to customer deposits and loan advances have been largely controlled by the People's Bank of China. The net interest margin between loan and deposit was established at about 3.00 percent, which is comparatively higher than other countries. Since over 70 percent of net operating income is generated from interest income, it is unsurprising that China's banks could keep earning high profits in these few years.

However, China's banks do face several challenges over the next few years, which may hinder their growth. First, the release of Basel III would increase the capital and liquidity requirements of banks, limiting the expansion of high yield loans and encouraging low yield bond portfolios. Moreover, the People's Bank of China has cut the interest rate for loans and deposits twice and widened the floating zone, which further affirms liberalization of interest rates. The liberalization surely threatens the subsistence of high interest income. In addition, economic turmoil also poses the threat of deterioration of asset quality of the banks. The recent increase of non-performing loans (NPL) coverage ratio of banks indicated this phenomenon; it is discussed below.

1.1. History of the Chinese banking sector and foreign involvement

The Chinese banking and financial sector started to develop more than 3,000 years ago, in the West Zhou period (from 1100 to 771 BC) when money and credit started playing a role in China's economy. It gained importance during the Qin period

(221–206 BC), when small-scale deposit taking and credit extension became frequent. After paper money was introduced during the Song Dynasty (AD 960–1279), until the Ming Dynasty (AD 1380–1600) small family or community-owned money shops were founded, which steadily expanded the business. This included deposit taking, lending, trade finance, money exchange and remittances. These small "quasi-banks" became the dominant financial institutions during the Opium War. After the Opium War, several Western banks entered the Chinese market quite successfully. The Qing government in the early 1900s set up a quasi-central bank, which was later named Bank of China. During these years, few regulations existed and many private banks were established. When the Nationalist government took over, tighter restrictions were imposed. By 1936, the big four government controlled banks (Central Bank of China, Bank of China, Bank of Communications and Farmers Bank) accounted for 56 percent of the total deposits in the Chinese banking system and their share rose to 80 percent during the Second World War and it went further up to 96.5 percent in the post-war period (Hu 2006). These figures show that China's banking industry had moved from free and open competition to heavy government involvement that resulted in a few dominant players.

During the next era, starting in 1949, private banking came to a full stop in China. Shutting down the Bank of Communications and limiting the Bank of China to a few foreign exchange transactions, the central government established the People's Bank of China (PBoC) as basically the country's "one and only" bank. It took care of all the important central and commercial banking processes simultaneously, from issuing notes and coins to collecting household deposits and setting the interest rates. At the end of the central-planning era in 1979, China's banking industry was primitive and fairly uninteresting.

The year 1980 marked the beginning of reforms in China, which also impacted the banking industry. The first step of the government in reforming of the system was to break up the mono-bank dominance. The government set up two specialized banks: China Construction Bank (CCB) and China Agriculture Bank (ABC). Furthermore, PBoC functioned as the country's new central bank, while the commercial banking operations were spun off, resulting in the foundation of the Industrial and Commercial Bank of China (ICBC) in 1984. The second step of the government was to relax barriers of entry and thus foster competition. This led to the creation of the Bank of Communications and several banks with smaller equity bases in the late 1980s as well as a rapid expansion of rural credit cooperatives in the early 1990s. Another important change in the banking policy took place in 1993, when specialized banks were freed from the burden of policy lending, which was transferred to the newly set-up China Development Bank, China Export-Import Bank and China Agricultural Development Bank.

Involvement of foreign financial institutions in China started slowly after 1979. Operational foreign banks were allowed in the Special Economic Zones, leading to the first license in Shenzhen in 1981. Several other coastal and eastern Chinese cities followed in the early 1990s, Shanghai being the first to let in foreign financial institutions. In 1996, the PBoC allowed foreign banks meeting certain requirements to conduct business in RMB in Pudong and Shanghai under a pilot project.

The government also passed the Commercial Banking Law in 1995 which recognized banks as profit-seeking institutions and paved the way for market-oriented operations in the banking industry. It furthermore established supervision departments at the PBoC to oversee all banks and set up stock and government bond markets. The 1997 Asian crisis impacted China too, though not as hard as other countries. After the collapse of the Hainan Development Bank, fears of a financial crisis rose and the government decided to abolish the "National Credit Plan" giving banks greater autonomy in an attempt to improve their loan portfolio. Subsequently, the big banks adopted a cautious attitude and smaller banks increased their market shares by taking higher risks. In order to improve risk management in banks, the newly set-up China Banking Regulatory Commission (CBRC) imposed rules on capital adequacy, loan classification and corporate governance, which successfully improved banking supervision in China. The big banks were able to get their non-performing-loan-problem under control to some extent through injection of additional capital by the government in 2003, which further stabilized the Chinese financial sector.

Additionally, the Chinese government took a step towards reforming the banking sector by opening it up to foreign strategic investment, hoping to attract the much-needed banking experience as well as capital. However, ownership of any single foreign investor is still limited to 20 percent and all foreign investors together can hold a maximum of 25 percent equity in a bank. Despite these limitations, banks have attracted significant amounts of foreign investment.

The latest wave of opening up started in June 2005 with the successful IPO of Bank of Communications, which attracted USD 2.2 billion in overseas offerings. In October 2005, China Construction Bank followed, marking the world's largest IPO since 2001 with USD 9.2 billion. Bank of China and ICBC then followed in 2006. Bank of China broke yet another record, making the largest IPO in the world since 2000, and the fourth largest IPO in the world ever, raising USD 9.7 billion. This record, however, did not last for long. In October 2006, ICBC marked the world's largest IPO to date, raising a total of USD 21.9 billion in Hong Kong and Shanghai simultaneously (Bremner 2006; Chandler 2006).

1.2. The Chinese banking sector: players and structure

The development of the Chinese banking sector led to the emergence of four large, state-owned players that dominate the industry today: Bank of China, China Construction Bank, Agricultural Bank of China and Industrial and Commercial Bank of China, called the "Big Four". In addition to that, there are three major policy banks, carrying out the government's policy financing: Agricultural Development Bank of China, Export-Import Bank of China and China Development Bank. Besides these large players, there are 12 joint-stock commercial banks (JSCBs), about 120 domestic commercial banks and around 36,000 credit cooperatives, as well as many non-banking financial institutions.

To date, foreign banks still do not play a major role in the Chinese banking industry, however, it is expected that the opening of China's banking sector will very likely increase their share in the years to come.

We will therefore analyze the domestic players in the Chinese market, before shedding light on foreign involvement in the Chinese banking sector. We conclude with highlighting the opportunities and challenges for FDI in the Chinese banking industry from a supply-side perspective, before completing the analysis from the demand-side in part three of this chapter. The policy banks are not included in our analysis, as they neither compete in the private banking sector nor do they represent potential opportunities for involvement of foreign players.

The "Big Four"

After the reforms and opening up of the Chinese banking sector, the extreme domination of the market by the Big Four has very slowly started to diminish. At the end of the year 2007, they held 53 percent of the total assets of the banking sector (Hansakul et al. 2009), compared to about 60 percent in 2003 and as high as 77 percent in 1995 (García-Herrero and Santabárbara 2004). However, to put these figures into perspective, the Big Four range among the largest banks in the world in terms of assets, employees and number of branches. The recent decline in market share is expected to continue, at a pace that is unlikely to worry the Big Four. This development is considered somewhat normal and has been observed in other countries and industries that opened up the once quasi-monopolistic markets (e.g. Deutsche Telekom after the reform and opening of the German telecommunications market).

Other issues are more pressing for the Big Four. As often is the case with state-owned companies in a centrally planned economy, the Big Four have been subject to government influence in the past, which is now hurting the companies as the markets have opened up. In the case of the banking industry, the issue has been soft constraints on lending, especially for large state-owned enterprises, thus leading to high NPLs (non-performing loans) on the Big Four's balance sheets. These continue to constrain their profitability (García-Herrero and Santabárbara 2004). Even though the share of NPLs in total assets has been significantly reduced in recent years (Hansakul et al. 2009), some people argue that this is cosmetic. Chovanec (2009) pointed out that "the bulk of bad debts were not written off as losses by the banks, but off-loaded onto state-run Asset Management Companies (AMCs)". Hence, it is not yet clear how these former NPLs will affect the Big Four in the future. As for now, they pay the interest on these to the AMCs, although interest payments are not as frightening as potential large-scale write-offs.

Joint-stock commercial banks

JSCBs are the second largest category of banks, after the Big Four, holding 14 percent of the banking sector's assets at the end of 2007 (Hansakul et al. 2009). Their assets grew by 33 percent in 2007, clearly outperforming the average industry growth of 20 percent.

JSCBs are partially owned by local governments, state-owned enterprises and partly the private sector. Currently, there are 12 JSCBs licensed in China, the biggest ones being Bank of Communications, China Minsheng Bank, China Merchants Bank, Shanghai Pudong Development Bank and Shenzen Development Bank. While China Minsheng Bank is the only entirely privately owned bank, five of them are listed on stock markets. JSCBs have focused more on private consumer loans as well as small and medium-sized enterprises, as the Big Four already have a strong footprint with larger corporate clients such as the state-owned enterprises. Their market-oriented mindset has brought them success and they are expected to continue gaining market share and importance in the Chinese banking sector. The main impediment to rapid growth is their still local focus and the disadvantages they face in terms of branch networks compared to the Big Four.

City commercial banks and credit cooperatives

The smallest domestic players in the Chinese banking sector are city commercial banks and credit cooperatives, who together account for more than 6 percent and 10 percent of total assets, respectively.

While city commercial banks have outperformed the average market growth by growing 29 percent in 2007 (Hansakul et al. 2009), the share of credit cooperatives in total banking sector assets declined sharply from 16 percent in 1995 (García-Herrero and Santabárbara 2004) to about 10 percent in 2006. However, this trend is not surprising, as city commercial banks were created in the 1990s to take over urban credit cooperatives. Hence, many have merged into city commercial banks with only rural credit cooperatives maintaining their position for agricultural financing and individuals. However, due to the localized set-up they are often subject to local government influence on their lending policies; the share of NPL in their portfolios is estimated to be extremely high. City commercial banks furthermore are limited to their respective regions as their license does not extend to national levels. This is a clear disadvantage compared to the state-owned commercial banks (SOCBs) and JSCBs.

Foreign banks

As the Chinese banking sector has only recently opened up and still has some restraints and regulations for foreign banks, their influence in the market is not very significant. Two milestones in policy reforms strongly affected foreign direct investment: first, in 2003, the Chinese government opened up the banking sector for foreign strategic investments, where foreign banks could hold minority shares in Chinese banks. However, despite tight regulations, FDI in banking has rapidly grown to USD 14 billion in 2005 (Hu 2006). Second, since late 2006, as a follow-up of China's World Trade Organization (WTO) accession, foreign banks are allowed to conduct RMB business with individuals. Nevertheless, to date foreign banks account for only about 2 percent of total banking assets in China. In the next paragraphs we discuss opportunities and challenges for foreign investment in China and thus touch upon some reasons why the share of foreign banks is still this low.

1.3. China domestic banks

Current NPL situation of China's domestic banks

On the surface the asset quality of the domestic banks appears to be very good and improving, however, there are concerns on debts to local governments and the potential increase of NPLs due to a possible big drop in property prices.

The good appearance of the asset quality

According to a research report published by DBS in August 2010, the asset quality of China's banks is good and new NPLs formation will be low, going forward. They only expect a moderate rise in NPLs (before write-offs) of 25 percent to 26 percent p.a. during 2010 and 2011. After the write-offs, NPLs should rise 11 percent and 14 percent in 2010 and 2011. NPL ratios should decline to 1.2 percent in 2010 and 2011 diluted by the continued and relatively fast loan expansion.

The Local Government Investment and Finance Platform

According to Ba Shu Song, the head of the Institute for Finance Research of the State Council Development Research Centre, the Local Government Platform has become the most actively growing debtor.

Starting from November 2008 when China started enforcing active fiscal policy and appropriately loosened monetary policy to respond to the financial tsunami, the growth in credit has been extremely fast. Outstanding credit was RMB 9.6 trillion in 2009. Among the debtors of these loans, Local Government Platform is the most active, most eye-catching and deserves the most attention and concern.

The so-called Local Government Platform broadly includes different types of city construction investment corporations, city construction development corporations and city construction asset operation corporations, etc., organized and set up by local governments. These corporations make use of allocation of assets such as land to organize and set up corporations assets and cash flow of which can more or less reach the standard of financing, and if necessary they are patched by repayment guarantees and financial subsidies, and the key is to invest the proceeds of the financing into projects of city construction, public business, etc.

Since the end of 2008, financing of the Local Government Platform has shown a fast growing trend. According to initial statistics, there are more than 3,000 such platforms of all and different levels of local governments, of which more than 70 percent are at county and district levels. In early 2008, the total debt of all levels of platforms was more than RMB 1 trillion; in mid-2009, it rapidly rose to more than RMB 5 trillion. *Financial Times* reported in July 2010 that according to its information from a senior Chinese official, the total debt had reached RMB 7.7 trillion then and 20 percent of that had a high risk of default; most of such loans were bank loans from China's domestic banks. The huge loans not only increased the burden of local governments but also put significant pressure on banks' operational risks. In November 2010 Jia Kang, the Head of the Institute of Financial Science of MoF, stated that the local government loans had gone up to more than RMB 8 trillion of which 23 percent had obvious risk.

How much damage can the platform cause?

Using the data in the DBS report, and the assumption that the total net new bank loans in China in 2009 and 2010 are RMB 7.5 trillion and RMB 7 trillion, respectively, we can assume the total loan outstanding at the end of 2010 to be around RMB 47 trillion.

If we assume the worst scenario that 20 percent of the RMB 7.7 trillion will become NPL, then the additional NPL due to the platform = 7.7 trillion x 20 percent = 1.54 trillion.

The ratio of this additional NPL to total loan = 1.54 trillion / 47 trillion = 0.0377.

Then making use of the financial data from Q3 2010 reports of the above-mentioned three big domestic banks, we can compile the ratio of the additional NPL to equity and profit before tax for the three banks, assuming the above ratio of additional NPL due to Local Government Platform is applicable for all the banks:

B/RMB	*Equity*	*Annualized PBT*	*Total loan*	*NPL*	*NPL/equity*	*NPL/annualized PBT*
ICBC	760	222	6572	248	0.33	1.12
CCB	598	192	5368	202	0.34	1.05
BOC	598	143	5555	209	0.35	1.46

Source: China Banking Regulatory Commission

The back-of-envelope estimate is that the worst scenario could be more than 30 percent of the equity or more than one year of profits of the banks might vaporize. Maybe this is the reason why the banks have been instructed to increase their CAR and they have been making second offerings of equity.

The quick conclusion is that the Local Government Platform will not kill the banks but the shareholders may suffer much from it if it turns sour one day, and it may hurt the Chinese economy for several years.

Impact of property price fall to NPL

China's central government has been suppressing property prices in China. The government has been setting up and enforcing new rules for this and the market believes the central government will even impose new property taxes. Although the transaction volume has been lowered much, property prices have not declined significantly. It has even been reported that property prices have been increasing slowly in many cities. So this may provoke the central government to enforce more and much harder measures and the market, the banks and CBRC are worrying that property prices may finally drop substantially and that may increase greatly NPLs of the banks and even lead to a huge and damaging systemic destruction of China's banking system.

CBRC has instructed the banks to perform stress tests to forecast the potential damage a fall in property prices may cause at the end of July 2010. CBRC did explicitly instruct the merchant banks to perform stress tests based on the scenarios that the property prices will drop 50 percent to 60 percent.

On 20 August 2010, www.stnn.cc reported that one senior executive of a joint-stock bank commented that it was possible property prices would drop 50 percent under the increasingly tightening policy and the price after such a drop would be at the same level as that in the first quarter of 2009; we believe that the worst scenario could be a price drop of 50 percent.

According to the media reports, domestic banks had released the results of their stress tests and said impact on NPLs (as released by major domestic banks) was expected to be very mild. The following were the reported results upon 50 percent property price drop released by several domestic banks.

	% NPL increase to total mortgage loan	*% NPL increase to total property development loan*
Minsheng	1.2%	2.1%
CMB	1%–2%	1%–2%
BoCOM	1.2%	1.6%
BoC	2%	4%
CCB	Insignificant	Insignificant

Source: China Banking Regulatory Commission

The figures look too mild to be believable and the media also doubt them because the banks themselves did the stress tests, i.e. there were no third-party referees for the tests and their results.

Theoretically the highest damages should be on banks which were the most aggressive in lending the two types of loans during the property boom in 2009, some media reviewed the published loan figures of the banks and concluded that the most aggressive major domestic bank in that period was BoC, and the figures in the previous table also show that BoC's NPLs on the two types of loans would rise the most under the stress test scenario. It was also reported that the situation for the Beijing Branch of BoC was even worse: under the 50 percent price drop scenario, the mortgage loan NPLs would be 7 percent of its total mortgage loan outstanding!

If we take BoC's data in the above table as the worst case, and take its financial data from its 2010 Interim Report, we can compile the worst scenario for BoC as follows (as at 30 June 2010):

Property development loan (M RMB)	425051
Mortgage loan (M RMB)	1016620
Increase of NPL due to 50% property price drop (M RMB)	37334
Ratio of NPL increase to annualized profit before tax	0.27
Ratio of NPL increase to equity	0.07

Source: Bank of China Interim Report 2010

This does not look good, but compared to the potential damage of the Local Government Platform, this is much smaller, if the stress tests results given by the banks themselves are correct.

1.3.2. ***Future opportunities***

Responding to the challenges and difficulties in the PRC banking industry, the domestic banks are proactively implementing different strategies.

Penetration in county areas

Driven by China's fast-paced urbanization and industry's migration to county areas, the economy in these areas is skyrocketing and is deemed to be more important to domestic banks' business development in the future. In accordance with National Bureau of Statistics of China, the county areas had a total population of 928 million, which accounted for 95.2 percent of China's total land mass and 69.8 percent of China's total population as of 31 December 2008; it accounted for 49.6 percent of China's total GDP in 2008.

In response, most domestic banks have decided to intensify their market expansion efforts and speed up the penetration in the county areas. For example, as of 30 June 2010, ABC has already established 2,072 branches in the county areas. Meanwhile, BoC and Temasek Holdings have set up a joint venture called BOC Fullerton Village Bank (中銀富登村鎮銀行) with the aim of opening 400 branches in these areas in the coming years. CCB will also join hands with Banco Santander Central Hispano Sa (西班牙桑坦德銀行) for establishing branches in county areas as well as implementing new operational systems. The initial registered capital has reached RMB 3 billion.

New market establishments outside China

More banks are going abroad either by setting up overseas branches or through cross-border M&A. To cite an example, ICBC, the world's largest bank by market value, has entered the markets of Vietnam, Malaysia and Canada and has applied for establishment of six branches in Europe, including Paris in the first half of 2010. In fact, ICBC has already acquired 20 percent stake in South Africa's

Standard Bank Group Ltd for USD 5.4 billion and it bought Thailand's ACL Bank for USD 545 million in October 2008 and September 2009, respectively. Howard Davies, former deputy governor of the Bank of England and adviser to the Chinese banking regulator, called the acquisition of Standard Bank Group Ltd "strategic logic" as ICBC can take advantage from the growing economic links between China and Africa.

Meanwhile, CCB has been approved to set up the Sydney Branch and the Moscow Representative Office in August and September 2010, respectively. John Foley of breakingviews.com has pinpointed that overseas expansion is likely to continue as Chinese banks are seeking to build their global presence. As further explained by Xiao Gang, the Chairman of Bank of China, Chinese banks that have the ability should hasten their pace in going abroad and increase their international competitiveness.

Cross-selling

In face of intense competition in the Chinese banking industry, domestic banks are targeting revenues from credit cards, wealth management services, financial leasing and fund management and insurance businesses through improving cross-selling efforts.

- Credit card

From 2001 to 2008, issued credit cards soared by 514 percent to 142.3 million and became one of the major consumer financial products for Chinese commercial banks. This growth can be attributed to rising household incomes and the resulting life-style change. Moreover customers are much better educated in regard to their investing and financing options. As such retail banking is presented with significant growth opportunities associated with increasing demand for consumer financial products.

As the domestic banks fully recognize the potential of this market, they are ready to intensify their marketing efforts and fight hard to attract customers. In fact, most domestic banks offer special promotions to attract new customers on a regular basis. In addition to waiving the annual fees permanently, some domestic banks have even offered lifetime bonus point programs to attract new customers. In short, we fully expect that the stiff competition will be in parallel with the market growth in the future.

- Wealth management and private banking

Recently, a new market for wealth management services has emerged as a result of the rapid increase in household wealth and an expanding class of wealthy individuals. In fact, China's household savings reached RMB 20 trillion in 2008 which was equivalent to 72.5 percent of China's GDP in that year. The combined wealth of China's millionaires overtook that of the UK; China ranked fourth worldwide in

2008. Hence, there is no doubt that wealth management and private banking have promising prospects in China. In response to these growth trends, domestic banks have begun to offer customized and professional wealth management services to mid- to high-end customers, such as asset allocation, dynamic wealth management and corporate finance advisory services. Besides, domestic banks have set up their own private banking departments and started to expand their market penetration in private banking services to high net-worth individuals in the PRC.

- Financial leasing and fund management

Besides credit card and wealth management businesses, domestic banks have diversified into other financial products / services also, such as financial leasing and fund management. As of 31 December 2008, seven domestic banks have already invested in or established financial leasing subsidiaries while eight domestic banks have established fund management subsidiaries. As of 31 December 2008, bank-owned fund management companies commanded a market share of 12.4 percent in terms of the total net assets under management in China.

For example, in 2008, Industrial Bank (興業銀行) set up a financial leasing unit with RMB 2 billion (or USD 283.5 million) in registered capital and bought a 20 percent strategic stake in Jiujiang City Commercial Bank, based in central Jiangxi Province to expand into the fund management and leasing businesses and invested in a smaller lender.

- Insurance

Traditionally, domestic banks were prohibited from underwriting insurance products and services. However, investments in insurance business have grown steadily since 2008, when CBRC designated four banks including ICBC, CCB, BoC and Bank of Beijing to take part in a pilot program allowing domestic banks to take stakes in insurance companies. Subsequently ICBC (Asia) has been approved for holding a 12.45 percent stake in Taiping Insurance; CCB has applied to take a stake in Beijing-based Happy Life Insurance Company; the Bank of Communications (BOCOM) has received China Insurance Regulatory Commission (CIRC) approval for the purchase of a 51 percent stake in China Life-CMG Life Insurance Company and Bank of Beijing has been approved to take a stake in ING Capital Life Insurance Company, Ltd.

In November 2009, CBRC promulgated the Pilot Administrative Measures for Commercial Banks to Make Equity Investments in Insurance Companies, permitting commercial banks to invest in the insurance industry. By leveraging their extensive distribution networks and customer base, this should become a significant business opportunity for domestic banks in the future. For example, as of 31 December 2009, ABC had 23,624 domestic branch outlets, covering all cities and 99.5 percent of the counties in China with approximately 320 million retail customers and 2.6 million corporate customers. Thus its potential sales revenue from insurance premiums is substantial.

1.4. Interest rate development and liberalization in China

Background of interest rate cut

People's Bank of China (PBoC) has long controlled the deposit and loan interest rate of all banks in China. In mid 2012, PBoC cut interest rates twice in less than a month. It was also the first interest cut in three-and-a-half years, which reflected that the growth of China's economy faced a great challenge.

On 7 June 2012, the PBoC cut the one year benchmark deposit and lending rate by 25 bps. At the same time, it also raised the cap on deposit rate to 10 percent premium and lowered the floor of lending rate to 20 percent discount. Previously, deposit rate did not have a floating area and lending rate only had floor of 10 percent discount. The flexibility allowed to banks implied further interest rate liberalization.

The second interest rate cut was in 5 July 2012 when the PBoC further cut the one year benchmark deposit rate by 25 bps and one year benchmark lending rate by 31 bps. The central bank further lowered the floor of lending rate to 30 percent discount to provide relief to sectors with high debt burden. It reflected growing government support for the economy at the expense of bank profitability. Details are shown in Table 1.1.

Table 1.1 CNY loan and deposit benchmark interest adjustment summary

%	*Before adjusted*	*Adjustment (7 June 2012)*	*Variance pp (vs previous adj)*	*After floating*	*Adjustment (5 July 2012)*	*Variance pp (vs previous adj)*	*After floating*
Retail deposit							
Current deposit	0.50	0.40	−0.10	0.44	0.35	−0.05	0.39
Fixed deposit							
3 months	3.10	2.85	−0.25	3.14	2.60	−0.25	2.86
6 months	3.30	3.05	−0.25	3.36	2.80	−0.25	3.08
1 year	3.50	3.25	−0.25	3.58	3.00	−0.25	3.30
2 year	4.40	4.10	−0.30	4.51	3.75	−0.35	4.13
3 year	5.00	4.65	−0.35	5.12	4.25	−0.40	4.68
5 year	5.50	5.10	−0.40	5.61	4.75	−0.35	5.23
Loan and advance							
6 months	6.10	5.85	−0.25	4.68	5.60	−0.25	3.92
1 year	6.56	6.31	−0.25	5.05	6.00	−0.31	4.20
1–3 year	6.65	6.40	−0.25	5.12	6.15	−0.25	4.31
3–5 year	6.90	6.65	−0.25	5.32	6.40	−0.25	4.48
> 5 year	7.05	6.80	−0.25	5.44	6.55	−0.25	4.59

Source: China Banking Regulatory Commission

Reasons behind the rate cut

The first purpose of the rate cut was to cope with the less rapid local GDP growth due to Europe's debt crisis. China has faced increasing pressure of sluggish GDP growth because of debt issues in US and Europe, with its GDP growth rate continuously declining from 2010 onwards. As of September 2012, the GDP growth rate was only 7.4 percent, which was even below the critical point of 8 percent as shown in Figure 1.1.

Besides, China's manufacturing PMI has declined to its lowest point of 49.2 percent in August 2012, a figure below the critical level of 50 percent (Figure 1.2), implying that the manufacturing sector was shrinking in the period.

In the 12 Five-Year Plans and 18th Big Meeting, leaders of China have repeatedly emphasized the importance of stable growth of the economy. Therefore, China would try to increase the extension of macro-adjustment and adopt new policies to expand demand for consumption and investment. PBoC has lowered deposit and loan interest rates twice to increase the confidence of investors and stimulate demand for borrowing and investment as a result.

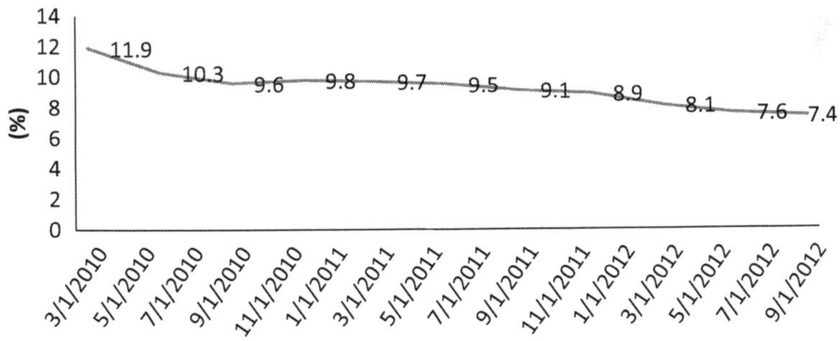

Figure 1.1 China's GDP growth rate from 2010 to 2012

Source: National Bureau of Statistics of China

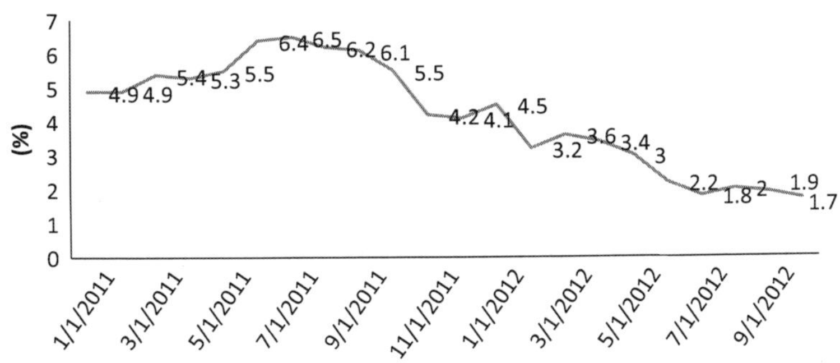

Figure 1.2 China's PMI in 2012

Source: National Bureau of Statistics of China

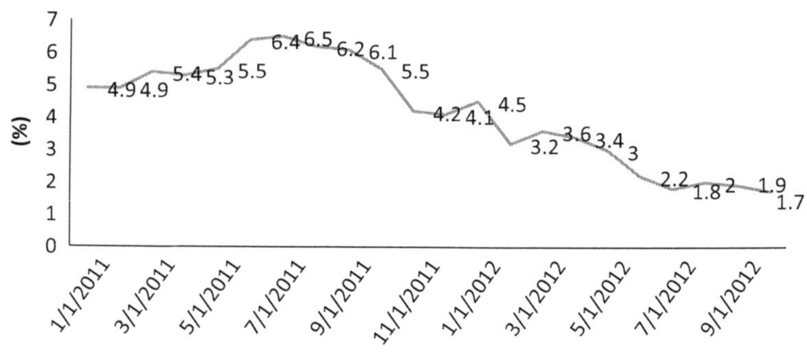

Figure 1.3 China's CPI year-to-year growth rate from 2011 to 2012

Source: National Bureau of Statistics of China

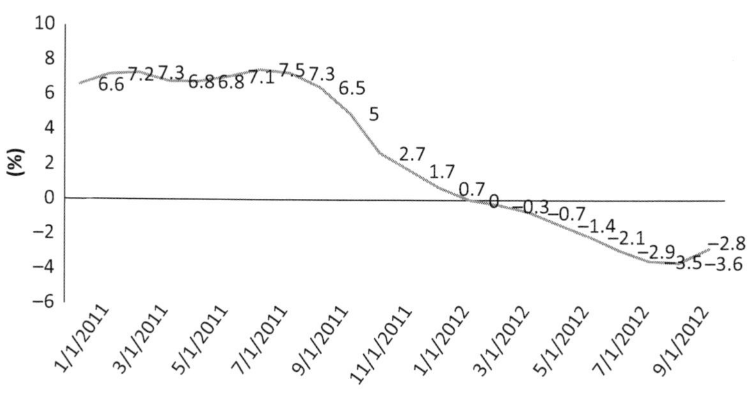

Figure 1.4 China's PPI year-to-year growth rate from 2011 to 2012

Source: National Bureau of Statistics of China

Another reason for the cut was that the decreasing inflation rate has provided the opportunity to reduce deposit and lending rates. As the debt crisis of the US and Europe has caused economic growth to slow down globally, making the investment sentiment more risk averse and causing commodity and oil prices to drop accordingly, China's CPI growth rate has also decreased to 2.2 percent on June 2012 as shown in Figure 1.3 and the real interest rate has turned from negative to positive, which provided an opportunity to lower the deposit rate.

In addition, China's PPI dropped 2.1 percent in June 2012 and the extent of decline increased in following months (Figure 1.4). This reflects that the real financing cost of corporations was high, thus decreasing the lending rate may help act as a relief for them.

Impact of interest rate cut and rate floating expansion

The first rate cut appeared to be symmetrical, the extent of the rate cut for both deposit and lending rates was about the same for tenures of one year or below. The interest rate cut was about 25 bps; and deposit rates for two years, three years and five years, the interest rate cuts were 30 bps, 35 bps and 40 bps, respectively. However, the interest rate cut was implemented simultaneously with interest rate liberalization which made the interest rate intrinsically non-symmetrical.

As mentioned before, the first rate cut allowed a premium of 10 percent on the deposit rate. Owing to the keen competition for deposits, banks were already using other deposit-related investment products to circumvent the limit. The recent drop in bank deposits implied that banks would raise deposit rates by offering the 10 percent premium immediately to attract more funds, despite the slow rise of long tenor deposit rates due to the expectation of continuous cutting of interest rates by PBoC.

On the other hand, the lending rate will also be dropped due to the decreasing debt financing demand in order to maintain the loan market share. Although lending will still be priced according to assessment of credit risk of customers, it was believed that most loans will be priced at the floor of the 20 percent discount on the benchmark rate in the long run. Therefore, because of the keen competition for loans and deposits, one year deposit and lending rates will be changed from 3.25 percent and 6.31 percent to 3.58 percent and 5.05 percent, respectively. Compared with the rate cut before (deposit rate: 3.50 percent; lending rate: 6.56 percent), the deposit rate was raised by about 8 bps and the lending rate was cut by about 150 bps. Thus it could be seen that the deposit rate was increased eventually under this rate cut.

If the second rate cut is viewed as a standalone action, it seems closer to a symmetrical rate cut than the first. Under the second rate cut, the deposit rate still had a cap of 10 percent premium and the lending rate had a lower floor of 30 percent discount. According to the keen competition assumption mentioned above, the one year deposit rate and lending rate would be changed from 3.00 percent and 6.00 percent to 3.30 percent and 4.20 percent, respectively. Compared to the intrinsic rate before the cut, both the interest rate, deposit and lending rates appeared to have dropped. In short, it could be found that the one year deposit rate has dropped 20 bps and one year lending rate has dropped 236 bps, which was much greater than the deposit rate after the two interest rate cuts.

The interest rate cut has multiple impacts on the banking industry and the macro-environment. First, the interest rate cut and the expansion of the benchmark rate's floating zone could further reduce the financing cost of individuals and corporations. As discussed previously, the one year intrinsic lending rate will most likely be decreased 236 bps to 4.20 percent after the two rate cuts. The reduction of financing costs will further stimulate investment decisions, property markets and even consumption which in turn help economic growth.

In addition, expansion of the benchmark rate's floating zone will decrease banks' net interest spread which would suppress their profitability. Taking one year deposit and loan as an example, the net interest spread before the rate cut was

3.06 percent, decreasing to 1.47 percent after the first cut and liberalization and to 0.90 percent after the second cut. Net interest income has long been the major income of Chinese banks so the reduction of net interest spread would force them to transform their business model to expand their non-interest income, such as insurance and unit trust commission income. Besides, banks would target small and medium enterprises due to their lower bargaining power, hoping to prevent the sharp drop in the net interest spread in loan portfolios. Yet on the other hand, better credit assessment of companies is needed to prevent deterioration of asset quality which would further erode banks' profit.

Expansion of benchmark rate's floating zone was the main implication of the change from planned economy to market driven, which helped to better allocate the resources among different counterparties. A partial free floating of interest rates gave banks more power to decide deposit and lending rates, thus larger and higher credit quality corporations could enjoy better lending rates which in turn lowered the financing cost and made the entire economy more efficiently financed. Besides, lowering the lending rate also helped reallocate the profit between banks and corporations by reducing the profit of banks to an appropriate level and translated it into profits of corporations. This overturns the phenomenon that banks always earn good profits even under economic downturns.

Peer banks comparison

Having discussed that interest rate cuts will shrink the interest margin and hence the profit of China's banks, real statistics of the banks are described and discussed to confirm these findings.

Sector Q3 net interest margin surprisingly raised by 4 bps, contrary to market expectations (Figure 1.5). It was believed that this was mainly driven by large banks' NIM expansion, given they had relatively long loan durations but very liquid deposit bases. PBoC's interest rate cuts in June and July almost immediately helped large

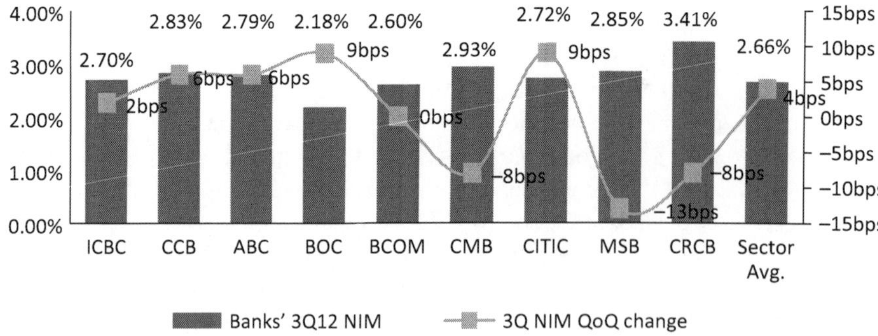

Figure 1.5 Banks' Q3 NIM and change in Q3

Source: China Banking Regulatory Commission

banks realize lower funding costs while it took longer to re-price loan portfolios. All Big Four banks realized some net interest margin expansion in Q3 while most small banks experienced some net interest margin contraction, as shown in Figure 1.5.

For banks other than the Big Four, the net interest margin was rather limited and was shrinking. The main reasons behind the shrinking net interest margin included the continuous rate deregulation, which further pushed up small banks' funding costs and the weaker loan demand from retail and private customers, which weakened banks' pricing power.

In short, the rise in net interest margin in Q3 was unsustainable. 1Q in 2013 could be a challenging quarter for large banks' net interest margins, given most of their mortgage loans and a sizeable portion of long-term infrastructure lending got re-priced in accordance with prevailing benchmark rates on 1 January 2013.

Future direction of interest rate policy

Originally China's banks were willing to lend money only to city governments or large corporations. Small and medium enterprises found it very difficult to raise funds in China. The one method for them was to lend money from juice dealers, but the juice loans were always charged high interest rates, which was out of regulation. One of the main purposes of interest rate deregulation was to force banks to reach out to small and medium enterprises and enhance their credit risk assessment in order to sustain the high loan interest spread. If China's banks still insisted on lending to traditional large corporations, their net interest income must be hard hit by the interest rate cuts. Through this transformation, the growth of China's economy can be efficiently supported by encouraging growth of small and medium enterprises. However, the transformation of the customers segment will be a long-term revolution.

In the short term, banks will try to raise their non-interest income. Compared with Hong Kong banks, Chinese banks have paid less attention to fee and commission income. For instance, fee for remittance was charged only to the transferor and this too was far below Hong Kong banks. One way for China's banks to increase the operating income was to increase the fees for traditional services to compensate for the reduction of net interest income.

1.5. BASEL III impact on China banking

BASEL III introduction

In September 2010, global consensus was reached on the BASEL III Accord after the serious financial tsunami. BASEL III aims to strengthen regulation of the banking industry through multiple ratios requirements and standards, herein summed up as follows:

Capital Conservation Buffer is newly proposed so that banks can absorb losses during periods of financial and economic stress. Banks that do not follow this

Regulatory Element	Ratio Standard	
	BASEL III	BASEL II
Tier 1 Capital Requirement	6%	4%
Tier 1 Common Equity Requirement	4.50%	2%
Capital Conservation Buffer	2.50%	
Contercyclical Capital Buffer	0%–2.5%	
Liquidity Coverage Ratio	100%	
Net Stable Funding Ratio	100%	
Leverage Ratio	3%	
Total Capital Ratio	8%	8%

Source: China Banking Regulatory Commission

Note: The phased schedule requires banks to meet the requirements by 2019.

rule will face restraints on revenue distribution while the Countercyclical Buffer serves as an extension to the conservation buffer. Besides, the Liquidity Coverage Ratio is to ensure high-quality liquid resources remain available for banks' one-month survival in stress and Net Stable Funding Ratio is to promote banks to provide stable funding for their activities.

BASEL III also introduces rules to cover Credit Value Adjustment risk, Central Counterparty risk and higher capital requirements for derivatives.

Starting from BASEL I

The Chinese banking industry has followed BASEL I requirements since February 2004, when China Banking Regulatory Commission (CBRC) promulgated Regulation Governing Capital Adequacy of Commercial Banks. It stipulates capital adequacy ratio (CAR) shall not be lower than 8 percent and core capital adequacy no lower than 4 percent. It then introduces several stipulations to cover the three pillars in BASEL II (yet it only stresses on credit risk and market risk with disclosure requirements lower than BASEL II). Those measures greatly improve Chinese banking conditions. By far state-owned commercial banks and some joint-stock banks have established Internal Ratings-Based Approach; based on the 2010 annual report, most banks have met the core requirements of BASEL II.

Stepping into BASEL III

In April 2011, CBRC introduced several ratios like CAR, leverage ratio, NPL coverage ratio and liquidity ratio in the newly issued *Guidance on Implementation of New Regulatory Standard on China Banking;* in June 2012, it issued *Administrative Measures on the Capital of Commercial Bank,* implying China's move towards enforcement of BASEL III. Some key elements are as follows:

Ratios	*Banks of Sig. Imp.*	*Banks of Non-sig. Imp.*
Core Tier 1	5.0%	5.0%
Tier 1	6.0%	6.0%
Tier 2	1.0%	0.0%
Capital Conservation Buffer	2.5%	
Contercyclical Capital Buffer	0%–2.5%	
Total	8.0%	
Leverage Ratio	4.0%	
Provision Coverage Ratio	2.5%	
NPL Provision Coverage Ratio	150.0%	
LCR	100.0%	
NFSR	100.0%	

Source: China Banking Regulatory Commission

Note: 1. Banks of Significant Importance shall meet the above requirement by the end of 2013.
2. Banks of Non-significant Importance shall meet the above requirement by the end of 2016.

I. CAR: China's requirement on capital comprises Core Tier 1, Tier 1 and Tier 2, and its required schedule (by 2016) is much earlier than the 2019 stipulated in BASEL III. Besides, China's definition of CAR is similar to BASEL, but varying risk weights of the RWA elements reflect efforts to adapt the industry to the domestic economy:

   i. Risk weight of debt claims on domestic banks increase from 20 percent to 25 percent, to prevent risk accumulation in the banking system;
   ii. Risk weight of debt claims on microenterprises from 100 percent to 75 percent, to help enterprises with financing and improve banks' loan structure;
   iii. Risk weight of individual loans decrease from 100 percent to 75 percent, for the above reason;
   iv. Mortgage loan is differentiated in that risk weight of first mortgage is lower;
   v. Risk weight of claims on overseas debt is determined by third-party rating; and
   vi. Favorable risk weight to overseas companies and domestic public facility enterprises is cut, mainly because of the weaker financial status of overseas institutions after the crisis.

II. Leverage Ratio: Leverage ratio is one of the biggest amendments in BASEL III as its calculation involves derivatives and out-of-balance-sheet assets. China follows this ratio but the standard (4 percent) is higher than the 3 percent in BASEL III.

III. Loan Provision Ratio: BASEL III doesn't cover this aspect while in China, Provision Coverage Ratio and NPL Provision Coverage are aimed to measure banks' risk exposure:

Provision Coverage Ratio (PCR, no less than 2.5 percent) = Loan Loss Reserves / Loan Balance

NPL Provision Coverage (no less than 150 percent) = Loan Loss Provision / Non-performing Loan

Banks are required to meet the higher standard of the two ratios, among which PCR of small-medium banks may be lower than 2.5 percent with reasonable loan structure, low NPL rate and good risk management system. Besides, if expected loan loss exceeds the provision, banks are required to compensate with their revenue for such difference.

IV. Liquidity Ratio: CBRC employs the same Liquidity Coverage Ratio and Net Stable Funding Ratio as BASEL III (both as 100 percent), only that China set the deadline by 2013 while BASEL III set 2015 (LCR) and 2018 (NSFR).

Apart from the above elements, CBRC also sets up ratios like liquidity proportion, loan / deposit ratio, liquidity gap ratio, reliance on core liabilities, the top ten deposit ratio, etc. to construct an all-round liquidity risk monitoring system.

Implementation

By Q1 2012, average CAR of China's commercial banks had reached 12.7 percent and CCAR 10.3 percent. Most banks have already met BASEL III requirements without considering the countercyclical capital buffer.

China's challenge under BASEL III

Capital gap

As far as CAR is concerned, listed banks have met the basic BASEL norms. However, under the new measures, requirements including the Countercyclical Buffer of 2.5 percent, Tier 2 of 1 percent for banks of Significant Importance exert great capital stress on China's banking industry. It is predicted that capital gap of the whole industry is RMB 1 trillion; capital gap of listed banks reached an estimated RMB 0.5 trillion (by far the total shareholder's equity of all listed banks is RMB 4.52 trillion). Under the CAR requirement, short capital will prevent banks from engaging in higher risk-return businesses, like derivatives and property loans. This has worried the capital market for the last few years and is partly attributed to banks' low valuation multiples.

Liquidity gap

Though China stipulates a liquidity coverage ratio (100 percent) and a Net Stable Funding Ratio (100 percent) for banks, by far, the most important reference for liquidity management in practice is Loan / Deposit Ratio. The government had introduced this ratio in Law on Commercial Banks since 1995, while the standard of 75 percent was set in October 2011 when it issued *Administrative Rules on Liquidity Management of Commercial Banks* (draft). Though it is a draft version, banks have to follow the rules by January 2012.

By September 2011, 64 commercial banks had exceeded the standard with total liquidity gap (within 90 days) of RMB 774 billion. Since the loan / deposit ratio is monitored on a monthly basis, to meet the standard, banks often need additional cash at month-end. Therefore market rate always jumps at that time. Therefore, banks design financial products to attract cash which usually offers much higher yields than term-deposits. On one hand, it is easy to attract risk-averse clients to buy these products for generating large volumes of deposits and on the other hand, these deposits as financial products help banks reduce reserve deposits they are supposed to hold with the central bank. Popularity of banking financial products stem from the loan / deposit requirement but now it has become a great concern for the regulator. By Q3 2011, outstanding balance of financial products had reached RMB 7.7 trillion i.e. more than 10 percent of deposits, exerting great repayment pressure on banks.

There have been calls for repeal of this standard. Some argue that this standard implies banks need approval to use loans to generate deposits. As in 2009 when the government released liquidity, RMB 9.6 trillion bumped into the market; 1.89 trillion was released in March. If banks did not turn these loans into deposits and then recycle them to generate loans, there would not be so much of credit in the market. Some also propose that loan / deposit ratios of Western banks are higher than 100 percent: 117 percent in US, 114 percent in EU and 85 percent in Hong Kong. China's 75 percent is obviously lower than international practice.

Besides, in China liquidity usually stems from two sources: funds outstanding for foreign exchange and credit loans. In the past few decades, export boom has provided more-than-sufficient liquidity for the economy and banks, therefore, bear no burden on this aspect but the export industry is not so good after the financial crisis. Therefore it is expected that credit loans will play a more important part in liquidity and the 75 percent standard may no longer be viable for economic development.

1.6. Non-performing loan (NPL) and asset quality

China's credit risk is rising and is probably much higher than what the official non-performing loans (NPL) statistics indicate. This is worrying as this is only the beginning of the NPLs cycle. Though it is expected that the government would intervene, concerns are still being voiced because the massive excess capacity of many Chinese industries contributes significantly to NPLs and after years of aggressive expansion that ran way ahead of demand growth, many of them had to eventually be rescued by the government. During this process, faster depreciation in the form of deleveraging and consolidation is likely to occur and while expectations of an imminent hard landing may be overstated, nevertheless it will be spread over a number of years and continue to fluctuate.

From the trough in Q3 of 2011, total NPLs of China's commercial banks rose by 11.9 percent at the end of Q2, reaching RMB 456.7 billion and 4.2 percent q-o-q, according to the China Banking Regulatory Commission (CBRC). Because of a similar growth in loans, NPLs remained unchanged at 0.9 percent. Yet, the total loan loss reserves set aside were RMB 1.3 trillion while estimates of special-mention loans which were doubtful but still performing were raised to RMB 1.5 trillion. According to *China Securities Journal,* NPLs increased by RMB 11.983 billion from the beginning of the year to RMB 20.678 billion by the end of August, while the NPL ratio remained at 3 percent.

More NPL woes ahead

The history of banking crises suggests there is no definitive linear correlation between the peak of NPL ratios and the scale of the pre-crisis credit boom as it also depends on how the situation is contained and resolved. In the sample of 42 crisis episodes compiled by Laeven and Valencia (2008), average annual credit growth as a proportion of GDP prior to the crisis was about 8.3 percent. In 2009 and 2010, this same ratio for China reached 27.8 percent and 20 percent, respectively. It is hard to see how China's NPL ratio could stay at the current level.

There is also a structural element in China's NPLs cycle. Many industries have massive excess capacity after years of aggressive expansion that ran way ahead of demand growth.

Eventually, China has to eliminate these inefficient capacities. This process will take some time, during which faster depreciation in the form of deleveraging and consolidation will be unavoidable.

The impact of NPLs

It is difficult to predict the exact trajectory and the end point of the NPL issue. Economies with less government intervention, such as the US, usually see NPLs peaking one or two quarters after growth troughs. In contrast, Japan was very slow in recognizing and resolving its NPL problem which started in the early 1990s. The NPL ratio didn't peak until 2002 and much damage was done in the meantime to the banking system and indeed to the overall economy.

China, where the government is even more involved in the economy, is running a clear risk of a prolonged NPL cycle. Local governments have poured millions of capital into rescuing failing corporates.

NPL problem in Zhejiang-Wenzhou and beyond

The real estate market of Wenzhou is one of the very few that have not "recovered" in terms of prices this summer, unlike its peers elsewhere in China. The money which companies borrowed from a variety of sources has been reinvested in the real estate market through speculation.

Wang (2012) reported in *China Daily* that the CBRC remains skeptical about the true NPLs of Chinese banks as many of them tend to be disguised or not accurately reported to the CBRC. He also expressed his concern that if the economic growth remains slow, NPLs would surge because the banks would not be able to write off their bad assets. Wang's view is also shared by a well-respected financial publication, *Caijing,* which also predicted that for every 1 percent increase in NPL ratio, there will be RMB 1 trillion in non-performing assets.

The PricewaterhouseCoopers International Limited 2012 report, however, shows optimism towards NPLs in China. It believed that the government would eventually intervene to control the NPLs. One example of this is when the CBRC instructed banks to invest in local government investment vehicles so as to avoid defaults. It pointed out that rather than relying on government intervention, the Chinese banks should actively seek restructuring of debts of their borrowers rather than relying on liquidation and foreclosure. Yet, the practicality of this suggestion remains doubtful since banks perceive the bankruptcy reorganization process as hard to control and time consuming.

1.7. Globalization of China's banking system

According to the July 2012 PricewaterhouseCoopers (PwC) study of foreign banks in China, there were 181 foreign banks from 45 countries and regions in China at the end of 2011. These "foreign banks" are in the forms of joint-ventures with local banks, wholly foreign-owned banks or locally incorporated banks. Besides, all of the four state-owned banks have successfully listed in regions or countries outside Mainland China and it is without doubt that the Chinese currency, the RMB, is gaining increasing popularity and is being used in trade. All these facts indicate that the Chinese banking system is gradually becoming more globalized.

Working towards the globalization of the Chinese banking system is a two-way process. It is important for the government to create a level playing field for foreign banks to enter the market and conduct their business and it is equally crucial for Chinese banks to expand outside the local market into the international arena. In order to strive for a level playing field, the Chinese government has set up regulatory bodies and regulations to govern foreign banks operating in China. It is, however, arguable whether these measures have provided these banks a level playing field.

All banks in China are regulated by the China Banking Regulatory Commission (CBRC) to ensure that they abide by the relevant regulations and laws. It also has the power to authorize establishment of banks and their business scope, as well as to audit the banks. With such extensive powers, the decisions and measures taken by the CBRC have a major impact on the banking system. However, it has been pointed out in the MPRA 2007 paper that the CBRC has not been given enough independence from the State Council and the Chinese Communist Party to efficiently carry out its functions. It is not difficult for one to doubt the neutrality of the CBRC and it is prone to the suspicion that the Chinese government is exerting its influence over the banking system through the CBRC.

The powers of the People's Bank of China (PBoC) were viewed as excessive by the US trade representative in a paper submitted to the US Congress in 2011 on China's WTO compliance. First, the PBoC has the power to set the benchmark interest rates for RMB-denominated deposits and loans, which means interference in setting of the interest rate which is then to be followed by other banks. Second, the PBoC can allocate credit limits to Chinese banks, which in turn acts as a tool to control the money supply within the market. These powers can hinder globalization of the banking system as this extensive level of interference falls far behind international standards.

The influence exerted by the Ministry of Finance (MoF) is also substantial as it is required that all major banking policies must gain prior approval of the MoF. Besides, it continues to have authority over some banks in China because it either has equity holdings or has a representative on the banks' governing boards. One example is the 50 percent equity MoF holds in the Agricultural Bank of China. The close ties between the MoF, the State Council and the Chinese Communist Party (CCP) imply that these representatives may push MoF agendas within the banks and indeed Martin (2012) has pointed out that local government officials frequently attempt to exert influence over operations of Chinese banks. Thus, the interference is considered detrimental in a truly globalized banking system.

Aside from governing bodies of Chinese banks, appointments of personnel in banks are also viewed with suspicion and are sometimes inappropriate. The boards of supervisors in all Chinese banks often include individuals appointed directly by the CCP. This issue has been raised in the 2012 *China's Banking System: Issues for Congress* paper as something that the United States considers inappropriate and it has expressed its concern over whether the Chinese banks are operating under maximum autonomy, which is a crucial requirement for achieving full globalization.

It is suggested from the above that the Chinese banks are subject to undue scrutiny that can result in negative perceptions as they try and become globalized. Yet, the PwC 2012 survey report has identified the regulatory requirements and management of human resources as the two major obstacles for foreign banks operating in China. The survey was conducted in the form of one-hour-long interviews with representatives from both foreign (12 Asian banks, 21 European banks and 8 North American banks) and locally incorporated banks.

Decree No. 478 of the *Regulations of the People's Republic of China on Administration of Foreign-funded Banks* stated that a minimum of RMB 1 billion in registered capital and a minimum of RMB 100 million in non-callable operating capital is required for foreign-funded banks to establish themselves in China and the banks need to possess a minimum of RMB 20 billion in assets at the end of the year prior to the submission of an application for opening a branch(es). Both of these requirements are considered a barrier by many foreign banks. Even local incorporation requires a minimum registered capital of RMB 1 billion (with an additional RMB 100 million for each branch). It is also required that a 75 percent loan-to-deposit ratio is maintained by the banks once they have incorporated locally.

The approval process for entry of foreign banks or their expansion in China is also considered onerous and slow. There are two steps to the process: an initial application is made to China's banking regulatory agencies and when approved, the bank has to submit additional information within six months for a final decision. When final approval is granted, the bank then has to register with the appropriate departments. The whole process can take a maximum of eight months before registration and along with the capital requirement; the process often makes foreign banks wishing to enter the Chinese market hesitant.

The "Three Measures, One Guideline" (3M, 1G) introduced in 2011 has further impacted foreign banks' operations in China. It is a regulation on fee income which states that fixed assets, shareholding and project financing cannot be financed by capital loans. It requires that the purpose of the loan be stated by both the lender and the borrower prior to its grant, and deviations from this are subject to penalization. This poses a burden on foreign banks with limited staff resources and they worry that they will be held responsible for deviation made by their clients, as reported by the PwC 2012 survey report.

The regulatory control no doubt has extensive influence on the ways that foreign banks operate in China. Foreign banks have revealed in the PwC 2012 survey report that Chinese regulations have restricted the introduction of new products and has affected the breadth of scope of their business. In fact, 27 of the surveyed banks reported having made fundamental or major adaptations to their work culture or processes in order to operate effectively in China, thus suggesting lack of fair competition for a variety of banks, which is essential for creating dynamics in a truly globalized banking system.

Sourcing human capital is another major obstacle that has to be overcome by foreign banks when seeking to expand in China. According to the PwC report, turnover of employees in foreign banks is 20 percent to 40 percent and the percentage is expected to increase in the foreseeable future as more foreign banks plan to get their due share in the Chinese market. This may result in salaries going up further, impacting costs of banks. Besides, sourcing of human capital amongst the local population is challenging, especially when banks hope to expand in rural and remote areas.

The legal infrastructure is considered critical in the role of banking globalization as it is the means through which ultimate rights and interests of banks and individuals are protected, should disputes arise. However, the Chinese government and legal bodies have long been seen as allowing inadequate disclosure and access to information in many aspects, ranging from the Wenzhou train accident to arrest of individuals associating with political bodies and it is unsurprising that foreign banks continue to express their concerns regarding the Chinese legal system, arguing it lacks transparency and some decisions made are arbitrary. One interviewee of the PwC 2012 survey questioned the neutrality of the legal bodies and showed his lack of confidence in the arbitration and litigation processes, which are heavily relied on in commercial disputes.

Another issue that may hinder full globalization of the Chinese banking system is the non-performing loans (NPL) in China. Although the NPL rate in China is reasonably low for a developing country, Martin (2012) has pointed out that NPLs in China are expected to rise due to the "local government funding platforms" policy, whereby the local governments establish separate entities for incorporating and financing local projects and can obtain loans from banks or issues bonds that are often purchased by local banks when they raise funds to finance these local projects. It is doubtful whether these loans can be repaid and some are transferred to Asset Management Companies (AMCs) and are then released back into the market and later purchased by banks as stocks.

Despite the negative factors that may impact full globalization, there is some visible and potential positivity that catalyzes and aids the process. First, the PBoC is currently upgrading China's National Advanced Payment System (CNAPS) to enhance the status of RMB as a global trade currency and facilitate cross-border trade. With the increased use of RMB in international trade, foreign banks and investments would certainly be interested in expanding their businesses in China and China's banks would have a more significant role to play in RMB denominated overseas businesses, thus enhancing the necessary dynamics for globalization.

Second, the Chinese government seems to have loosened constraints placed on foreign banks in China by introducing interest rate liberalization. When banks have the autonomy to determine their own interest rates to suit market demand and supply for funds, they have a better competitive edge as they can tailor products and policies that can better cater for market needs (Song 2001). This allows fairer competition between banks of all hues and this level playing field is exactly what is needed to achieve full globalization. Besides, with the implementation of BASEL III, foreign banks are optimistically expecting reliefs for their operations in China, although the details and timeline of related policies are yet to be released.

Finally, with the Chinese government's desire to portray Shanghai as an International Financial Centre (IFC), there is a longing for accelerated globalization. Elliott (2011) listed some attributes that are "necessary or quite desirable" when building a financial centre and these should be followed if Shanghai were to become one. They include appropriate regulation for financial stability, core infrastructure, openness to foreign entry, availability of high quality of finance professionals and legal infrastructure. As can be seen, concerns have been raised regarding some of these aspects. Given China's ambition and persistent efforts, as displayed in the establishment of the international board for listing in the Shanghai Stock Exchange, it is possible that Shanghai will be able to transform itself into an IFC. Globalization of the Chinese banking system would most certainly be catalyzed as it would then have a critical role to play in handling the increased amount of money in China and RMB as a widely used trading currency.

To conclude, it can be said that the Chinese banking system is on its way to full globalization despite the many obstacles faced by foreign banks and the control exerted by regulatory bodies on the banking industry. However, with the gradual decentralization of controls due to pressures from different nations and appropriate catalytic factors, one should remain optimistic about full globalization of the Chinese banking system in the near future.

References

Accenture report (2011). Albert Chan, Ying Wan, and Jacky Yang. Beyond Basel III: The future of high performance in Chinese banks. www.accenture.com/us-en/Pages/insight-beyond-basel-iii-future-high-performance-chinese-banks.aspx

Areddy, J.T. 2009. China wants Citigroup to expand. *The Wall Street Journal Asia*, 30 September. http://online.wsj.com/news/articles/SB125425605841450345

Asia Monitor. 2009. Rapid loan growth poses significant risks to banking sector. *Asia Monitor: China & North East Asia* 16 (6): 1, 4. Business Source Complete, EBSCOhost

Bills, Steve. 2008. Citi China strikes TSYS deal to support consumer debit cards. *American Banker* 173 (172): 7. www.americanbanker.com

Bremner, B. 2006. China's ICBC: the world's largest IPO ever. *Business Week*. September 26, 2006. www.businessweek.com

Hua Zhang,. 2009. Corporate banking in China: opportunities for entry. Celent. January 20 www.celent.com

Chandler, Clay. 2006, 17 May. Wall Street's war for China. *Fortune*. money.cnn.com

China Banking Regulatory Commission. 2006. *Background information for the regulations on administration of foreign-funded banks*. China Development Gateway. chinagate.cn

China Daily. 2008. Moody's: banking outlook remains stable. *China Daily*, 18 June. www.chinadaily.com.cn

China Daily. 2009. Challenges face China banking industry in 2009. *China Daily*, 2 January, www.chinadaily.com.cn

Chovanec, P. (2009). China's real estate riddle. *Far East Economic Review*, 172.

Economist Intelligence Unit. 2009. Banking on the countryside. *Business China* 35 (6): 3–4. Business Source Complete, EBSCOhost

Elliott, D.J. 2011. Building a global financial center in Shanghai: observations from other centers. www.brookings.edu/research/papers/2011/06/10-shanghai-financial-center-elliott

Euromoney. 2009. Bank of China: private banking pioneer builds on its strengths. *Euromoney, Sep2009 Guide to Private Banking*. info.euromoney.com

Gray, Joanne. 2005, February. The inside story: Margaret Ren. *Asiamoney*. asiamoney.com

García Herrero, A., & Santabárbara, D. 2004. Where is the Chinese banking system going with the ongoing reform? *EconWPA*.

Hansakul, Syetarn, Steffen Dyck and Steffen Kern. 2009, 16 March. China's financial markets – a future global force? *DB Research*. www.dbresearch.com

Hu, Fred. 2006. Chinese banking industry – past, present and prospect. *Tsinghua University* (draft in progress). Business Source Complete, EBSCOhost

Hu Yuanyuan. 2009. Report: China's retail banking expects fast growth. 23 January, *China Daily*. www.chinadaily.com.cn/bizchina/2009-01/23/content_7425154.htm

Info-Prod Strategic Business Information. 2009, 10 November. *Moody's says prospects for retail banking in China are encouraging*. iStockAnalyst, www.istockanalyst.com

KPMG and Reuters. 2007. *Retail banking in China: New frontiers*. www.kpmg.com.cn

Kudrna, Z. 2007. Banking reform in China driven by international standards and Chinese specifics. Working paper. http://papers.ssrn.com/sol3/papers.cfm?abstract_id=1026854

Laeven, L., & Valencia, F. (2008). Systemic banking crises: a new database. *IMF Working Papers*, 1–78.

Lanzeni, Maria L. 2004, 24 August. Foreign direct investment in China – good prospects for German companies? *DB Research*. www.dbresearch.com

Lilai Xu. Foreign banks in China: Market segmentation and expanded presence in the post-WTO environment. Edward Elgar Publishing, Inc. Cheltenham, UK. www.elgaronline.com/view/9781848442146.00013.xml

Martin, M. F. (2012, February). China's banking system: Issues for Congress. Congressional Research Service, Library of Congress. http://assets.opencrs.com/rpts/R42380_20120220.pdf.

Rules for the implementation of the law of the People's Republic of China on foreign-funded enterprises. Revised on April 12, 2001, approved on October 28, 1990 by the State Council of China, issued on December 12, 1990 by the Ministry of Foreign Economic Relations and Trade, PRC.

Song, L. 2005. Interest rate liberalisation in China and the implication for non-state banking. *Financial Sector Reform in China*, Cambridge, MA: Harvard University Asia Center, 111–30.

UN World Investment Report 2009. www.unctad.org

White, Lawrence. 2009, September. Citi makes a China comeback. *Euromoney* 40 (485). info.euromoney.com

Wikipedia, the free encyclopedia. en.wikipedia.org.

Xiuying Jin and Richard Lung. 2007, May. *China's new foreign bank regulations.* Country Analysis Unit, Federal Reserve Bank of San Francisco.

Li, Y., & Tang, S. 2007. The Challenge of Removing Administrative Barriers to FDI in China. China in focus: economic, political and educational issues, 47. Zhou Yan. 2009. China all alone in Asian M&A growth. *China Daily*, 6 January.

Mainland China Banking Survey. 2009. KPMG. www.cbrc.gov.cn

DBS Group Research – China Banking Sector 20

星島環球網: "房贷压力测试加码 房价跌50%谁先倒下23 August 2010, finance.stnn.cc

China Daily 財經頻道 : 交行房贷压力测试结果乐观 房价跌50%对银行影响有限 20 August 2010.

Reuters.com: 中国银行业对房价下跌50%进行风险压力测试 警示意义大于实质 10 August 2010.

ChinaReviewNews.com: 銀監會 : 房貸壓力測試不代表房貸政策可能變動 6 August 2010.

Ifeng.com: 銀監會下令壓力測試 : 若房價下跌50%–60% 6 August 2010

ce.cn: 房貸壓力測試加碼 三高考驗房地產信貸 8 August 2010

XinHuaNet.com: 新一輪壓力測試:樓價跌50% 銀行房貸無風險? 25 August 2010

JRJ.com: 银监会将推动开展房地产贷款压力测试 31 August 2010

ccvic.com: 银行将按季度进行房地产贷款压力测 21 April 2010

Reuters.com: 银监会要求银行按季进行房地产贷款压力测试 21 April 2010

Hong Kong Economic Times: 中央緊盯樓價波動 銀監研風險 23 August 2008

Financial Times. FTChinese.com: 中国官员警告地方政府融资平台贷款风险 27 July 2010

Finet.hk: 【息差走勢】建行 : 6月底地方政府融資平台貸款額為5,778億,不良貸款6.7億 23 August 2010

Chinadaily.com: 银行不良贷款反弹当警惕 17 August 2012

Reuters. 2010, 6 July. China bank I.P.O. raises $19 billion.

ICBC Third Quarter 2010 Business Report www.icbc.com/news/2011nov28-05

China Construction Bank Q3 2010 Business Report

Bank of China Q3 2010 Business Report

Bank of China Interim Report 2010

PwC Report (June 2011), Foreign Banks in China

PwC Report (July 2012), Foreign Banks in China

MPRA 2007 annual report

BOCOM International, China Banking Sector Report. (2011, May). Guideline on new banking regulation standards. www.bocomgroup.com/mediafiles/documents/p2_6532_en.pdf
Wang Xiaotian. 2012. NPL ratio grows in the third quarter. 23 October, *China Daily*. www.chinadaily.com.cn/china/2012-10/23/content_15837696.htm
American Chamber of Commerce White Paper – Banking Section April 2011.
European Business in China Position Paper 2010/2011: Banking and Securities.
China Banking Regulatory Commission (CBRC) annual report.
The Future of Banking in China
USTR Release of the 2011 Report to Congress on China's WTO Compliance
HSBC Holdings plc, Interim Report 2010: Strong, steadfast, sustainable
HSBC Bank (China) Company Limited (July 2011), Fact Sheet
HSBC Bank (China) Company Limited (July 2010), Fact Sheet
BCG Report, Banking on China (May 2006), Successful strategies for foreign entrants
The value of China's emerging middle class_Mckinsey Global InstitutePreparing for China's urban billion_Mckinsey Global Institute: www.mckinsey.com
Statistical Data / National Bureau of Statistics (NBS) 1982–2010: www.stats.gov.cn
Internet World Statistics: www.internetworldstats.com/asia.htm
Latest Q3 financial statement of big four banks
China Macro-economy statistics, Bloomberg
Summary of Basel III, www.bis.org/bcbs/basel3.htm
BA, Shusong, BASEL III in China, July 31, 2011.
BA, Shusong, China Implementing BASEL III: Progress and Future, June, 2011.
Moody's Analytic, Basel III New Capital and Liquidity Standards – FAQs, October 2012.
Foreign Banks in China. (2012).
Foreign Banks in China. (2011).
Bad news for bad loans in China. www.pwchk.com
China's true level of bad debts are not yet recognized by banks. www.alsosprachanalyst.com
NPL ratio grows in the third quarter. www.chinadaily.com.cn

2 The bond market in China

2.1. History of the bond market in China

Before 1949: Qing Dynasty and Republic of China

The bond markets in China can be traced back to the late Qing Dynasty when the government faced huge indemnities resulting from a series of wars with the West and was in need of further funds to finance more wars against various invaders. The Qing Government was controlled by the royal family which was unwilling to borrow from its own citizens, so it relied almost exclusively on issuance of bonds abroad for financing. Collaterals for the foreign government bonds were mainly maritime customs initially and were finally extended to other government revenues: taxes on commodities like salt, alcohol and tobacco, internal provincial transfer taxes and revenues of the railways, for instance. In other words, the Qing Dynasty had lost almost all of its fiscal income before it collapsed.

After the fall of the Qing Dynasty in 1911, the Republic Government agreed to honor the previous government's foreign debt so as to gain the West's recognition of the new regime and it then continued to rely on foreign debts secured by fiscal revenue. However, as it was more difficult to raise debt overseas while the government was short of cash, the Republic Government also started to issue domestic government bonds. In 1914, a new agency, Internal Debts Bureau, was established to overlook the issuance of domestic public debts. Furthermore, the development of the domestic government bond market triggered some development in the domestic corporate bond market in China during that period of time.

The development of the domestic bond market of China afterward was not smooth. The domestic government bonds were insufficiently secured as foreign bondholders held senior claims to the same security. In addition, due to poor government financing and constant change of power in the country, the Republic Government was not able to establish its image as a trustworthy borrower. The government defaulted on its debts repeatedly and used its power to reset terms of the bond contracts for its own benefit, without consideration of the bondholders. Last but not least, real value of domestic government bondholders' investments decreased by 90 percent because of inflation in the 1940s and the subsequent issuance of a new currency under the "Currency Reform" in 1948 effectively wiped out most of the government's domestic debt at the expense of the bondholders.

Consequently, the domestic government bond market was hurt, which in turn damaged the whole image of the China bond market. The problem was intensified by the adverse development of the domestic corporate bond market. Given the unstable government and poor bond contract enforcement, corporate bondholders' interests were not adequately protected while returns for their investment were unjustifiably low. As a result, it further hurt the corporate bond financing's credibility and its long-term development in China.

Post–1949 and modern China's bond market

After the People's Republic of China (PRC) was established in 1949, there was almost no development in the bond market for three decades as the country's economy was under centralized planning and budget allocation. In the early years, few bonds except for treasury bonds were issued through administrative apportioning of incomes rather than voluntary investment, and there was no secondary market for the bonds which were issued as an alternative form of savings instead of investment. Further, the PRC government decided not to have any internal and external debts for about 20 years following the break-up of its relationship with the Soviet Union in the late 1950s. Needless to say, there was no development in the China bond market during that period.

In 1979, the PRC government launched the economic reforms and reopened the country's economy to foreign markets again. Development of modern China's bond market commenced at that point in time. As a tool to finance the economic reforms and to control inflation, government bonds were issued again. However, the bond issuances were still done through administrative apportioning and there was still no official secondary market for bond trading until 1988 when spot transactions among bank counters were approved in 61 cities around China.

Set out below are significant milestones for the development of the bond market in modern China during the last three decades:

Year	*Milestones*
1982	➢ The first issuance of international bonds in the international capital market (Japan) by China's financial institutions (China International Trust and Investment Corporation, i.e. CITIC).
1988	➢ Official establishment of China's secondary bond market upon approval of spot transactions among bank counters in 61 cities.
1991	➢ Introduction of repo in the treasury bond market. ➢ Listing of treasury bonds on the Shanghai Stock Exchange and among securities business counters of Shanghai. ➢ Pilot distribution of government securities via distribution syndicates (vs. administrative apportioning in the past).
1992	➢ Introduction of bond futures in China.
1993	➢ Launch of scripless issue pilot scheme.

(*Continued*)

Year	*Milestones*
1994	➢ Establishment of policy bank and initial issuance of policy bank financial bonds through administrative allocation.
1995	➢ Closure of bond futures market.
Late 1996/ 1997	➢ Establishment of Government Securities Depository Trust & Clearing Co. Ltd. (GSDTCC) to undertake the official responsibility of bond custody and settlement for China's interbank bond market. ➢ Establishment of interbank market.
2002	➢ Completion of issuance of fixed rate 30-year bonds.
2003	➢ Creation of China's first bond index (Chinabond Index) and yield curve (Chinabond yield curve) by GSDTCC. ➢ Initial issuance of USD bonds by China Development Bank in China. ➢ Initial issuance of commercial banks secondary bonds by Industrial Bank.
2005	➢ China's first introduction of Qualified Foreign Institutional Investor (QFII) into the interbank bond market by granting strategic QFII direct access rights to the market. ➢ Official commencement of bond forward transaction in the interbank bond market. ➢ Issuance of Panda bonds by approved foreign institutions (International Finance Corporation and Asian Development Bank) in China. ➢ First asset-backed securities (ABS) and mortgage-backed securities (MBS) were issued by China Development Bank and China Construction Bank, respectively.
2007	➢ Enforcement of new provisional rules governing the credit rating of fixed income securities and listed companies by China Securities Regulatory Commission (CSRC).

Source: Chinabond and the People's Bank of China

2.2. Present Chinese bond market overview

Market structure

The bond market started to emerge in China after the government resumed bond issuance in 1981 and the market experienced rapid growth through restructuring of the trades after 2005. At the current stage, the China bond market consists of three markets: the interbank bond market, the over-the-counter (OTC) market and the exchange market. Under the current structure, China Government Securities Depository Trust & Clearing Co. Ltd (CGSDTCC takes the responsibility of the General Custodian as China's central securities depository of the bond market. CGSDTCC is also a general depository for second-tiered bond depositories. Commercial banks and China Securities Depository and Clearing Co. Ltd (CSDCC) take the roles of second-tiered bond depository for the OTC market and the exchange market, respectively.

Until now, the interbank market is by far the most active and important one among the three bond markets. The interbank bond market provides a market for bond transactions and repurchases of institutional investors such as commercial banks, rural credit cooperatives, securities companies, insurance institutions and other financial institutions. Most book-entry Treasury bonds, policy financial bonds are listed and traded in this market. As of November 2011, RMB 19.8 trillion worth of bonds are traded in the interbank bond market which accounts for 94.6 percent of total bond market trading in China. Hence currently, bonds trades made by non-financial institutions and individuals through the OTC market and the exchange market account for only a very small proportion of the bond market in China.

Regulatory framework

The rules and regulations created obstacles in the development of the bond market. However, the Chinese government has introduced several new regulations and modifications to further develop the market in order to build a strong capital market.

China's bond market supervision and regulation is shared by several agencies that require cross-sector regulatory cooperation, joint consultations on decree promulgation and alignment of administrative guidelines. The People's Bank of China (PBoC), as the central bank of China, leads the monetary authority and supervises the interbank market and the OTC market. PBoC, together with associated government agencies, approves the sale of short-term corporate bills and commercial paper issued by securities companies. On the other hand, the China Securities Regulatory Commission (CSRC), the executive arm of the State Council Securities Commission, supervises the exchange market. In 2007, CSRC released new rules on listed firms' corporate debt issuance in order to support a major expansion in the corporate bonds sector. CSRC now takes charge of vetting issuances. The Ministry of Finance (MoF) undertakes the role of establishing and implementing strategies, policies and guidelines for public finance, together with scheduling of public borrowings. Together with the State Administration of Foreign Exchange (SAFE) that approves the Qualified Foreign Institutional Investor (QFII) investment limits, MoF also approves RMB bond offerings by foreign development institutions.

According to AsianBondsOnline, the PBoC announced that margin deposits such as payment for banker's acceptances, letters of guarantee and letters of credit would be included for the purpose of required reserves calculation. Large banks will be asked to set aside the reserves over three stages and small banks over six stages. The government estimates the increase in reserves to be the equivalent of a 50 bps–100 bps hike in the reserve requirement ratio.

Market overview

Market size

For the past 10 years, the market size has grown continuously and the value of outstanding local currency bonds in China reached RMB 20.7 trillion as of

September 2011. From 2002 to 2010, the average growth rate of bond issuance was 42 percent and the average growth rate of bonds outstanding was 33 percent, which is relatively huge (See figure 2.1). Compared to 2009, bond issuance increased 10 percent to RMB 9.1 trillion. Spot-trading volume increased 23.9 percent to RMB 6 trillion and repo trading volume increased 18 percent to RMB 8.6 trillion. The number of issues increased 24.8 percent to 1,167 compared to 2009, of which 847 were credit bonds (i.e. corporate bond, short-term financing bills and mid-term notes) amounting to 1,167 issuances.

Since the maturity of government bonds is long and there is a continuous increase in issuance, we think the deposit balance will continuously increase. For corporate bonds, even though the size is not yet large, this sector is showing steady growth in volume and thus we expect robust growth in the future. Moreover, the Chinese government is well aware that the capital market of China cannot grow further without a developed bond market. Therefore, the government is planning for growth in the corporate bonds sector with the necessary modifications in regulations and approval procedures.

Bond type

The total bond depository balance increased 4 percent (year-on-year) to RMB 21 trillion as of November 2011. This percentage resulted from an increase in various bond types. For government bonds such as Treasury bonds, savings bonds and local government bonds, the balance increased 11.9 percent to RMB 7.3 trillion, compared to a year before. For policy bank bonds, the balance increased 24.4 percent to RMB 6.4 trillion, and corporate bonds increased 15.2 percent to RMB 1.6 trillion. However, the bond balance for policy bank bonds including China Development Bank, Export-Import Bank of China and Agricultural Development

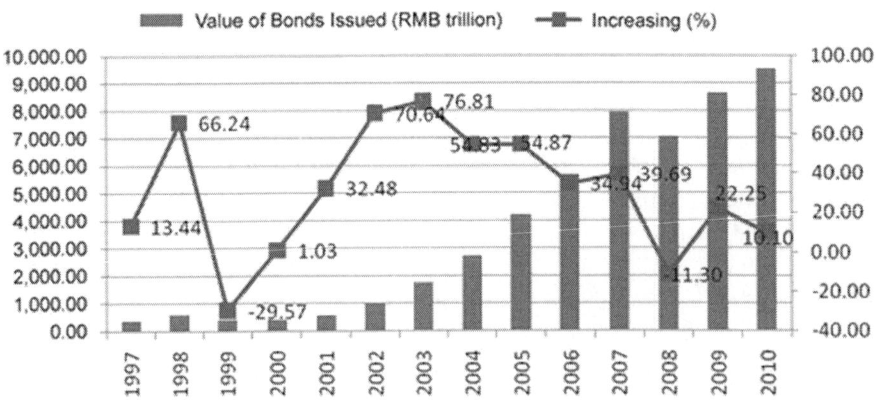

Figure 2.1 Bond issuance and the amount increasing between 1997 and 2010

Source: Chinabond.com.cn

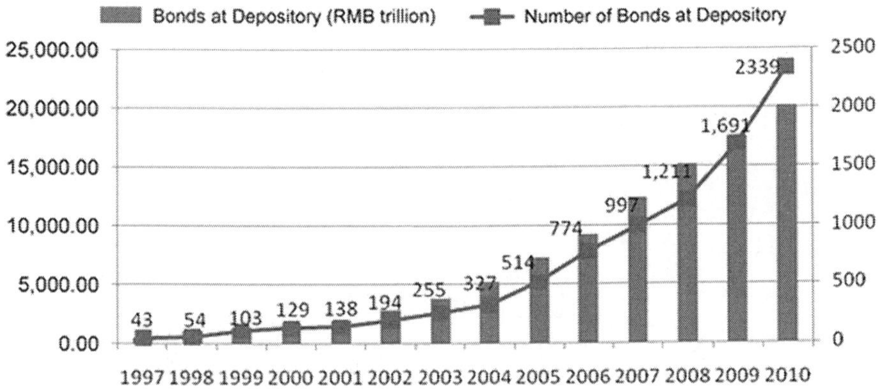

Figure 2.2 Bonds at depository between 1997 and 2010

Source: Chinabond.com.cn

Bank of China decreased 52 percent to RMB 6.5 trillion compared to 2009 (See figure 2.2).

2.3. Bond supply and demand

The Ministry of Finance and the PBoC are responsible for China's fiscal and monetary policy and the three policy banks – China Development Bank, Import-Export Bank, Agricultural Development Bank – play important roles in executing government economic policies. Total issuance in 2009 was RMB 8.6 trillion and by the end of 2009, the total amount of bonds outstanding (in the interbank and exchange markets) was RMB 17.8 trillion. Government bonds, central bank bills, financial bonds and non-financial corporate bonds represented 32.2 percent, 23.8 percent, 28.6 percent and 14.8 percent of the total market, respectively.

Segments of the bond market

There are three segments in the secondary bond market: the interbank bond market, the exchange market and the over-the-counter (OTC) market (See figure 2.3). The interbank bond market formed back in 1997 is the most important and active among the three. It is driven fundamentally through bid-ask quotes between two trading counterparties. This market relies on the National Inter-bank Funding Center and the Central T-bond Registration and Settlement Co Ltd and provides a platform for bond transactions. Most book-entry Treasury bonds and policy financial bonds are listed and traded in this market. The interbank market plays a key role in ensuring the economy's health, transmission of monetary policy and allocation of financial resources. This market promoted the development of

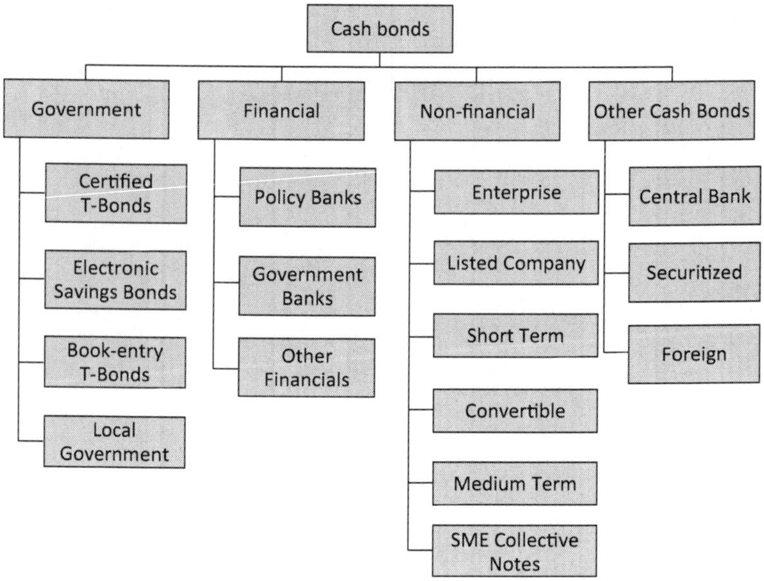

Figure 2.3 Bond types

direct financing and has reduced the economy's reliance on credit and has also facilitated market-based interest rate reform. As a result, China now has a bond yield curve that provides a benchmark for price-setting and price-quoting in the primary and secondary markets. The central bank conducts its open market operations directly in the interbank bond market and the development of this market will provide more scope for the central bank. Finally the most important play that the interbank bond market offers is that it allows companies to manage their liquidity, by providing a platform to adjust their excess reserves levels to better manage their risk.

On 27 April 2005, the PBoC announced the *Measures Governing the Issuance of Financial Bonds on the National Inter-bank Bond Market,* which went into effect as of 1 June 2005. This event signifies China's central bank's initiative to standardize the activities of issuing of financial bonds on the national interbank bond market. These measures are aimed at improving the market-based framework as well as the effectiveness of market regulation.

Government bonds

Government bonds are underwritten by the four stated-owned banks while other commercial banks and securities companies focus on financial and corporate bonds. Most of the bonds are held by banks, insurance companies, securities firms and corporations and the interest earned is tax exempt. There are two types of bonds: electronic savings bonds and book entry bonds. Electronic savings bonds are targeted at individual investors and funds are channeled directly into national expenditure. Book entry bonds make up the majority of the bond market and are targeted at the institutional investors. These bonds are mainly traded on the interbank and exchange markets. The majority of the Chinese government bonds are long-term, with maturities of about 7 to 10 years. In recent years, faced with increasing capital inflows and inadequate supply of Ministry of Finance bonds, the PBoC has conducted open market operations to "sterilize" the large capital inflows. In December 2008, the total outstanding amount of government bonds was RMB 4.875 trillion.

Central bank bonds

Central bank bonds are issued by the PBoC to members of the interbank bond market. They are typically short-term in nature, most having maturities from 3 months to 3 years. Over 77 percent of central bank bonds have maturities of less than 1 year and are the central bank's favorite tool for open market operations. Central bank bonds do not enjoy the same tax exemptions that Treasury bonds do but are of the same credit quality as Treasury bonds. This instrument has become one of the preferred instruments for liquidity management in money markets and institutions. Central bank bonds are the second-most actively traded bonds in the interbank market. They have become popular instruments for money market funds and other institutional investors for liquidity management. The rates on central bank bonds provide benchmark rates for the Chinese money market. The interest rate is set by MoF, and the rate is usually higher than the after-tax savings deposit interest rate, but lower than the rate of Treasury bonds. By the end of 2008, outstanding central bank bills had reached RMB 4.812 trillion, just shy of government bonds.

Financial bonds

Financial bonds are issued by commercial banks and non-banking financial institutions to raise mid- to long-term capital. Policy banks' bonds are the main type of financial bonds, having slightly higher liquidity than government bonds and representing about 24 percent of the market. Most policy banks' bonds have a short- to medium-term duration and are traded only on the interbank market. Issuance of policy and financial bonds must be approved by the State Council and PBoC and they issue bonds at much lower cost than commercial banks due to their bonds being sovereign debt. The three government-backed policy banks are China Development Bank, which focuses on national infrastructure funding and industry support, Export-Import Bank, which focuses on financing exports and imports of high-tech products and foreign construction contracts and investments and Agricultural Development Bank supporting agriculture and rural development. Funds raised via these bonds are usually used to finance key national projects not covered by the country's fiscal budget. Of the three policy banks, China Development Bank is the main issuer; it issued 25 bonds worth RMB 670 billion in 2009 alone.

In 2004, commercial banks that met certain qualifications were allowed to issue subordinate bonds. These bonds had durations of 10 to 15 years and were mainly created to improve capital adequacy. The amount of subordinated bonds that each bank can issue is capped at no more than 50 percent of its core capital.

In December 2005, after the commercial banks used up their subordinated bond quotas, the PBoC authorized issuance of hybrid capital bonds for improving capital account liquidity. These bonds have a maturity of 15 years. Hybrid bonds allow deferment of interest and principal repayments if certain conditions are met. Banks can issue hybrid bonds only to the extent of 100 percent of core capital. By the end of 2009, nine hybrid capital bonds had been issued, by China Minsheng Bank and Shenzhen Development Bank, China Industrial Bank and Huaxia Bank, with a total of RMB 18.8 billion outstanding.

Non-financial bonds

Currently, there are four types of non-financial corporations' bonds: enterprise bonds, convertible bonds, short-term corporate financing bills (CPs and MTNs) and listed company bonds. Enterprise bonds were the first type of corporate bonds issued in China and they are traded in both the interbank and exchange markets. They have lower coupon rates than company bonds as they are backed by the state-owned banks and have a 7- to 10-year maturity period. Insurance companies and commercial banks are the main holders of this type of bonds. Corporate CPs and MTNs are also traded on the interbank market and are issued by large corporations. These instruments have a much shorter application process and provide more flexibility for corporations to raise debt without the necessary bank guarantees. All corporate bond issuances have to be approved by the National Development Reform Commission (NDRC) and must be guaranteed. Furthermore, only firms of the highest credit rating have access to the corporate bond market. Convertible bonds on the other hand have a maturity of 5 years with coupon payments. Mutual funds, insurance companies, QFIIs and securities companies are the main buyers of such bonds. Given that the central bank owns many of the large industrial institutions, it is understandable that the central bank sets such restraints for corporate bonds. Even though state-owned enterprises (SOEs) can benefit from bond financing, there is always the risk that ownership of state-owned assets may pass on to foreign creditors, which is a threat to the central government. Until very recently, only firms with very sound financial conditions were granted access to the bond market, leaving companies that truly need the bonds out of scope. At the end of 2008, the size of CPs and MTNs reached RMB 420 billion and RMB 167 billion, respectively.

The *Administrative Rules for Short-term Financing Bills* were published 23 May 2005 and this stimulated the recent growth of the bond market. Short-term corporate bills are issued on the interbank market, which is regulated and supported by the People's Bank of China. These bills are restricted to companies with extremely good credit ratings and mature within 91 days.

Panda bonds

Panda bonds are China's local currency denominated foreign bonds issued by international agencies. In February 2005, the central bank permitted international development institutions to issue RMB-denominated bonds and this provided an alternative method (aside from QFII and QDII) to balance capital inflows and outflows. There are only four issues outstanding (total par value RMB 4 billion), which were issued by International Finance Corporation (IFC, 2005 and 2006) and Asian Development Bank (ADB, 2005 and 2009). This market in comparison to the other China bond instruments is very small. Investors are usually expected to hold Panda bonds until maturity as the market is rather illiquid. However, Panda bonds offer a new financing venue for overseas institutions and they can also help promote the RMB's position in the international financial market. This way, China's lenders can invest in overseas assets denominated in RMB.

Repo

There are three types of repos traded on the Shanghai Stock Exchange: new-style collateral repo, old-style collateral repo and buy-sell repo. By 2007, the interbank repo market had been extended to cover all aspects of the financial system. There are three main differences between the old and new repo. In a new repo, collateralized cash bonds are claimed and moved to a "collateral storehouse" by the repo sellers. New repo transactions are monitored and settled by security accounts rather than by securities firms. The new repo clearing system checks collateralized bonds and only approves transactions with sufficient collateral. Repo trading mainly occurs in the interbank market, similar to where the old collateral repo and buy-sell repo are traded. In 2000, the interbank repo market was opened to include securities firms, fund institutions, insurance firms and other financial institutions, which greatly improved the capital flow between commercial banks and non-banking financial institutions. Access was also extended to non-financial institutions in 2007 and they can now conduct repo transactions through their settlement agents.

QFII

Foreign investors can access the China bond market by obtaining Qualified Foreign Institutional Investor (QFII) quotas. Approved QFIIs can invest in government and corporate bonds and convertibles listed on the Shanghai and Shenzhen stock exchanges. In late 2002, China relaxed regulations on foreign investors investing in Treasury bonds and launched the Qualified Foreign Institutional Investor (QFII) program which allowed foreign capital to invest in the Chinese bond market. In 2005, the International Finance Corporation (IFC) and Asian Development Bank (ADB) were allowed to issue RMB-denominated bonds in China. As of 30 September 2009, there were 78 approved QFIIs with a total quota of USD 15.72 billion. According to the latest SAFE regulation announced in September 2009, the maximum accumulated investment quota for one single QFII is now USD 1billion.

Bond demand

Despite China overtaking Japan and becoming the world's second-biggest economy in early 2011, China's bond market lacks the scale and liquidity compared to countries that have a comparable economic size. Instead, the banking industry provides a majority of domestic credit to businesses, especially to state companies. Research has shown that China's bank lending was 140 percent of GDP while its bond market was only 0.7 percent of GDP in 2004. Its bond market was as small as India's. The limited assets and investors in China's bond market fail to attract investment from institutional investors. This further dampens retail investors' demand for bonds in spite of high household savings in China.

Bond market participants

Major investors in the China bond market include commercial banks, insurance companies, mutual funds, foreign commercial banks, securities firms, non-financing institutions and foreign financial institutions holding Qualified Foreign Institutional Investor (QFII) licenses. National commercial banks and city commercial banks are among the most active investors in spot trading and repo markets. National commercial banks and city commercial banks accounted for 36 percent and 26 percent of spot trades in 2009, respectively. In the repo market, they accounted for 46 percent and 19 percent of repo trading volume in 2009.

National commercial banks are also major holders of Treasury bonds. As of the end of November 2011, the Treasury bond market was approximately RMB 6.40 trillion. National commercial banks held over RMB 3.35 trillion worth of Treasury bonds. Special members, which include People's Bank of China, Ministry of Finance and policy banks, are the second-largest group of investors in Treasury bonds. They held a total of RMB 1.55 trillion worth of these bonds.

Insurance institutions and fund companies play only odd roles in China's bond market. Insurance institutions had an insignificant 1 percent share in the spot trading volume and 3 percent share in the repo trading volume in 2009. Fund companies accounted for 4 percent and 6 percent of spot trading volume and repo trading volume, respectively, in 2009.

The investor base of bonds in China is significantly different from that in the West, where major investors are fund managers such as pension funds. Banks are among the biggest underwriters and investors in corporate bonds. Many other investors are enthusiastic about purchasing bonds with yields higher than the bank deposit rate due to the limited number of investments available in China and overseas. Meanwhile, investors are relatively insensitive to the risk, and as a result, bonds issued by state-owned enterprises seem most issuance. In a market where defaults are rare to none, investors expect the government to bail out enterprises when they go bust.

Foreign investors in China's bond market

Foreign financial institutions have access to the bond market by way of approved QFII quotas. The total QFII quotas currently amount to about USD 20 billion, although a majority of the QFII quotas is invested in equities. In 2009, foreign banks accounted for only 8 percent of spot trading volume and 2 percent of repo trading volume. These foreign institutions can invest in government and corporate bonds and convertibles listed on the Shanghai and Shenzhen stock exchanges.

In 2005, strategic foreign institutional investors were allowed to invest in the interbank bond market, which is the most active in China, for the first time. The Pan-Asia Index Fund and the China Index Bond Fund of the Asian Bond Fund invested in bonds there. Since these strategic investors had a mature investment philosophy and advanced knowledge of bond market operations, their participation brought in more competition among institutional investors. However, the interbank bond market was still closed to a majority of foreign funds until 2010.

New participants in the interbank market

In August 2010, the People's Bank of China began allowing foreign financial institutions and RMB clearing banks in Hong Kong and Macau to participate in the interbank bond market. This policy was later expanded to foreign central banks and monetary authorities to invest their RMB holdings in the interbank bond market. Foreign banks need to first apply for investment quotas on the interbank market. Each bank also needs an account with a local lender for debt transactions clearing. Foreign central banks are required to disclose funding sources and investing plans in their applications when applying for this program. By 2 May 2011, the central bank had approved 20 foreign institutions to invest in the interbank bond market.

Foreign financial institutions approved to enter the interbank bond market include offshore branches of Chinese-funded commercial banks, foreign corporate banks and Hong Kong– and Macau-based branches of foreign banks. The central bank of the Republic of Austria and that of Malaysia are examples of central banks that have been approved to invest in the interbank bond market.

The main objective of this policy is to broaden the use of RMB and spur currency flows from abroad. Due to the increasing offshore RMB deposits, especially in Hong Kong, PBoC created this new channel for banks to invest directly in China. Meanwhile, it has indirectly encouraged bond investments and increased the liquidity in China's bond market. This was an important step to open the once-closed domestic bond market to foreign investors. Some had estimated that foreign institutions may have bought more than RMB 10 billion worth of bonds on the interbank bond market.

2.4. Impediments to and supports of China's bond market

Without a doubt, the Chinese bond market to date has been predominantly an outcome of government interventions. Despite a track record of three decades, its development is falling behind other Asian peers in both breadth and depth. After an unsuccessful experience in opening up the financial markets as a whole in the 1990s, the Chinese government opted for calculated measures to expand the debt market. However, this maneuver undeniably increased systemic risk of the already fragile financial system. Below are the five impediments that are hindering the growth of the bond market in China.

Impediment I: Bankruptcy laws

The Chinese Central Government must put in place stronger bankruptcy laws that protect the rights of senior debt holders and provide a mechanism that allows investors to seek compensation for damages. These laws will need to rely on strengthened financial disclosure regulations, in order to give comfort to investors that they have the ability to determine if losses on debt were caused by financial misrepresentation and seek damages.

The lack of strong bankruptcy protection is a major contributor to the high level of regulation in the bond market. The Company Law of 1994 is designed to protect investors of bonds as the bankruptcy process in the judicial system is incapable of addressing concerns of default resolution. The law restricts bond issuance to firms that meet solvency, revenue and capitalization criteria and have a net asset value of at least RMB 30 million. It also takes the decision of interest allocations away from managers by setting out the ratio of distributable profits to interest payments. The law stipulates guidelines on the purposes of corporate debt and includes criteria to invest in industries that comply with the policies of the state. Bonds also cannot be utilized to cover losses or non-productive expenditures, including those of R&D. Interest rates may not exceed the limit set by the State Council, limiting the competitiveness of bond issuance. Finally, the issuer must also comply with any other ad-hoc conditions that the State Council may impose on issuance of debt.

The Company Law of 1994 imposes major restrictions on yield and credit quality of bonds in the market, making it difficult to match bond issuances with the risk and return demands in the market. The regulatory bodies in China should consider relaxing these restrictions to allow smaller firms and those in weaker financial position to raise high yield debt. While this form of debt will be inherently more risky for investors, it will yield higher returns to investors. Additionally, the rates on this high yield debt will likely be lower than the prevailing rate on commercial loans being offered to non-SOE institutions, lowering the cost of borrowing for firms looking to expand.

Impediment II: Capital account convertibility for Panda bonds

The Chinese government, through its regulatory bodies, should work with the international community to encourage the issuance of debt in China via Panda bonds and bonds offered through subsidiaries of foreign companies. As the nation's currency is not current account convertible at this time and the expectations of convertibility in the next decade are low, many foreign companies are hesitant about issuing debt in China as they have very little recourse to withdraw funds from the country if required. As only one foreign subsidiary has been involved in a bond issuance, the Bank of Tokyo-Mitsubishi UFJ's 2010 issuance of 1 billion yuan of notes, we see that the issue of non-convertibility has hurt the development of the domestic bond market.

In September 2011, the PBoC, the Ministry of Finance, the National Development and Reform Commission and the CSRC made a joint announcement that

China would allow international organizations to send proceeds of RMB bond sales abroad to encourage bond market development. This initial experiment covered only debt issued by the World Bank and Asian Development Bank and allows them to convert proceeds into another currency with the approval of the State Administration of Foreign Exchange.

The experiment has laid the groundwork for regulations on the transfer of capital raised by bond issuance out of China, provided the debt is rated AA or above by at least two credit ratings firms, one of which must be registered in China to rate RMB-denominated bonds. This framework should be used to enact laws that assure multinationals with subsidiaries in China the confidence that they can reallocate funds raised in China outside of the country if required.

Impediment III: Limited private placements

CSRC regulations permitted in 2007 only listed companies the right to issue corporate bonds, giving them and a small number of major state-owned enterprises permits to issue bonds. This limits the corporate bond market to only companies trading on the Shanghai and Shenzhen exchanges to bring corporate debt to market. The government may experiment with allowing privately held companies (including joint-stock companies and partnership with unit shares) of suitable size to offer corporate bonds. This will in effect allow expanding companies an alternative to more expensive bank loans and allow them to obtain financing to grow prior to an IPO.

Impediment IV: Risk management products

The fixed income market in China should also begin to mimic some aspects of the Western markets in terms of products offered. For instance, different structures of bonds should be available based on the type of corporation that is issuing the bonds. This will allow for bonds and their rates and maturities to more accurately capture the funding needs of the issuing firm. Additionally, more developed derivatives products should be brought to the market to transfer risk of owning bonds to match risk return profiles. This would include the introduction of Credit Default Swaps (CDS) as a mechanism of limiting the exposure of investors to a particular issuer.

China again has the advantage of learning from the missteps of the Western financial markets in the context of these products and has an opportunity to build laws and market infrastructure for regulating these products before they become a risk to the system.

Impediment V: Domestic credit rating agencies

Last, the private sector must step up to develop credit rating agencies that can properly evaluate creditworthiness of debt issuers. Private companies, like Moody's and S&P, should be developed in China and independently rate the quality of debt. Currently, the PBoC has approved two national-level securities ratings agencies: China Chengxin Credit Management Co. and Dagong Global Credit Rating. There are also approximately 80 other rating institutions operating without approval, many of which are consulting or accounting firms that provide rating services. However, currently the ratings presented by both nationally sanctioned and independent companies lack the confidence of some investors. Learning from the mistakes of credit rating agencies in the West, the government can work to ensure stronger oversight of these agencies in order to ensure that ratings are not manipulated. The combination of these measures will bring down the high risk premiums investors in the fixed income market demand based upon factors that are not part of the issuer's creditworthiness.

Support from the central government

One objective of the 12th Five-Year Plan and the detailed economic development guidelines to be implemented by the Chinese government is to improve the ratio of direct financing. As indicated in the earlier part of this chapter, domestic credit (direct financing) still constitutes 56 percent of all financing activities in China. This indicates the effort of the central government towards continued financial reform, particularly targeting the domestic financial markets. Given that currently the national banking system is bulging with unreported bad debts, continued heavy reliance on bank loans could prove detrimental to the Chinese economy. Therefore, the central government is attempting to diversity sources of financing.

The detailed plan to achieve the target stated in the 12th Five-Year Plan was further reiterated by Premier Wen's work report, targeting the problems impeding bond market development. First, steps are to be undertaken to gradually unify not only bond trading currently dominated by the interbank market but also the multiple-regulators supervision system. Second, credit accountability is to be enhanced through enforcing disclosure requirements on bond issuers, and developing domestic credit rating agencies. Third, market-oriented innovation is to be promoted. In this respect, the recent relaxation of approval procedures for small and medium enterprises and increasing issuance of convertible bonds demonstrate the much-needed progress. Last but not least, regulators are committed to strengthen investor protection through implementation of a bond insurance mechanism and possibly adopting sinking fund provisions to better protect the interests of bond investors.

In March 2009, the central government endorsed the transformation of Shanghai into an international financial center by 2020. To achieve this ambition, the policy makers need to undertake aggressive strategies to be ready for inflow and outflow of capital. Regardless of whether Shanghai will become a global financial center within the specified timeframe, the bond market will be the first to benefit. The tearing down of the "Great Financial Wall" (RMB convertibility) means internationalization of the currency, which is planned for 2015. At the same time, legal and supervision infrastructures related to financial markets are expected to mature in the coming decade. Combining the former and the latter means easier access to surplus savings for issuers and fixed income investments for investors, leading to a more matured bond market through product diversification and liquidity.

Efforts by industry regulators

Aside from the planning by the central government and attention from the current administration, industry regulators are steering the bond market towards further growth, particularly in the corporate bond sector. The China Securities Regulatory Commission, in 2001, pledged to simplify issuance procedures for corporate bonds. On the other hand, the National Association of Financial Market Institutional Investors pledged efforts to aid small and medium enterprise in raising bond financing. Though currently a small segment of the overall market, short-term commercial paper, medium-term notes and SME pool bills are expected see the fastest growth as a result of these commitments. The NAFMII also plans to aid SMEs to issue high yield bonds, convertible bonds and asset-backed securities.

Structural changes in the investment landscape

Due to the ongoing shift towards a market economy, the rise of institutional investors such as pension funds is inevitable. Given the pension system reform, the three pillars of the pension system, state pensions, occupational pensions and private pensions, will increase their holdings of fixed income products. A report by University of Paris showed state pensions at the end of 2006 held almost half of their portfolios in bank deposits, with deficient returns. As the government shifts away from state pensions and dilution of investment mandates, pension asset managers would demand higher yield bond investments. The same report estimates that financing of retirement is expected to reach 5 percent of GDP by 2015.

Another structural change is the healthcare and social welfare reform. As the government starts rolling out nationwide health insurance coverage and payments to the underprivileged, institutional inventors and their roles in asset-liability management emerge. This could be another growth driver for the bond market, as fixed income products are utilized to manage future payments in matured bond markets.

The national savings rate and household savings rate are 46 percent of GDP and 24 percent of disposal income, respectively. This is much higher than most countries. Due to underdeveloped financial markets, these surplus savings could not be channeled into investments. Therefore, most is held in bank deposits, yielding less than 2.52 percent. Especially given the gyrations in equity market returns and inadequate personal retirement pensions, the savings rate is likely to remain high. The problem of a high savings rate is also amplified by lack of diversification in investment products, fixed income in particular.

References

Areddy, J.T. 2009. China wants Citigroup to expand. *The Wall Street Journal Asia*, 30 September, www.wsj.com

Asia Monitor. May. 2009. Rapid loan growth poses Significant risks to banking sector. *Asia Monitor: China & North East Asia*. www.asia-monitor.com

Cao, Belinda, Henry Sanderson and Kevin Hamlin. 2010, 17 August. Central bank opens interbank bond market to Hong Kong banks holding yuan. *Bloomberg News*. www.bloomberg.com/news/2010-08-17/central-bank-opens-interbank-bond-market-to-hong-kong-banks-holding-yuan.html

Chen, Andrew H., Sumon C. Mazumdar and Rahul Surana. 2011, September–October. China's corporate bond market development – security design implications of information asymmetry. *The Chinese Economy* 44 (5): 6–33.

Liu, Gigi and Ou-Yang, Hui and Zhang, Jessica, China bond market overview (June 15, 2010). *Quantitative Portfolio Strategies*, June 2010. Available at SSRN: http://ssrn.com/abstract=1633879 Heaton, Cris Sholto. 2011, 26 April. China's capital controls continue to keep foreign cash at bay. www.indexuniverse.eu/europe/features-a-news/7782-chinas-capital-controls-keep-foreign-cash-at-bay.html

Hui, Sui. 2011, September. Factors influencing the development of China's corporate bond market and relevant suggestions. *International Journal of Business and Management* 6 (9), p258

Huaipeng, M. (2006). The development of China's bond market. BIS Paper 26/Developing Corporate Bond Markets in Asia, 56–60.

12th Five-Year Plan, www.chinabond.com.cn

AsianBondsOnline (www.asianbondsonline.adb.org)

Bloomberg (www.bloomberg.com)

China Bond (www.chinabond.com.cn)

China Central Depository & Clearing Co., Ltd (www.chinabond.com.cn/d2s)

China Foreign Exchange Trade System (www.chinamoney.com.cn)

China Statistical Yearbook 2010 (www.chinabond.com.cn)

International Monetary Fund (www.imf.org)

National Audit Office of the People's Republic of China (www.cnao.gov.cn)

National Bureau of Statistics of China (www.stats.gov.cn)

The People's Bank of China (www.pbc.gov.cn/publish/html/kuangjia.htm?id=2012s18.htm)

World Bank (www.worldbank.org)

3 Analysis of China's stock markets

3.1. Development of China's equity markets

In September 2012, the famous hedge fund investor George Soros said, "the growth model that has been driving it (China) has been exhausted. They have to change."

This year is a watershed for China equity. China's new political leadership and government have adopted a lower growth rate target and listed companies recorded the worst earnings performance in the past 10 years; foreign and local investors have never been so bearish on Chinese equities. To understand the past and the future, we first investigate the history and system of Chinese equities in the mainland and overseas. Then we discuss the bubble and crisis of China's equity markets during 2007–2012. Finally, we will discuss the future of China's equity markets in a global context.

History and development of China's stock markets

The original stock market was shut down by Mao Zedong during the Cultural Revolution as capitalism was viewed as an idea of the West. In 1978, Deng Xiaoping launched the "open door" policy, the first cautious step towards free-market reform. Before an official exchange was established, securities were traded in the black market without any regulations and protection for investors. In early 1990s, China opened the Shanghai Stock Exchange (SSE) and the Shenzhen Stock Exchange (SZSE) and shut down many OTC markets in an effort to centralize market activity in the two exchanges. In 1992, the China Securities Regulatory Commission (CSRC) was formed in response to the 810 incident in Shenzhen when rioting broke out due to a lack of subscription forms and suspected corruption from the People's Bank of China (PBoC). In 1999, China promulgated securities laws to put the markets under more control in response to the Asian financial crisis. The markets boomed in the first few years of the 21st century until hit by the global financial crisis of 2008. As part of the stimulus package to keep the markets from going into recession, the Ministry of Finance cut the share trading stamp tax giving companies more equity.

With liberalization of the national economy, the securities market of China has developed rapidly in the last two decades. As of June 2012, market capitalization of SSE had already breached USD 2460 billion and SZSE had market capitalization of over USD 1106 billion. In terms of market capitalization, SSE ranked number 3 in Asia and number 7 in the world. SZSE ranked number 7 in Asia and number 15 in the world.

Stock types and some facts

In China, stocks are divided into two classes, A-shares and B-shares. A-shares are Renminbi-denominated shares of China-incorporated companies traded in SSE and SZSE (See Figure 3.1 and 3.2). It represents the largest class of Chinese shares; Qualified Foreign Institutional Investors (QFII) and Renminbi Qualified Foreign Institutional Investors (RQFII) are able to trade. B-shares on the other hand are quoted in US dollars on the SSE and HK dollars on the SZSE.

Prior to April 2005, China's stock markets had a two-tier share structure, non-tradable versus tradable shares. Only about one-third of the shares of listed companies were traded freely on the exchanges. The remaining two-third shares were those of state-owned enterprises and were kept off the markets. These shares were made non-tradable to let the government retain control of listed companies, lest they fall into the hands of private or foreign parties.

In Hong Kong, there are H-shares and Red chips. Both are denominated in HK dollars. H-shares are shares of China-incorporated companies that are traded on the Hong Kong Stock Exchange. Some A-share companies also have H-shares trading in Hong Kong. Red chips are mainland Chinese companies incorporated outside China and listed in Hong Kong. The actual business is based in mainland China and controlled by the central, provincial or municipal governments (See Figure 3.3).

Yearly Summary for 2012			
Yearly	*Total*	*A-share*	*B-share*
No. of listings	2,035	944	54
No. of New Listings	432	26	0
Issued Volume	946,409,437	244,470,419	1,359,240
Market Value	2,085,602,031	1,375,435,449	6,827,666
Tradable Volume	892,958,680	191,363,579	1,359,240
Market Value of Tradable Volume	1,859,956,454	1,150,132,848	6,827,666
Turnover in Volume	192,384,818.09	166,024,745.79	686,610.86

Figure 3.1 Shanghai Stock Exchange statistics

Source: Shanghai Stock Exchange

Statistics By Securities 2012-12-06

Securities	*Amounts*	*TradingValue*	*Trading Volume*	*Issue Capital*	*Market Value*	*Negotiable Capital*	*Negotiable Value*
Stocks	1582	44,363,468,282	5,174,382,165	721,955,033,739	6,255,482,000,506	525,171,432,364	4,149,757,275,107
A-share	472	21,210,809,666	2,773,781,770	405,455,469,699	2,911,843,117,826	338,193,837,319	2,375,373,541,310
B-share	54	140,575,912	29,567,770	16,238,743,331	79,781,987,320	16,118,681,959	79,126,143,849

Figure 3.2 Shenzhen Stock Exchange statistics

Source: Shenzhen Stock Exchange

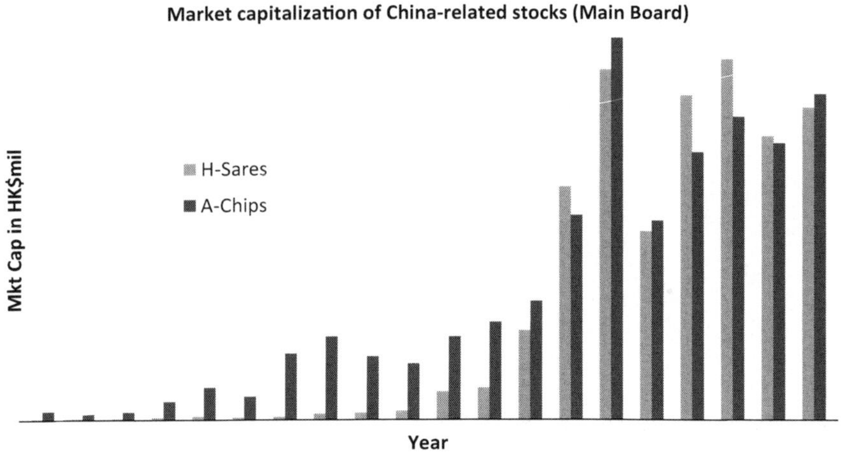

Figure 3.3 Hong Kong Stock Exchange statistics

Source: Hong Kong Stock Exchange

3.2. Market players in China's stock markets

There are mainly two types of market players in China's stock markets. Domestic individual retail investors and domestic institutional investors dominate the total market capitalization of China's stock exchanges. The reason is mainly related to the Qualified Domestic Institutional Investor (QDII) scheme. It is a scheme approved by the China Securities Regulatory Commission. It relates to the capital market set up to allow financial institutions to invest in offshore markets such as securities and bonds with limited investment quota. As of September 2012, USD 84.3 billion (only 3 percent of SSE market capitalization) of QDII quota was approved by the China State Administration of Foreign Exchange. With the limited QDII quota, domestic investors are strongly bound to investment opportunities in local markets instead of offshore markets.

Figures 3.4 and 3.5 below show the shares of total market capitalization and annual stock trading volume in 2010; over 99 percent of market capitalization and trading volume in China's stock markets are accounted for by the domestic investors. This is quite different from other emerging markets, as shown below.

China's investor behaviors

Investors in China's equity markets share some common features with investors from other locations. On the other hand, they have distinct behaviors which are different from other investors. In the following section, behavioral biases suffered by Chinese investors are discussed.

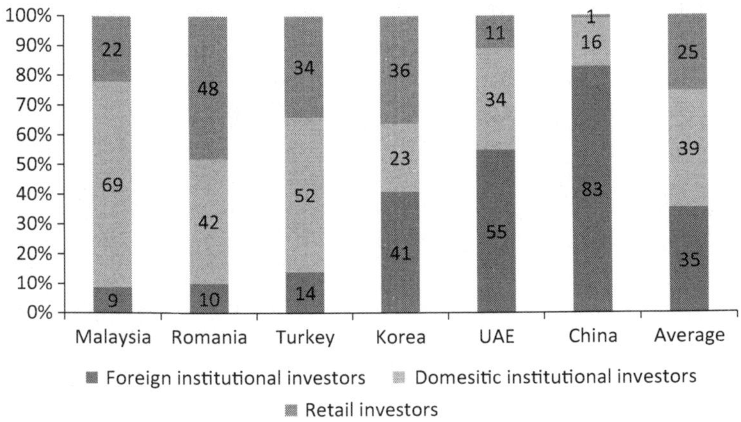

Figure 3.4 Share of total market capitalization in 2010

Source: IOSCO survey data

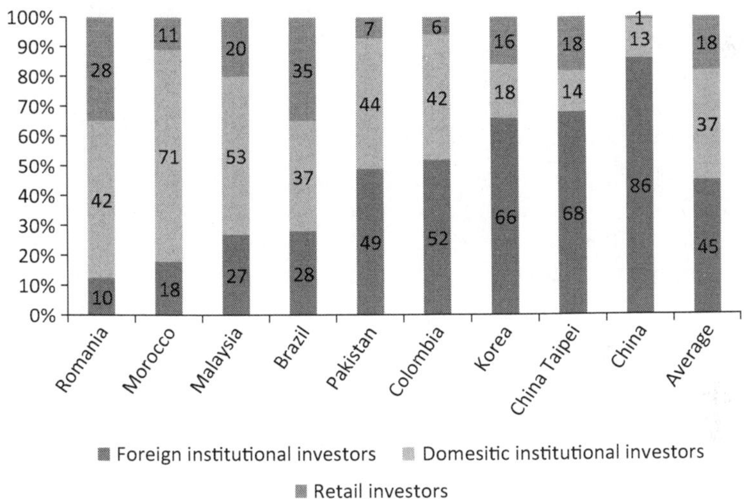

Figure 3.5 Share of annual stock trading volume in 2010

Source: IOSCO survey data

Overconfidence

Overconfident investors feel certain about their knowledge and investment skills. Odean (1998a) says this overconfidence causes them to trade too much and hold under-diversified portfolios. Chinese investors own few stocks in general. Chen, Kim, Nofsinger and Rui (2004) found that mainland China investors hold stocks of only 2.6 different companies on average. In comparison, US individual investors hold an average of 4 stocks. Chinese investors hold under-diversified portfolios compared to other investors.

Besides, Chinese investors appear to trade frequently. Mean monthly turnover of Chinese investors is 27.3 percent whereas monthly turnover of US investors is 7.59 percent. Chinese investors trade at a rate about four times higher than US investors. They underestimate the associated risks of under-diversifying and active stock investing. Many Chinese investors blindly chase high prices without gathering much financial information about the companies. They trade more aggressively after market gains. Overconfidence is more obvious in the Chinese stock market with short-selling constraints.

Disposition effect

Disposition effect refers to the likelihood of investors selling stocks when prices increase, while keeping stocks that have dropped in value. Chinese investors are inclined towards the disposition effect. They are more likely to realize gains than losses. Chen et al. (2005) reported that the Proportion of Gains Realized (PGR) of Chinese investors is 0.519. It is larger than the Proportion of Losses Realized (PLR), which is 0.310. Odean's (1998b) results for US investors show PGR of 0.148 and PLR of 0.098. Comparing both results, disposition ratios are higher for Chinese investors than US investors.

Dual listing between China's and Hong Kong's stock markets

With the geographical advantages and the direct investment in Guangdong Province, Hong Kong has established close linkages with China's economy for a long time, especially after the sovereignty handover. With the strong economic ties, interrelations between stock markets in Hong Kong and in China are getting more visible and are strengthening.

Since June 1993, the Hong Kong Stock Exchange has accepted listings of Chinese companies after regulatory bodies of China and Hong Kong signed the Chinese-Hong Kong Memorandum of Regulatory Cooperation. The first listing of an H-share stock in Hong Kong was Tsingtao Brewery Co Ltd (0168.HK) on 15 July 1993. By the end of November 2012, there were 172 H-share stocks listed in the Hong Kong Stock Exchange, accounting for about 28 percent of total market capitalization and about 41 percent of total market turnover in the Hong Kong Stock Exchange. Among the 172 H-share stocks, 78 stocks are listed in both China and Hong Kong stock markets, while the rest of the stocks are listed in Hong Kong only.

The advantages of dual listing are as follows. First, it allows unrestricted access to capital to Chinese companies. Domestic retail investors dominate the total market capitalization in China's stock markets. With listing as an H-share, it provides a platform for global investors to participate and insert capital in Chinese companies. The wider investor base allows risk sharing among investors and lowers cost of capital. Besides, stocks listed in Hong Kong require strict disclosure requirements and regulations compared with rules in China. This provides more protection to global investors and limits the use of private benefits associated with concentrated ownership in Chinese companies. This results in lower cost of capital and thus higher stock return.

Updated: 30/11/2012

Main Board

Year-end	*H shares*	
	Market capitalization *(HK$mil)*	*% of market*
1993	18,228.70	0.61%
1934	19,981.32	0.96%
1995	16,463.77	0.70%
1996	31,530.63	0.91%
1997	48,622.01	1.52%
1998	33,532.66	1.26%
1999	41,888.78	0.89%
2000	85,139.58	1.78%
2001	99,813.09	2.57%
2002	129,248.37	3.63%
2003	403,116.50	7.36%
2004	455,151.75	6.87%
2005	1,280,495.01	15.78%
2006	3,363,788.46	25.39%
2007	5,056,820.09	24.62%
2008	2,720,188.76	26.53%
2009	4,686,418.75	26.37%
2010	5,210,324.73	24.88%
2011	4,096,659.80	23.47%
2012*	4,516,176.08	21.54%

GEM

Year-end	*H shares*	
	Market *(HK$mil)*	*% of market*
1999		
2000		1.47%
2001		3.10%
2002		4.58%
2003		7.21%
2004		9.56%
2005		9.64%
2006		16.82%
2007		14.09%
2008		25.57%
2009		25.76%
2010		14.97%
2011		5.45%
2012*		6.54%

(Continued)

Updated: 30/11/2012

Main Board

Year	*H shares*	
	Turnover	*% of*
	(HK$mil)	*equity turnover*
1993	33,037.82	3.01%
1994	34,208.97	3.32%
1995	17,291.65	2.27%
1996	24,890.36	1.93%
1997	297,769.58	8.48%
1998	73,538.68	4.61%
1999	102,788.51	5.80%
2000	164,309.62	5.74%
2001	245,201.03	13.47%
2002	139,711.41	9.50%
2003	501,496.87	22.12%
2004	933,860.83	27.49%
2005	949,155.23	26.46%
2006	2,521,764.08	39.26%
2007	7,748,899.57	46.93%
2008	6,130,592.75	48.53%
2009	5,152,805.63	44.56%
2010	4,700,842.42	38.29%
2011	4,662,787.32	38.84%
2012*	3,342,703.30	38.72%

GEM

Year	*H shares*	
	Turnover	*% of*
	(HK$mil)	*equity turnover*
1999		
2000	6,868.59	8.15%
2001	6,155.01	15.62%
2002	3,897.80	8.86%
2003	4,652.71	12.20%
2004	7,195.46	27.93%
2005	4,154.00	18.60%
2006	14,860.02	34.02%
2007	23,632.65	14.84%
2008	7,861.73	15.09%
2009	15,501.38	20.46%
2010	16,933.86	12.67%
2011	4,072.46	6.47%
2012*	704.88	2.33%

Source: Hong Kong Stock Exchange. hkex.com.hk

Spread between prices of A-shares and H-shares

With the efficient-market hypothesis, assuming both markets are strongly efficient, values of dual-listed stocks should be indifferent in the two markets. However, it's known that there are pricing differences between A-shares in China and H-shares in Hong Kong, with A-shares of the same company trading at prices higher than its H-shares.

Below is a graph of Hang Seng China AH Premium Index from 1 March 2006 to 6 December 2012. Hang Seng China AH Premium Index (with Base = 100) tracks the price difference between A-shares and H-shares. The higher the index, the higher is the premium on A-shares over H-shares, and vice versa. The graph below shows that A-shares were mostly traded at a premium over H-shares, which was especially significant for years 2007 and 2008. Recently, prices of A-shares and H-shares are converging to the base level. We will further discuss its impacts on valuation in Section 3.4.

Factors of A–H spread

Limited investment opportunities

One of the reasons is higher trading volume for A-shares in China. A-share is the dominant investment instrument in Chinese stock market, whereas H-share is one of the various investment instruments for global investors. The A-share market is more speculative than the H-share market. A-shares investors are more willing to take risk with the same level of expected return. The Chinese stock market is an emerging market and its country risk is higher than the Hong Kong market's. Hence, prices of A-shares are usually higher than prices of H-shares.

Restricted short-selling policies

With restraints on short-selling for all stocks in China's stock markets until March 2010, prices of A-shares tended to have an upward bias due to the reflection of opinions of optimistic investors only. On the other hand, short-selling has been quite prevalent in the Hong Kong Stock Exchange. That's why the A/H spread existed. Recently, the China Securities Regulatory Commission (CSRC) relaxed short-selling in A-shares markets allowing investors to sell short the index stocks of the Shanghai Stock Exchange and the Shenzhen Stock Exchange. Relaxation of short-selling is likely to reduce the stock overvaluation and lead to convergence of prices of A-shares and H-shares.

3.3. China's bubbles in the past 20 years

One glance at the chart of the Shanghai Index over the past 20 years shows a roller coaster. The index peaked at the end of 2007 and slumped from 2007 onwards. However, if we look back carefully, there were difference phases of ups and downs in China's equity markets. Some investors may call these boom and bust cycles or bull and bear markets; however, Walter and Howie (2003) concluded that "a better description would be to say that China doesn't have bull markets, only bubble markets." This chapter discusses the history of bubbles in China's equity markets and its recent development, which brings out the driving factors and problems of China's equity markets.

The 10 early years

After the Shanghai Stock Exchange was founded, the Shanghai Index started trading at 99.98 in 1990, on 19 December. In the following six trading days, it jumped 30 percent. After Deng Xiaoping's visit to South China in February 1992, retail investors started to rush into stock markets. On 21 May 1992, the Shanghai Index jumped 105 percent in one single trading day after all trading limits were lifted from the Shanghai exchange. The market crashed in the next 6 months. It was the early development stage of A-shares, market liquidity was thin and the trading system was immature. The bubble with high market volatility was clearly driven by government policy and retail investors' liquidity.

In mid-1995, due to high corporate profits and the government's clear signals on curbing inflation and a significant rate cut, China's A-shares experienced another bull run. Walter and Howie (2003) claimed this period clearly reflected manipulations of stock trading in the market; Shenzhen Development Bank (SDB) was the best illustration as its share price jumped 177 percent in five months.

China's Internet bubble 1999–2001

Although China's A-share market was almost a closed market due to controls on foreign capital, it followed global markets between 1999 and 2001 during the tech bubble. In 2000, more and more institutional investors entered the market and many companies with the "new economy" concept were listed in the US, such as Sohu (April 2000), Netease (June 2000) and Sina (July 2000). China's equity markets were full of excitement and were fuelled by these tech companies.

The big bear 2001–2005

After the Shanghai Index reached its peak in 1999, China's government attempted to liquidate 10 percent of equities of state-owned companies to meet pension obligations. The market was in a panic again and A-shares went into a bear market for four years, until 2005.

During this big bear market, the government implemented endless failed policies to encourage investors and NSSF and the state-owned insurance company pumped money to support the market but all these actions ended in failure. Wentao (2007) suggested this wild bubble and bear market is an important time for China's equity market, as authorities are more likely to find the appropriate methods to solve the problems.

The biggest bubble and bear market

After a four-year-long bear phase, the China Securities Regulatory Commission (CSRC) announced a company reform which is called Guquanfenzhi reform (股權分置改革), in April 2005. The reform received negative response at the beginning. In September 2005, CSRC, State-owned Assets Supervision and Administration Commission (SASAC), Ministry of Finance (MoF) and Ministry of Commerce (MoC) and People's Bank of China (PBoC) announced jointly the reform framework and details. Different from the previous reform in 2001, the government tried to ease market concerns over possible share declines due to market expansion and holders of non-tradable shares promised not to sell their shares in the secondary market for a certain period of time. After the significant policy, market sentiment improved and mainland retail and institutional investors started to pump money in equity markets.

It is worth noting that during this recent market bubble, there were several important factors. First, Chinese equities attracted global liquidity after PBoC allowed RMB appreciation in 2005. CSRC allowed foreign investors to participate in A-shares through Qualified Foreign Institutional Investors (QFII) quota in 2002, but foreign investors did not feel enthusiastic about Chinese equity markets until RMB appreciation. Second, the wild speculation reflected China's high savings rate and lack of investment channels. Zeng and Wan (2008) agreed that the government's measures for cooling down the housing market pushed funds to flow into the equity market. Third, IPOs of many well-reputed state-owned enterprises attracted investors, such as Ping An Insurance (2006), China Life (2006), China Bank (2006) and PetroChina (2007).

As rampant speculation created another bubble, SCRC stopped new mutual fund issuance, MoF raised the stamp tax, PBoC raised the interest rate six times and required a reserve ratio of 10 times. After PetroChina's A-share IPO was listed, the Shanghai Index reached 6,092 in October 2007 and its P/E multiple exceeded 60, it reached the peak and entered another bear market.

Echo of A-share: China's bubbles in Hong Kong

Although the Hong Kong stock market provides a better regulatory framework and more sophisticated institutional investors participate in this market, there have been a few bubbles which echo A-shares speculation.

Red chips gambling

With the background of the housing bubble and equity market speculation in Hong Kong in 1997, one key feature was red chips speculation. It was significant as it was the first China story and equity speculation in an offshore market. Before Hong Kong's handover to China, a lot of investors expected China's economy to boom and thought Hong Kong would continue to flourish after coming under Chinese rule. In addition, some foreign investors argued that investing in red chips constituted exposure to China's free market reform. As most red chips were window companies of Chinese local governments, investors expected asset injections from the central government. During 1996–1997, there were many red chips listed in Hong Kong. The local demand had created excess liquidity and most IPOs were 300 to 400 times oversubscribed. The most extreme case was Beijing Enterprise, whose IPO was 1,200 times oversubscribed. However, the red chips bubble ended with the Asian crisis in August 1997.

China bubble 2006–2007

During 2006–2007, it was another bull market for global equities. With the high economic growth and consumption and the demand for resources, China's GDP growth rate was 12.7 percent and 14.2 percent in 2006 and 2007, respectively. Meanwhile, the State Council approved many state-owned enterprises listing in the Hong Kong Stock Exchange. As a result, China's equity bubble in Hong Kong shared many common features like the red chip mania 10 years ago, such as IPO oversubscription. Chinese equities attracted global liquidity to Hong Kong and the Hong Kong China Enterprise Index (HKCEI) jumped 94 percent and 56 percent in 2006 and 2007, respectively.

If we look back in history, this speculation of Chinese equities in Hong Kong shared a similar path with A-shares. We want to point out that the interaction of A- and H-shares in this period was particularly strong, as evident from IPOs and liquidity. The IPO boom in Hong Kong attracted retail and institutional investors locally and internationally.

In the second half of 2006, many large-sized H-shares had a dual listing of A-shares in the Shanghai Stock Exchange because of the Chinese government's intention to expand and reform the stock market. These IPOs of A-shares boosted H-share prices. Second, since the QFII quota for foreign investors was limited in 2006, Chinese companies' shares listed in Hong Kong provided an avenue for investment, i.e. a substitute to A-shares.

Anti-China climate 2011–2012

China's equity markets have been concerned about corporate governance but most investors pay attention to growth and profits rather than the governance. However, while China's economic growth slowed down in 2011, one research company, Muddy Water Research, published a report that accused Sino Forest, a Chinese company listed in Canada, of being a Ponzi scheme. It marked the beginning of an anti-China climate in the following months. Trading in shares of many small capital Chinese companies was suspended by US SFC and most of them were delisted at the end. In Hong Kong, many P chips were sold off by investors as they had lost confidence. One significant report was the Red Flag report published by Moody's in July 2011. Moody's particularly pointed out the weak governance, high risk growth model and weak quality of auditing and financial reporting.

As a result of the IPO boom in Hong Kong, China P chips accounted for 27.5 percent of market capitalization in April 2012. Following the anti-China climate in 2010, China P chips auditing and accounting fraud became another concern in 2012. Auditors' resignation and corporate governance reports brought another confidence crisis to Chinese companies listed in Hong Kong. Until April 2012, trading of shares of seven P chips had been suspended in Hong Kong and three of them involved accounting frauds.

What do these bubbles tell?

The past 20 years' history of China's equity markets, the ups and downs, bubbles and bear markets, offer many lessons for investors. First of all, it is all about politics. Government policies have impacts on investors' sentiment and confidence. Second, the basic market liquidity comes from local investors. An important cycle was during 2006–2007, when the government implemented the Guquanfenzhi reform and encouraged large-sized stated-owned enterprises to list their shares and local investors poured their money into equity markets due to the negative savings rate and housing austerity policies.

Third, we note that the Hong Kong equity market is playing an important in the China equity story. From red chip bubbles to P chips scandals, these bubbles were associated with the boom of IPOs by Chinese companies. There were some lessons for foreign investors to pay more attention to Chinese companies' governance, credit ratings and fundamentals rather than merely a beautiful growth story.

Fourth, we would like to point out that Chinese equities performance has been influenced by external factors also. The "new economy" concept in 2001 reflected the tech bubbles globally. Another significant factor in these two years was that while foreign investors worried about the hard landing of the Chinese economy and China's government adopted a slower growth target in 2012, some hedge funds attempted to short China's equities because of their bearish views. As a result Chinese equities lagged behind global markets, particularly the A-shares market.

Finally, since the bull market in 2006, A- and H-shares interaction has become an important factor to both markets. For institutional investors considerations, A/H premium or discount has also become a factor in valuation considerations.

3.4. Outlook of equity market in China – the new era

Change of leadership

On 15 November 2012, China concluded the First Plenum of the 18th Communist Party Congress and announced the new leaders of the Party. Xi Jinping was confirmed as the General Secretary of the Party, and the seven-member Politburo Standing Committee consists of Xi Jinping, Li Keqiang, Zhang Dejiang, Yu Zhengsheng, Liu Yunshan, Wang Qishan and Zhang Gaoli.

While the line-up of the new leadership presented little surprise, it is noteworthy that in addition to becoming the Party chief, Xi Jinping was also elected as the Chairman of the Party's Military Committee. This is in stark contrast to the past where both Deng Xiaoping and Jiang Zemin continued to hold the Military Committee chairmanship for a few years after they had retired from the position of General Secretary and from the Party's Politburo Standing Committee. This development is said to indicate a more clear-cut and smooth transition than in the past. With the dual appointments, it is believed that the Party's collective leadership will be able to achieve consensus more effectively and Xi Jinping will have the strong backing to immediately exercise his stewardship over internal policy debates.

The new leadership we believe will continue the path of reform and opening-up, which has been the country's central policy for the past 30 years. Such a sense of continuity is backed by the fact that these top officials have already played a large role in setting policy in recent years. Xi Jinping is the son of Xi Zhongxun, a former Politburo member and vice premier who was one of the architects of China's Special Economic Zones (one of the symbols of China's opening-up policy) in the early 1980s. For the past five years, Xi has been Hu Jintao's understudy as China's Vice President, Vice Chairman of the Central Military Committee and a member of the Politburo Standing Committee. Li Kaiqiang was confirmed as Premier in March 2013. For the past five years he has been Wen Jiabao's deputy as Vice Premier and member of the Politburo.

It is also expected that the reform policy is to be fine-tuned and carried out with a greater sense of urgency, in light of the many structural issues in the country's economic and social systems that have built up after decades of strong economic growth. The composition of the Politburo includes a good mix of those with "elitist" background as well as those with "populist" emphasis. It is broadly believed that the new leadership would continue the consensus-based management style typical of recent decades, to formulate policies that pay balanced attention to the economic growth as well as the well-being of vulnerable social groups.

So how should investors assess the changes that the new leadership is envisioning? In the speech at the First Plenum of the 18th Congress, President Xi Jinping pointed out:

> Our Party's responsibility is to unite all the people in the country, free up the minds, carry out reform and opening up, keep on improving social productivity, be steadfast in efforts to create wealth and well-being for all the people.
>
> Our Party needs to stand up to many challenges and pressing issues, especially the issues of corruption, isolation from the people, bureaucratism and formalism. We need to stay alert and assiduously combat these problems.
>
> We need to shoulder the responsibility for the nation . . . for the people . . . for the party.

The above statements send a strong message from top leadership that development and prosperity for all the people is of vital importance to the Party's legitimacy. The new leadership acknowledges the pressing urgency for strengthening the rule of law, which is the foundation for further economic reform and even political reform. President Xi Jinping's speech also emphasizes improving social welfare as a top focus for the new leadership, including education, jobs, income, social safety net, healthcare and housing, etc.

Therefore, it is expected that the new leaders are likely to focus more on quality than the pace of economic growth in coming years. During the 18th National Congress of CPC (8–14, Nov. 2012), Hu Jintao pointed out that the country aims to double GDP and household income by 2020, which translates into around 7 percent annual growth. Such a growth target might disappoint certain investors anticipating more aggressive economic stimulus but it may not necessarily be bad for the equity market. It is noted that the offshore China equity index MSCI China has barely kept up with S&P 500 index over the past three years; it has underperformed significantly over the past four years. Why is it the case? Despite the fact that China's GDP growth has been substantially faster than that of the US, overall earnings growth of Chinese public companies has lagged behind their US counterparts. China has recognized the drawbacks of previous aggressive stimulus plans that have caused a build-up of excess inventory and production capacity in the economy, besides creating the widening income divide as well as housing bubble pressure. Therefore, a less aggressive growth target, but a more balanced and sustainable growth model should benefit the Chinese equity market.

Obviously, it will be a priority for the new leadership to introduce a series of economic reforms designed to address the imbalances in China's economic structure. Some of the priority items should include land reforms, the Hukou reform (resident permit system), banking sector liberation, RMB internationalization, income distribution and accelerated development of the social welfare system. It is also expected that the new leadership will articulate more specific mid- to long-range macro policy targets and reform agenda in the coming 12 months to reflect the spirit of President Xi Jinping's speech as mentioned above. These events should shed light on the economic growth trajectory and structural investment opportunities for global investors.

Economic data of China

The Chinese equity market has slowed from the first quarter of 2012 due to the concern of the "hard landing" of China's economy. In the first half of 2012, various economic indicators were not doing good, resulting in lowering of the benchmark rate twice by the People's Bank of China in June.

However, the pessimistic sentiment was gradually faded out during the 3rd Quarter. China's fixed assets investment and retail sales bottomed out in Q3.

Also, the HSBC China Manufacturing PMI (Purchasing Managers' Index) has emerged from its bottom and stayed above 50 since October. A reading above 50 means the manufacturing industry is expanding in that period. See the graph below for the recent trend of China HSBC Manufacturing PMI.

The year-to-year growth of industrial production is on an improving trend. The 10.1 percent year-to-year growth in November has been the first double-digit growth numbers in six months.

With the updated number of CPI staying at 2 percent, it is commonly deemed that China's economy has soft-landed while the GDP in Q3 was reported to be 7.4 percent which met the market's expectation.

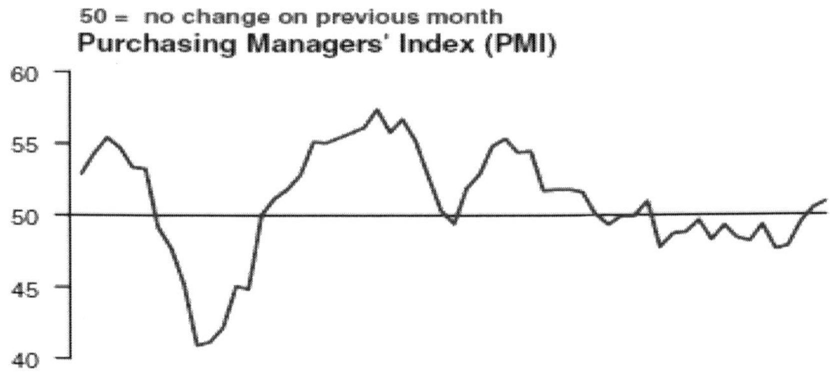

Source: HSBC

External economic outlook

Monetary-easing environment

US Federal Reserve announced the QE3 program in September 2012. The QE3 buying USD 40 billion mortgage-backed securities and the newly announced USD 45 billion monthly purchase of long-term Federal Debt securities will continue to increase the money supply and keep a low-rate environment in the US in order to boost its economic recovery. Together with the US, Japan and UK are undergoing an asset purchase plan which would also increase money supply in turn. Hot money has been created and it is moving around looking for higher yield. Asian markets including China benefit by capital inflow as the economies' growth in the region is generally more promising.

Key risk: Europe

Long-Term Refinancing Operation and Outright Monetary Transactions carried out by the European Central Bank have massively brought down the systemic risk of Europe. However, it is expected that the European debt crisis cannot be resolved in the short run. Therefore, any unpredicted events and changes in Europe, especially political issues, may lead to lower risk appetite. Emerging equity markets like China need a "risk-on" investment sentiment to support their rally. For China markets, the European debt crisis is still a key external factor that jeopardizes the upside of the stock market.

Valuation outlook

China A-shares are now having a record low valuation of less than 10 times forward P/E ratio. As the growth rate of the economy has stabilized and may regain strength, A-shares are said to have bottomed out. In fact, the Shanghai composite index is now at the level of one-third of the all-time high. See the graphs below.

The A/H premium has become an important factor in valuation of Chinese equities in both A and H-shares markets. The premium that investors allow A-shares over H-shares has narrowed since 2007, which mostly reflects that A-shares have underperformed compared to H-shares during the past five years. However, as both Hong Kong and mainland market liquidity are driven by different participants, A/H share prices converging also reflects that mainland local investors are bearish on equity while foreign investors are still holding and buying large state-owned enterprises stocks. A-shares in some sectors are being discounted to H-shares lately, meaning the A-shares are cheaper nowadays. These sectors are financial and infrastructure companies. Some market analysts argue that such A-shares are discounted due to foreign liquidity of QE3 buying China equity in the Hong Kong market. As a result, A-shares have become cheaper as some investors consider the price of the same company in two different markets.

3.5. IPOs in China

3.5.1. IPOs in China in a nutshell

Average return on China's IPOs is outstanding compared to other countries

Data on IPO performance in different countries, compiled by Professor Jay R. Ritter, highlights the unusually high firs-day returns in mainland China. With an average underpricing of 137 percent vs. only 16.2 percent in the United Kingdom or 16.8 percent in the United States (Ritter 2010), IPOs in China are outstanding. China's IPO underpricing appears extremely high even when compared to other emerging economies, such as Indonesia (26.3 percent), South Africa (32.7 percent) and Brazil (34.4 percent). It is interesting to note that the extreme underpricing only affects A-shares traded on mainland exchanges. Chinese companies listing B-shares, H-shares and N-shares do not experience such drastic underpricing. Traditional IPO underpricing theories which focus on information asymmetry and effects of reputation of the underwriting banks cannot really explain the degree of underpricing seen in the Chinese mainland markets.

Review of China's IPO financials shows high average across the board

The average P/E ratio of IPOs between 2006 and October 2011 was 61 with a high of 82 in 2007 and a low of 46 in 2011. The average abnormal initial return is 86 percent with 185 percent as a high and 22 percent as a low. During the same period, the market average return is 33 percent with 127 percent as high in 2006 and -65 percent as low in 2008; P/E as well as index returns show high volatility (See Table 3.1).

Both the P/E ratio and IAR (Initial Abnormal Return) for IPOs in 2007 were higher than in other years, whereas the bubble size represents the IPO volume. In 2006, 2008 and 2011, P/E levels are very close to each other and ranged from 45 to 50. In addition, the bubble size represents the IPO volume.

In addition China's IPO volume was about three times the volume of the US and if we include the Hong Kong market, Greater China's IPO volume was about 3.6 times the US. China's influence in the global capital market is therefore much bigger than it first appears. We also took the IPO volume as an index of new company formation and privatizations in one country to show China's position in the global capital market. The unprecedented scale of China's IPOs definitely implied the global corporate landscape is changing and will probably never be the same again.

China's IPO abnormal initial return decreased since 2007

From 2006 to 2011, China's stock market demonstrated a much more volatile behavior than before. Based on public information, the yearly volatility of Shanghai and Shenzhen stock markets was 44.76 percent and 47.50 percent, respectively. Most of the time IPO Abnormal Initial Return is much higher than index return while volatility is lower. This makes IPOs an attractive investment opportunity and often preferable to just buying market indexes. In 2007, IPO AIR was almost twice the market return. For 2008, 2010 and the first 10 months of 2011, the market returns were negative 65 percent, 13 percent and 16 percent, respectively, while the IPO AIR were positive 115 percent, 42 percent and 22 percent. In the year 2009, the two returns are almost of the same level. Altogether the graph clearly shows two things: First, IPO AIR is in most years higher than the index return. Second, IPO AIR decreased since 2007 dramatically from 185 in 2007 to 22 in 2011.

Table 3.1 IPO data from 2006 to 2011

Year	*IPO P/E*	*IPO Abnormal Initial Return %*	*IPO Volume Billion USD*	*Index Return %*
2006	49	78	26	127
2007	82	185	72	94
2008	49	115	17	–65
2009	72	74	33	74
2010	68	42	79	–13
2011	46	22	41	–16
Average	61	86	45	33

Source: Wind Information

IPO companies tend to underperform over the long term

Another interesting phenomenon in China's IPOs market is the tendency to underperform in the long term. Ritter (1991) was one of the first who proposed this problem. He also found out that IPO underperformance was more obvious for companies which went public during periods of high IPO activities.

Usually these researchers looked back at IPO companies' performance for three to five years. Because of the limitation of data, we just included returns of companies which went public from 2006 to 2010 over five different time horizons in our analysis. The graph shows that companies that issued capital in 2008 did show a very obvious declining returns trend. We think this is mainly because of the unfavorable market situation at that time. For the years 2007, 2009 and 2010, the curves are quite flat with slight upward as well as downward movements. For the year 2006, the curve is upwards. Altogether, we can see that depending upon the year of the IPO, long-term return tends to stay flat or even downward sloping. Over the long-term IPO companies tend to underperform.

Financial industries have highest IPO dollar volume

From 2006 to November 2011, the top five IPO industries by dollar volume are capital goods, banks, energy, materials and insurance. For the same period the telecom industry had the highest abnormal initial return compared to 9 other industries.

IPO activities in China are clearly concentrated in major cities

There is a severe imbalance between IPO volume percentage and GDP contribution for different provinces, especially Beijing. In 2010, 41.67 percent of all raised capital flew to firms registered in Beijing while Beijing only contributed 3.52 percent of GDP for the year 2010. This can be explained by the fact that most big public companies in China are state-owned companies with headquarters in Beijing. For example, in 2010 the Agricultural Bank of China went public in the mid-2010, with the world's largest ever IPO. ABC raised a total of $22.1 billion in both the Shanghai and Hong Kong stock markets. And because ABC's head office was in Beijing and the group went public as a single company, its IPO volume was treated as Beijing's IPO volume while GDP contribution calculation from ABC is based on locations of ABC's branches in different provinces all over China.

Why IPOs in China are different

Regulatory and structural explanations for China's A-share underpricing

Standard theories relating to IPO underpricing are insufficient to explain the degree of underpricing of China's A-shares. As a result, researchers from all over the world have put forward alternative theories to explain this phenomenon (Jie 2009; Tian 2005, 2007). Most alternative theories focus on China's unique regulatory structure, weak accounting standards and poor corporate governance as the drivers of extreme IPO underpricing.

IPOs in China have been dominated by privatization of large Chinese state-owned enterprises (SOE), while IPOs by smaller enterprises or entirely private firms have played a much smaller role. The Chinese government views IPO activity as part of its investment and capital formation goals set forth as part of its five-year plans. As such, IPO activity is driven by political considerations as much as by capital markets. Every year, Chinese regulators set targets for investment, including sub-targets for regions and industries, and then invite companies to seek capital through an IPO. While targets are set by regulators, they are not formally disclosed and aren't known outside of the policy-setting bodies. Each year, IPO demand exceeds the allocated capital-raising quotas, leading to long waiting periods for companies looking to go public. Since different targets exist for different industries and regions, the waiting period may vary depending on the company, with some enterprises being able to list quickly while others wait many years for getting listed. Corruption and unclear, non-transparent decision making further complicate matters, making it nearly impossible to know when a specific company will be given the right to make an IPO.

Historically, pricing of IPOs in China has been set by regulators, based on earnings multiples (P/E). Until 1999, regulators capped IPO pricing at a P/E ratio of 20, which greatly underpriced the shares relative to prices prevailing in the secondary market. Since then, regulators have been liberalizing pricing and introducing more flexibility, but the IPO pricing process still remains far from transparent. In the West, investment banks working on an IPO seek investors through a road show process, during which they explain the story and prospects of the company, and gauge investor interest. The investment banks can then adjust the IPO pricing based on investor feedback to price the IPO as close as possible to demand. No such mechanism exists in China and no market / investor feedback is allowed to impact the IPO pricing. This leads to more conservative underwriting and pricing of new issues.

There is often a very long delay between IPO offerings in China and the listing of shares for trading. This delay too results from the regulatory process in China, with authorities limiting the number of IPOs coming to market and trying to balance the growth and investment flows to different regions of the country. The delay between subscribing to an IPO and committing capital to actual listing can take several months and in some cases years. In addition, investors must commit capital equal to the amount of shares they wish to subscribe, even though in the end they are likely to receive a very small allocation due to vast IPO oversubscription. In other words, investors must commit a large amount of capital, for an unknown period of time, and wait for that capital to be returned after the shares have begun trading and being allocated a tiny percentage of the desired IPO amount. As a result, only huge returns on IPO allocations received can justify the long delays and capital commitments needed.

Finally, a number of China-specific factors relating to information and control asymmetry help underpricing of IPOs. First, accounting standards in China remain lax and less trustworthy than in many Western markets, leading investors to be suspicious and demand higher returns from new companies coming to market. Second, the initial public offerings in China tend to be minority share issuances which still leave the government as the majority shareholder. This means that even after the company is privatized, public shareholders are unlikely to be able to exercise much influence on the company's board. This gives rise to a corporate governance discount, as investors are buying an economic interest in the company, but without much voting or management control power. Third, in cases where companies are controlled by powerful insiders, the long period between IPO share subscription and public listing has given insiders the opportunity to steal assets from the company during this time period. After the company releases its financial statements and receives investor's money but before its shares are listed for public trading, there is an incentive for insiders to remove key assets from the company's books and transfer them to other entities they may control. This risk is referred to in the academic literature on China IPOs as "tunneling risk" and is another factor that leads to the large discounts seen on Chinese IPOs. Finally, China remains a country with restraints on capital accounts, meaning it is very difficult for the ordinary Chinese to transfer money and invest abroad. As a result, Chinese investment options are limited to bank deposits, domestic bonds, domestic equities and real estate. With bank deposits paying interest rates below inflation, bonds illiquid and real estate purchases made ever more difficult by the Chinese government concerned about a bubble, Chinese equities (A-shares) remain as one of the only investment outlets for the ordinary Chinese. This helps to explain the huge amounts of speculation in the stock market, IPO oversubscription and very large first-day returns.

Chinese companies raise funds on alternative markets

Chinese companies today can raise equity financing in a variety of markets. While the focus of this chapter is on the Chinese mainland A-shares market, important alternatives exist in the form of the Hong Kong Stock Exchange (HKSE) as well as the New York Stock Exchange (NYSE). Finally, there has been a recent spike in US listing of Chinese companies via reverse-merger IPOs – a dynamic that warrants attention.

While the Shanghai stock market today is the fifth largest in the world by capitalization, it is important to note that many Chinese companies are seeking listings outside of mainland China. NYSE has attracted the business of such giants as China Life Insurance (LFC) and China Mobile (CHL), while ICBC (1398) and Ping an Insurance (2318) are listed on the HKSE. Most interestingly, the two largest IPOs of recent years, Agricultural Bank of China (1288) and AIA Group (1299) both chose Hong Kong, not Shanghai, for their IPOs. By doing so, the companies are signaling that while China's mainland exchanges may be growing, large companies looking for significant liquidity and funding still choose more mature markets such as Hong Kong. The lower degree of underpricing found in Hong Kong means companies are able to raise more money than they would if they listed on the Chinese mainland, and that could be a factor explaining why large Chinese companies still prefer IPOs in non-mainland markets.

Reverse-merger IPOs as a unique vehicle

In addition to the mega IPOs of companies such as Agricultural Bank of China, recent years have seen a dramatic increase in the so-called reverse-merger IPOs of many Chinese companies seeking capital. A reverse-merger IPO is considered a simpler and cheaper way of going public, allowing many small companies to circumvent the compliance and road show necessary for a traditional IPO. In a reverse-merger transaction, a publicly listed "shell company" with little or no operating assets is first registered with the SEC via an S-1 registration. Such listing generally takes place in the over-the-counter or pink-sheets markets. Next, the publicly listed company acquires a privately held company, with shareholders of the private firm exchanging their shares for those of the public firm. The assets and directors of the surviving company are almost solely those of the former private firm. Finally, the public entity can issue additional shares to raise capital.

There are numerous US companies offering advice on going public via reverse-merger IPOs. While nothing about the process is specific to China, Chinese companies have dominated the US reverse-merge IPO statistics in recent years, with consultancy firms specifically set up to cater to Chinese clients.

A quick search on Google reveals such companies as "Go Public Institute – Public Shells for Reverse Mergers" (www.gopublic.com), "Dynasty Resources", (www.dynastyresources.net/corporate-finance.html), "Going Public Experts" (www.goingpublicexperts.com/), "Williams Securities Law Firm" (www.gopublicdirect.com), "How 2 Go Public.Com" (www.how2gopublic.com). When contacted, one of the firms claimed it could complete a reverse merger IPO process for a total of USD 40,000. Further research reveals the clients of the above companies and the S-1 filling they have made with the US Securities and Exchange Commission (SEC). All the companies we have found were exclusively Chinese, had little assets and consisted primarily of insiders looking to sell shares in their businesses. Examples of companies recently filing S-1 documents, along with information highlighting the business of each company, are presented in Table 3.2.

The business prospects, financial accounting standards and corporate governance of many of these companies appear weak. Similarly, reliability of the US law firms working on these reverse-merger transactions appears seriously doubtful. In fact, a significant number of such firms have been delisted, sued by shareholders and are being investigated by the SEC (Delfeld 2011). Due to the amount of reverse-merger IPO activity, the SEC has also considered imposing additional rules and checks for companies seeking a reverse-merger; a recent SEC announcement (SEC 2010) has said that reverse-merger IPO companies are prone to "fraud and other abuses" while many of the companies may "either fail or struggle to remain viable."

Table 3.2 Cases

Premier International Hotel Group, Inc.	Date: 2010-10-14
"The business purpose of the Company is to seek the acquisition of or merger with, an existing company. The Company intends to seek a merger with a company located in the People's Republic of China ("China") in the Hotel Industry. The Company reserves the right, however, to complete a business combination with a company in any industry, whether or not the Hotel Industry." www.sec.gov/Archives/edgar/data/1503508/000139390510000588/pihg_1012g.htm	
Advanced Pipe Fitting Technologies, Inc	Date: 2010-01-19
"We are a start-up stage company. We are a company without revenues; we have minimal assets and have incurred losses since inception. We will sell and distribute a series of pipefitting, pressure conduits and coupling products primarily used in oil and gas transfer, petroleum refinery, and sub-critical, supercritical power plant projects." www.sec.gov/Archives/edgar/data/1478490/000139390510000027/apft_s1.htm	
GHN Agrispan Holding Company	Date: 2009-10-14
"We are engaged in the provision of catering service and canteen sales and sales and distribution of agricultural products such as fresh fruits and vegetables and dry food products in the PRC." www.sec.gov/Archives/edgar/data/1472688/000101968709003659/ghn_s1-101409.htm	
Hyperera, Inc.	Date: 2009-11-10
"Our business is sale of hardware and software and customization of clinical information system software for medical clinics and hospitals in China and throughout Asia." "The Clinical Information System we sell was developed in China by Beijing ChaoranChuangshi Technology Co., Ltd ("Beijing Chaoran"). It was established in 2002 specializing in technology developed and service, sales of computer hardware and software, machine and electric equipment. Beijing Chaoran is located in No. 28 Mujiu Road, Mujiayu Town, Miyun, and Beijing, China. Beijing Chaoran is a Chinese Technology company owned 100% by Mr. Liancheng Li, the father of our Chairman Zhi Yong Li." www.sec.gov/Archives/edgar/data/1458868/000114420409057900/v165514_s1.htm	
Mega World Food Holding Company	Date: 2010-12-08
"Through our wholly-owned subsidiary Mega World Food Limited, referred to as Mega World Limited, our business will be the sale of frozen vegetables in all areas of the world except China. We have not yet sold any of these products. We sell the following types of frozen vegetables: frozen bamboo shoots, frozen mulberry, frozen white cauliflower, frozen lotus root, frozen green soy bean, frozen broccoli, frozen rape flower, frozen snow bean and frozen sward bean." www.sec.gov/Archives/edgar/data/1503161/000121465911001225/s410111s1a3.htm	

Implications for future IPOs in China

What (and what not) to expect for the upcoming years

Looking to the future is always a challenging exercise. When it comes to the Chinese context, it is even harder because the country is growing so fast and the government tends to be efficient in responding quickly to market issues. In the past five years, stock markets observed impressive first-day returns on IPOs in China. This phenomenon happened due to a set of structures, regulations and incentives that were in place at that particular moment. Thinking ahead for the upcoming years, it is important to understand what might change and what kind of impact the change is likely to have on IPOs' first-day returns.

Market structure: From a macro perspective, there are no significant expected changes in the market structure for IPOs over the next years. There are still many large SOEs that can benefit from raising capital through IPOs and these companies are very likely to receive preferential treatment from regulators for clearance of their listing applications. These companies are already big players in their respective markets and are very likely to follow China's overall economic growth, hence presenting attractive opportunities for investors.

Although improving over the years, these companies still present the same problems that existed in the recent past years which were part of the reason for underpriced IPOs (weak accounting, poor corporate governance and lack of transparency, etc.).

Regulations: There are many questions investors have nowadays that are on the government's agenda. Will there be a relaxation on foreign investment rules? Are the A- and B-shares going to be unified? While the answers to these and other questions are highly anticipated, it is hard to say precisely when the government is likely to address them (not to mention a larger issue, that is the Renminbi convertibility).

The Chinese government is currently trying to push companies to make their initial offerings more in mainland China than in Hong Kong (last year Hong Kong had the largest volume of IPOs by market capitalization and in 2011 the trend was the same), but both Shenzhen's and Shanghai's pipelines are full and it is up to regulators to maneuver the companies to be listed.

A new initiative that is going to take place in the Shanghai stock market is the "International Board", which will allow international companies to be listed in that stock exchange, providing local investors with new investment options (major multinationals operating in China are expected to be the first ones in the International Board).

Apart from that, there are efforts to make the Chinese stock market follow more international rules and it is expected that IPOs in China will eventually be organized through a registration-based system like in the US or Europe, but there is no clear deadline for this to happen.

Incentives: there are two different angles to analyze incentives: the government / company owners and the public perspective.

The largest IPOs are normally SOEs and since the government usually retains a large part of its shares in the company, a high first-day valuation return is welcome.

From the public's perspective, as stated before in this chapter, there are currently not that many interesting investment alternatives and the IPOs seem like a good opportunity because demand is far greater than supply and most people cannot buy the stock at its initial price (there are quotas and a lottery scheme most of the time).

Since China is likely to keep the trend of increasing the IPO market (by market capitalization, not necessarily by number of IPOs), it is possible that the public will have more chances to access initial prices. The International Board in Shanghai will also help increase supply of investment opportunities for the general public.

Other than the three main aspects presented (structures, regulations and incentives), it is possible to argue that the market is simply getting more mature (evolving over a learning curve). While that is highly debatable, data show that in 2010 and 2011 first-day returns were, on average, lower than the previous years. The debate is whether this was really a maturing evolution or it simply reflects the ongoing global economic crisis. Since there is a cap on foreign investments for A-shares, making supply lower than demand, the global crisis is probably not a major driver of China IPOs' lower first-day returns recently.

Very recently, GuoShuqing was nominated as the new chairman of CSRC. He has ambitious plans to develop China's capital markets, making it more competitive and more on par with its Western peers. His proposal is to build a comprehensive bond financing platform and promote innovation in financial services. Moreover, he promises to have "zero tolerance" on insider trading, assuring more transparency in the marketplace. Whether he will succeed or not, only the future will tell us, but one thing is for sure: China is pushing its capital markets towards Western rules and dynamics.

Considering market structure, regulations, incentives and evolution on a learning curve, we do not expect to see first-day returns reaching European standards but there is a market evolution in place and it is very unlikely that China's stock market is going to see abnormal first-day returns in the future. What is more likely to happen is that the market would follow the 2010/2011 trend with returns averaging between 20 percent and 40 percent.

Conclusion

China's openness to a market-driven economy is a recent process and the country has managed to change drastically over the past few decades. Profound changes have happened in the Chinese society as well as in the economy, and the stock market was no exception to that.

Just like the country as a whole, China's stock market is still on its way to becoming a sophisticated marketplace. The government is ensuring the transition takes place slowly; through the past decades, local investors were able to profit from the market's imperfections.

China is going irreversibly towards a Western style of stock exchange regulation and dynamics. It will increase investors' confidence; thereby increasing the flow of money into China, but it will also make the initial IPO returns lower. But the path to this future is tortuous and will take years. While China is not there yet, the days of 100 percent (or more) profit in one day are over and the average expected initial return is decreasing, but investors are still able to profit from above-average IPOs.

References

Charles, G. and Sun, L. 2010. Preliminary comparison between ChiNext and SME. www.chinalawandpractice.com/Article/2351745/Channel/7576/Preliminary-comparison-between-ChiNext-and-SME.html

Chen, G. M., Kim, K. A., Nofsinger, J. R., and Rui, O. M. 2004. Behavior and performance of emerging market investors: Evidence from China. Working paper, Washington State University (January).

Cheung, Y. L., Ouyang, Z., and Tan, W. 2009. How regulatory changes affect IPO underpricing in China. China Economic Review, 20(4), 692–702.

Delfeld, C. 2011, May 26. One of the best ways to limit your risk in China. Investment U. www.investmentu.com/2011/May/limit-risk-investing-in-china.html

Han-da, P. 2011. Strategic investors and IPO under-pricing: Chinese evidence.

Ernst & Young. 2011. Ernst & Young global IPO trends report. www.ey.com/GL/en/Services/Strategic-Growth-Markets/Global-IPO-trends-2011. Retrieved 28 November 2012.

KPMG, ed. 2007. The rise of China capital market: a study of China's stock, bond and derivatives markets. www.kpmg.com/CN/en/IssuesAndInsights/ArticlesPublications/Documents/rise-china-capital-mkt-0711.pdf

Lin, Ada. 2009. ChiNext: A touch of warm sunshine after the cold winter. www.pedaily.cn/Item.aspx?id=194148

Liu, Lillian. 2009. Shenzhen GEM debuts, with 28 firms. *China Daily* (HK Edition 29 October 2009, p. 4).

Liu, Yiyu. 2009. Don't fret over high PE numbers, says Greifeld. *China Daily.* (China Edition 29 October 2009, p. 10).

Moody's Report. 2011, July. Red flags for emerging-market companies: a focus on China. http://members.zkiz.com/storage/1610/6c2dPBC_134306.pdf

Odean, Terrance. 1998a. Are investors reluctant to realize their losses? *Journal of Finance* 53: 1775–1798.

Odean, Terrance 1998b. Volume, volatility, price and profit when all traders are above average. *Journal of Finance* 53: 1887–1934.

OICU-IOSCO. 2012. Emerging markets committee of the international organization of securities commissions. http://awareness.sca.ae/Arabic/IntReports/Report_2012_08.pdf

Reuters. 2009. Timeline – China launches Nasdaq-style market for start-ups. http://in.reuters.com/article/2009/10/23/idINIndia-43379720091023

Ritter, J. R. 1991. The long run performance of initial public offerings. *The Journal of Finance*, 46(1), 3–27.

Ritter, P. 2010. IPO data. http://bear.warrington.ufl.edu/ritter/ipodata.htm. Retrieved 26 November 2012.

Ritter, J. R. 2011. Initial public offerings: Tables updated through 2010. Unpublished working paper.

Tian, L. 2011. Regulatory underpricing: Determinants of Chinese extreme IPO returns. *Journal of Empirical Finance*, 18(1), 78–90.

Tian, L., and Megginson, W. 2007. Extreme underpricing: Determinants of Chinese IPO initial returns. Available at SSRN 891042.

Wai-yin Kwok, Vivian. 2009. The Nasdaq of China is coming. www.forbes.com/2009/05/06/china-second-board-markets-equity-shenzhen.html

Walter, C., Fraser, G., and Howie, F. (2003). *Privatizing China: A guide to China's stock markets and their role in corporate reform*. Wiley.

Wentao, Tan, ed. 2007. A history of China's stock markets, Chapter 8 in *China's financial markets: an insider's guide to how the markets work*. Neftci, S., & Ménager-Xu, M. Y. (Eds.). (2007). Access online via Elsevier.

Xi Jinping (President). 2012. Speech at the First Plenum of the 18th Congress. http://news.china.com/18da/news/11127551/20121115/17530532.html

Xinhua. 2009. China's growth enterprise board to shore up small businesses. http://news.xinhuanet.com/english/2009-04/01/content_11114849.htm

Xinhua. 2009. ChiNext: to boom or to doom? http://news.xinhuanet.com/english/2009-11/03/content_12373929.htm

Yan-Leung, Cheung. 2012. HK plays an irreplaceable role. *China Daily,* 29 June. http://usa.chinadaily.com.cn/opinion/2012-06/29/content_15534073.htm

Yuan, J. 2009. Alternative explanations of under-pricing of Chinese initial public offerings (Doctoral dissertation, University of Nottingham).

Zeng, Z., and Wan, X. 2008. Understanding the recent performance of China's stock market. China Economic Journal, 1(2), 213–225.

Zhang, Jiawei. 2009. GEB sparks different opinions among institutional investors. *China Daily.*22 Oct

Zhu, N. 2002. The local bias of individual investors. unpublished paper, Yale University, 1999(2000), 2001-0.235白韌. 2009.《紫荊》:深圳創業板對香港的利弊 www.hkcna.hk/content/2009/1030/30517.shtml

4 The real estate market in mainland China

Since it embraced economic reforms and free-market principles, China's economic boom has spawned a raving shopping spree with the affluent Chinese middle class buying up luxury properties in the mainland, pouring millions of dollars into the country's real estate market and driving up prices to unprecedented levels. In the decade to 2010, China's housing market is estimated to have doubled to roughly twice that of Spain or the United Kingdom. However, critics argue that behind these flourishing scenarios, dreams of ordinary Chinese people to own a house are being dashed by rising house prices and interest rates. With speculation around the impending real estate bubble growing and the threat of a slowing GDP, the future of the Chinese real estate market is uncertain.

As an essential component of fixed asset investment, real estate development investments accounted for about 14 percent of total GDP in the first nine months of 2011 and contributed significantly to China's economy. The upsurge of real estate and home prices has also contributed to the persistent increase in the Consumer Price Index from 2.4 percent in March 2010 to 5.1 percent in November 2010 which was beyond the 2011 target of about 4 percent set by the Central Government. Back in April 2010, the State Council of the People's Republic of China had already started to implement a series of measures to deal with a potential real estate bubble which could threaten social and economic stability and financial security, with the aim to control home prices and to cool the overheated real estate markets.

4.1. Evolution of the real estate market in the past decade

Thanks to high liquidity, depreciation of USD, favorable and stimulating policies and speculative demand coupled with inhibited purchase demand after the financial crisis, the real estate market has escalated strongly since 2008 with housing sales values and land area rising significantly. The figure below reveals that the price of residential property has nearly doubled from January 2009 to January 2011 and gradually dropped slightly due to austerity measures imposed by the Central Government (Figure 4.1). The CAGR of the total residential floor area was 12.3 percent per year from 2006 to 2011 (Figure 4.2).

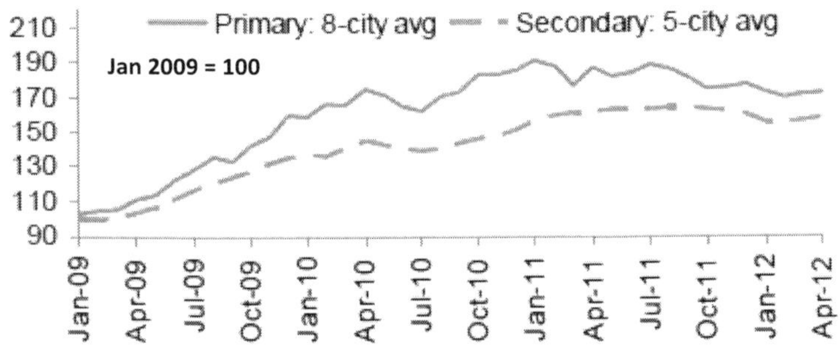

Figure 4.1 Residential properties price growth

Source: CEIC, CentaData

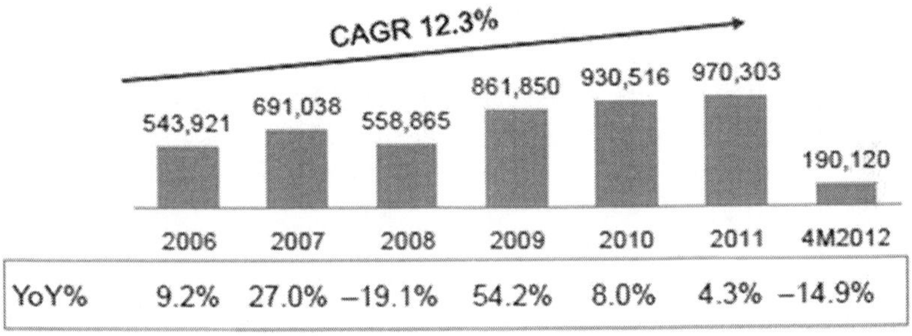

Figure 4.2 CAGR of total residential floor area from 2006 to 2011

Source: CEIC, CentaData

According to the National Bureau of Statistics, the average housing price in Shanghai rose over 150 percent from 2003 to 2010. The real estate investment growth remained very high until early 2012.

Residential / commercial property prices are on fire. What are the major reasons that give rise to the current phenomenon? What's pushing up housing property prices? There are essentially five forces that affect the real estate property market in China:

- Central Government – set property-related policy
- Local Government – raise revenue by selling state land
- Developers – buying land from state governments
- Consumers / Investors – buying properties from developers
- Banks – giving loans to developers and home buyers

As shown by Figure 4.3, the value chain of the real estate market can be summarized as follows.

First start with local government which sells land to the developers who mainly build three types of houses: (1) subsidized houses for the poor; (2) affordable

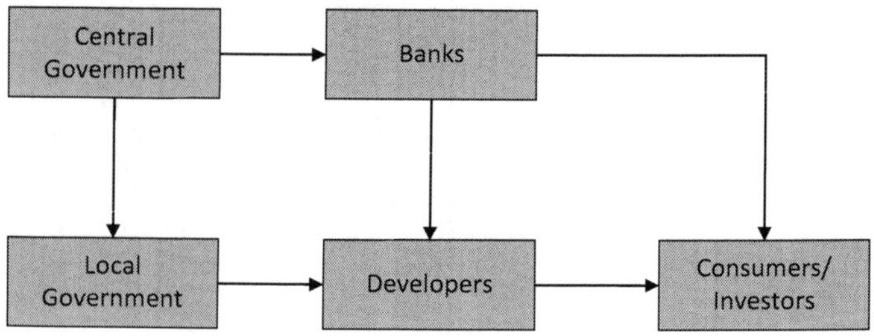

Figure 4.3 The forces of action in the real estate market

houses for people with average income; and (3) high-end residential properties. Since land is mostly sold via auctions to developers who can pay the highest price, developers who bid high prices for land will mostly go for building luxury residential properties which can generate the most lucrative profits. Moreover, all housing construction creates jobs and boosts the auxiliary industries such as steel and cement sectors, adding to the overall economic performance of government officials in the local economy; local governments are therefore very pleased to have more real estate construction projects in the provinces. In late 2008 when the global financial tsunami hit the world economy, developers had already slowed construction because of the series of tightening measures exerted by the Central Government since 2007 which partially reduced the supply of houses to the market during that period. With the release of the 4 trillion stimulus plan, market sentiment became strong again and the property prices began to surge.

Some of the buyers are average-income buyers who purchase flats for self-use and others are rich Chinese who purchase flats for speculative purposes because there are not many investment alternatives in China, which brings more business to the banks.

The Central Government normally instructs banks, mostly owned by the government, to lend more to boost the economy. In 2009, around RMB 9.59 trillion was lent out which was almost double than the previous year. The government also relaxed the regulations to make it easier for people to borrow money during that period which directly boosted the real estate market during 2009–2010.

4.2. Political, demographic, economic and institutional environments

Political environment

The year 2012 was an important but turbulent one. The US elected its president and China held its 18th National People's Congress in the second half of the year during which China announced its new political leadership. In his second term in office, President Obama has stepped up the US focus on Asia Pacific including China, partly with the hope to help pull the US out of its present poor economic situation and in particular, to reduce its high unemployment rate. In the APEC forum on November 12 in Hawaii and the subsequent visit to Australia, Obama outlined his plan to increase economic and military engagements in the region, widely taken to be a means to counterbalance the rise of China as a world power. To continue to exert pressure on China to reevaluate the RMB upwards more quickly and to open up its domestic markets to US businesses remain top priorities on the US agenda (Bloomberg, 14 November 2011).

The Central Government of China ensured a smooth and orderly transition. No major policy changes, including that for the real estate markets, were expected in the interim and any measures, which could include selective monetary easing or tax cuts in selective industries or areas such as consumption, agriculture and exports, are aimed at ensuring stability and maintaining targeted growth.

Demographic, economic and institutional environment

While the US is still slowly recovering from the 2008 financial crisis, the recent sovereign debt problems in a number of countries in Europe such as Greece and Ireland have become significant threats to the already fragile global economy, potentially dragging it into a long stagnation or even recession. Slowdowns in overseas markets have had an adverse impact on China's exports, which have already become more expensive due to rising production costs because of higher wages and materials costs inside China and a higher RMB exchange rate.

GDP, inflation and RMB

China has maintained the momentum of rapid economic growth in recent years, with GDP growth averaging over 9 percent per annum to become the second-largest economy next to the US (see Figure 4.4).

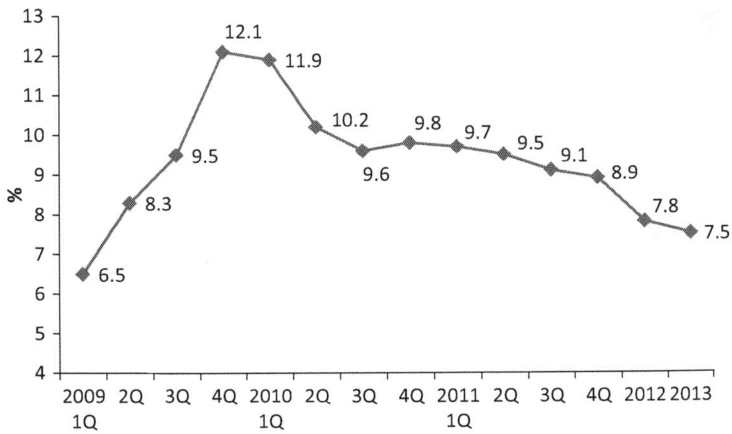

Figure 4.4 Quarterly GDP growth percentage in China

Source: National Bureau of Statistics of China

CPI has also risen quickly since 2006, and despite a severe drop caused by the financial crisis in 2008, has resumed its upward trend since late 2009 to reach a three-year high of 6.5 percent year on year in July 2011 before abating to 4.2 percent in November (see Figure 4.5 below).

One of the key strategies for China to maintain long-term sustainable and balanced growth will be a gradual shift away from heavy reliance on exports and infrastructure investments towards more domestic demand–driven growth. To facilitate this, China has gradually let RMB appreciate, making imports more affordable for Chinese consumers and also to help suppress inflation and reduce political pressure from the US.

On the other hand, inflation and RMB appreciation expectations have led to persistent flow of investments and hot money into China's fixed assets including real estate, which are often seen to be an effective hedge against inflation, causing their prices to rise quickly.

Urbanization

Unlike many emerging market countries, which have only a few major cities, China has over 100 cities with a population of over 1 million but economic development has been uneven among regions. For the 20-year period from 1990 to 2010, according to the National Bureau of Statistics of China, average GDP (nominal) per capita for the whole country increased from RMB 1,638 to around RMB 29,748, but there are significant income inequalities between the middle class in the eastern coastal cities and those inland, which has become a source of discontent regarding government policies and economic misdistribution.

While a significant part of China is still rural, its fast-growing consumer class is urbanizing quickly (see Figure 4.6); an estimated 14–15 million people per year in the coming years, an irreversible trend which has created a strong demand not

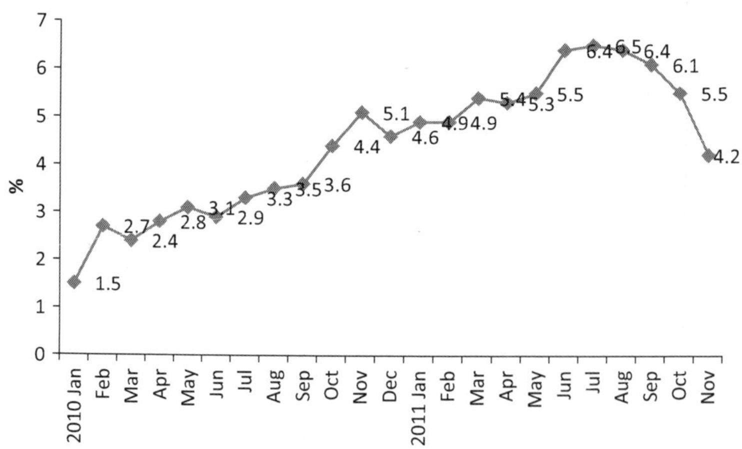

Figure 4.5 Monthly CPI growth percentage in China

Source: National Bureau of Statistics of China

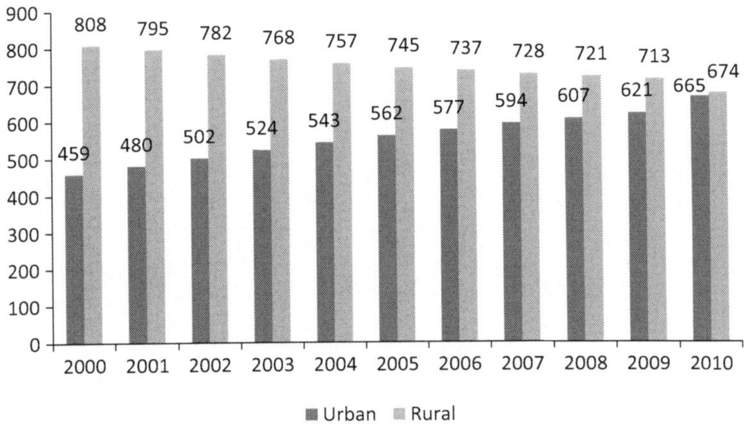

Figure 4.6 Journey to the cities – China's urban vs rural population, 2000–2010

Source: National Bureau of Statistics of China

only for retail properties, but also for residential housing, offsetting the potential drop in demand caused by an aging Chinese population.

It is therefore a priority for the Central Government to provide sufficient and affordable housing to increasing demand from home buyers, and to poor households to douse possible social unrest.

Infrastructure

The Chinese government has put great emphasis on development of the country's infrastructure in order to meet the demands of its booming economy. In his work report on 5 March 2011, Premier Wen reported that in the past five years, China had expanded its railway system by 16,000 km and its road system by 639,000 km, including 33,000 km of expressways (Ichainnel 2011). According to KPMG's analysis and report in April 2011, in the 12th Five-Year Plan, investments will continue to be made in railways and roads with the aim to increase the length of the expressway network to 83,000 km from 65,000 km at the end of 2010 and the length of operational high-speed railway to 25,000 km from close to 10,000 km in July 2011. China's telecommunication sector is also booming, from fixed line to mobile services. Based on the data provided by China's Ministry of Industry and Information Technology, at the end of September 2011, the number of phone users had exceeded 1.24 billion of which mobile phone users were over 950 million. Infrastructure is undoubtedly the backbone of real estate. Without adequate roads, railways and communications, real estate value will be greatly diminished.

Banking / trust sectors

Regulated by the CBRC, the four big Chinese commercial banks dominate the banking sector in China and all are listed in mainland and Hong Kong. The Central

Government is a major shareholder of each of the four institutions. As a result, to a certain extent they are instrumental in executing the Chinese government's directives and policies at various points in time.

Also regulated by the CBRC is a much smaller trust sector. Trust companies have the combined characteristics of private equity, asset management and banking and part of their businesses has been working with banks to provide financing through asset securitization to the real estate sector who cannot obtain bank financing under the tight restrictions imposed by the CBRC. Trust companies do not take on the risk of an investment themselves, but funnel funds from companies and wealthy individuals into a wide range of investments, including direct stakes in property developments. According to China Trustee Association's data, trust companies provided RMB 113.9 billion in new funding to property developers in the third quarter compared with RMB 136.7 billion in the second quarter and RMB 71.1 billion in the first three months of 2011.

Money supply

While the US, Europe and Japan have been pumping liquidity or maintaining quantitative easing to boost or support their troubled economies, China has been recently tightening its money supply to control inflation, escalating real estate prices and the risk of potential asset bubbles. Although the PBoC lowered banks' Regulatory Reserve Ratio (RRR) by 50 basis points with effect from December, it is more likely that the Central Government will continue its stance of prudent monetary policy in the foreseeable future while allowing banks to step up lending to targeted sectors such as low-cost housing, SMEs and selective infrastructure projects to maintain economic growth.

4.3. Market characteristics

50 fast-growing cities in China

Not every city or province has the same growth in real estate development. Some of them are more favored by investors or developers because of the well-developed infrastructure, while some are preferred because of high growth momentum. The chart prepared by Jones Lang LaSalle shows classification of 50 secondary and tertiary cities in China, which offer substantial real estate opportunities. This is named as China 50.

Tier 1 (Core Cities) – Beijing, Shanghai, Guangzhou and Shenzhen as they are characterized by a high level of economic and international business connectivity, high liquidity and transparent markets.

Tier 1.5 (Transition Cities) – Chengdu, Chongqing, Tianjin, Hangzhou, etc., as they have a high degree of infrastructure investment and FDI and have benefited from policy support from the Central Government.

Tier 2 (Growth Cities) – Xi'an, Qingdao, Ningbo and Wuxi as they have a high degree of wealth and strong underlying demographics to support the local economy.

Tier 3 (Emerging Cities) – Kunming, Harbin, Nanning as they are gradually being lifted off. Many developers are going in to establish "first mover" advantage.

Market segmentations

The revenue of the real estate industry can be broken down into four categories, namely, building sales, land development rights transfers, building leasing and others. Building sales was the largest market segment for the real estate industry, accounting for 93 percent of the industry revenue in 2010 (Figure 4.7). Around 75 percent of the sales are made to buyers who occupy it for self-use purpose, while others are for investment and speculation.

Building leases account for around 2 percent of the total market where clients are mostly corporate. This market is very small because the rental yield is not attractive compared to capital gain and there are higher risks when leasing property out.

Land development-rights transfers occur when the developer is not financially capable of completing the construction.

Standard residential buildings accounted for the largest portion of industry revenue in 2009. In terms of gross floor area (GFA), it accounted for almost 80.4 percent of the industry's total volume in 2011. Given the strong demand and rapid growth rate in the past years, this percentage is expected to increase further.

Low-income (affordable) dwellings only accounted for 1.5 percent of the industry revenue. With rising construction costs, developers find it unprofitable to build it and shift the focus to high-end residential housing. Furthermore, due to market speculation and lack of enforceable legislation, the original objective of building this type of property is lost.

The proportion of villas and high-end apartments escalated to 10.1 percent in 2009 because of the higher average prices where most large developers like to tap this market for better returns.

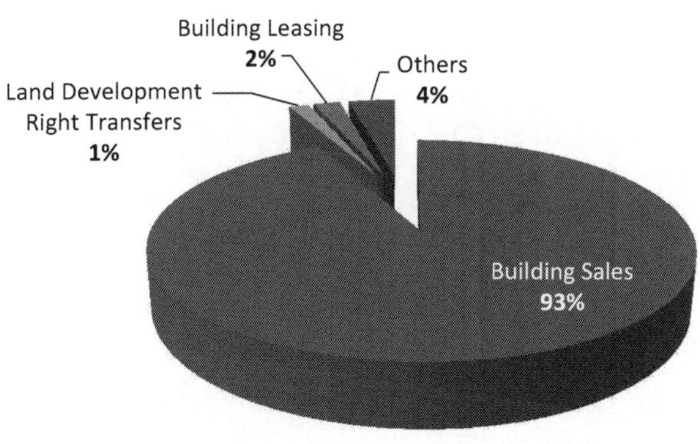

Figure 4.7 Breakdown of revenue contribution in the real estate market

Source: IBIS

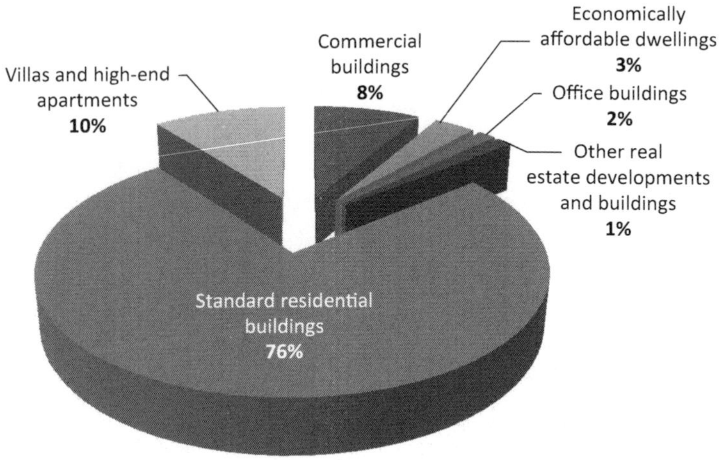

Figure 4.8 Real estate products and service segmentation (2009)

Source: IBIS

Office and commercial buildings accounted for 3.7 percent and 8.3 percent of the industry revenue, respectively. The development of this type of buildings is closely tied to economic activities and service sectors such as department stores, supermarkets, restaurants and entertainment parks which have been thriving in recent years (Figure 4.8).

Major players in the real estate market

As shown in Figure 4.9, the real estate market in China is quite widely spread among thousands of developers which range from SOEs to POEs and even some sole proprietors. The largest residential property developer in China – China Vanke – accounted for only 1.2 percent of the entire market in 2011 indicating the fierce competition in the market. The industry's top four firms were estimated to account for 3.6 percent of the industry revenue in 2011 and therefore the industry is subject to low concentration. Small players are having higher difficulties to enter the industry in view of the recent higher start-up costs and unfavorable government policy.

Barriers to entry

On one hand, rising property prices is the one of the processes of economic revolution. On the other hand, a severe real estate bubble or the deflation of the bubble would create social unrest, bringing about detrimental consequences. Central Government has enacted policies to raise barriers to land purchases to stop the bubble from worsening or prevent it.

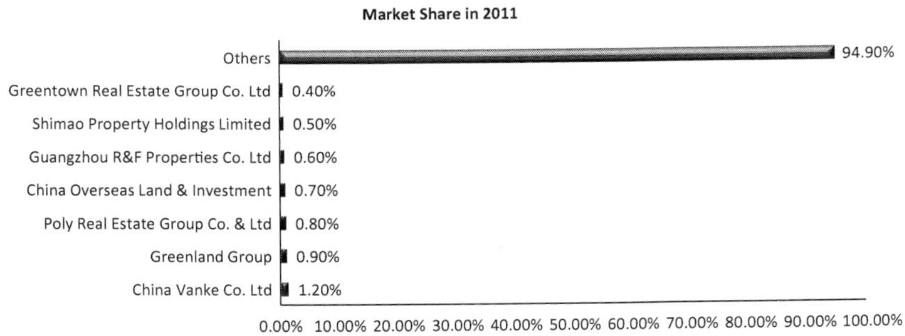

	China Vanke Co. Ltd	Greenland Group	Poly Real Estate Group Co. & Ltd	China Overseas Land & Investment	Guangzhou R&F Properties Co. Ltd	Shimao Property Holdings Limited	Greentown Real Estate Group Co. Ltd	Others
Market Share in 2011	1.20%	0.90%	0.80%	0.70%	0.60%	0.50%	0.40%	94.90%

Figure 4.9 Major players in the real estate industry

Source: IBIS

Tax regime

There are various types of taxes in the real estate industry which curb the lucrative business.

- Corporate Income Tax: 15 percent to 25 percent
- Value-added Tax (VAT): 17 percent
- Sales Tax: 5 percent
- Contract Tax: 3 percent – 5 percent
- Land Value Increment Tax: 30 percent – 60 percent
- City Construction and Maintenance Tax: 1 percent – 7 percent
- Education surcharge: 3 percent

Banks' appetite / raising interest rate

Between October 2010 and July 2011, the PBoC raised interest rates five times and also raised the Required Reserve Ratio (RRR) consequently to tighten liquidity which helped curb property speculation as this increased developers' costs.

In line with the government's goal to cool down the real estate investment boom, the top four state-owned banks have been more cautious and selective in lending to real estate developers and have gradually reduced real estate loans quota by 20 percent in 2010–2011.

Also, the government had raised the down payment for first-time buyers' mortgages to 30 percent from 20 percent and that for second homes to 60 percent from

50 percent. Mortgages for third home purchases are prohibited. This helped prevent the general public from leveraging bank financing for speculation.

Limiting land purchases

This prohibited developers from purchasing land easily and stopped some unqualified developers from operating in the industry. This indirectly imposed more challenges for developers in speculations. Banks were prohibited to provide developers with loans for land purchase.

Limiting foreign investment

Previously, foreign ventures could directly own real estate projects in China which created a competitive environment but also resulted in an overheated market. Starting from 2007, foreign ventures can only enter industry through joint ventures with domestic players or partnerships. This helped avoid hot money or capital from flowing into the economy to speculate on asset appreciation.

Local regulation such as home-purchase limits

In view of the competitive market and stringent government regulations, the key factors responsible for success of the players in the property industry include:

1. GOOD REPUTATION

In China, word of mouth is very important as people spread bad news easily via the Internet or other media channels. Good reputation instills confidence in customers about good housing quality and induces customers to recommend friends and relatives to buy properties with the same brand again in other regions.

2. BRAND NAMES

Large developers, especially those targeting the high-end market, establish their own brand names. This allows them to sell at higher prices than their peers in the same region even if the quality is similar.

3. STRONG FINANCIAL CAPABILITY

A strong financial capability is critical to ensure completion of a property project. Many small- and medium-sized developers have gone bankrupt or faced consolidation during 2007–2008 because of the tightened market liquidity and breakdown of the cashflow chain. Financially healthy developers with good liquidity can not only weather any ups and downs in the property market, but also seize opportunities to acquire distressed assets when rivals are having financial difficulties.

A recent example would be the Chinese property developer Greentown China Holdings which has agreed to sell a stake in the company to Hong Kong–listed conglomerate Wharf (Holdings) Ltd in June 2012.

4. RESPONSIVE ADJUSTMENT TO CHANGING REGULATIONS

Regulation by the Central Government has been intensified in recent years. Developers should possess the flexibility to respond to the rapidly changing rules and regulations in order to stay competitive in the market.

Industry phenomenon by geographic spread

As shown in the graph above (Figure 4.10), East China (including Shanghai), being the most prosperous economic zone, accounted for the largest share of industry revenue which was around 46 percent in 2008, followed by the mid-southern regions (including Shenzhen, Guangzhou) which is characterized by a higher level of service activities as well as per capita GDP. Probably due to the proximity to the Central Government, the residential market in Northern China (such as Beijing and Tianjin) is not particularly flourishing compared with other regions, except for some particular projects which hit record-high selling prices. The northern market is mainly focused on commercial / office buildings due to high volumes of business activities.

North East and North West regions account for approximately only 5.1 percent and 5.0 percent of the industry revenue, respectively, because of the relatively underdeveloped infrastructure as well as distance from the economic centers of China. It is interesting to note that South West region such as Chengdu has been

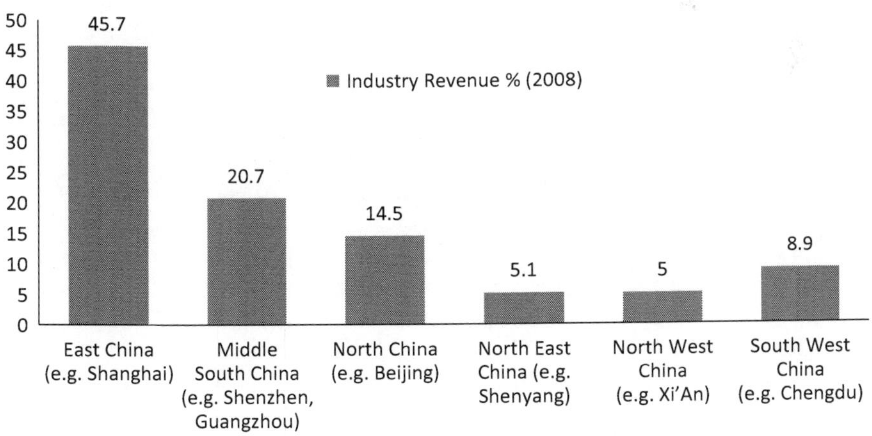

Figure 4.10 Geographical spread of the real estate market in China in 2008

Source: IBIS

gaining in popularity in recent years because of the huge population in the provinces and the growing average income of the people which encourages them to change flats or invest in property.

4.4. An impending bubble in the China real estate market?

China's economy has grown rapidly in the past decade and overtaken Japan as the second-largest economy in the world. The extraordinarily rapid growth drew global attention and the China bubble has become one of the hottest and most controversial economic topics lately. There have been rigorous discussions and analyses by economists, bankers and academia about whether China's economy is experiencing a Japanese-style bubble (that burst in the 1980s). China is significantly larger than Japan and the world economy today is far more fragile than it was in the late 1980s when the Japanese bubble burst, so the global consequences of a crash in the Chinese economy would be far greater.

China's economy appears to be following Japan's path. RMB appreciated by 22 percent from 2005 and money supply grew 47 percent in 20 months from 2008 to 2010. Shanghai Composite Index peaked at 2007, almost 4 times the level in 2005. House prices have increased 2.5 times since 2002. China recovered quickly from the crisis in 2008 and its real GDP has been growing by 9 percent to 10 percent per year. China is expected to overtake the United States to become the biggest economy in the world in the near future. The similarities between China's economy at present and Japan's bubble economy have raised fears of a bubble economy taking shape in China.

High property prices in China, in particular, are highly concerned by investors. The asset markets in China, namely, the stock market and the property market, are said to be overheated and on the same path of process as the Japanese asset bubble in the 1980s and 1990s.

In simple and superficial comparison, China's economy may look like a huge bubble that is going to burst anytime soon and collapse like Japan's economy did. However, the similar trends support nothing but just speculation. With more details, we can figure out the differences between Japan in 1980s and China in 2000s. Even though the stock market indexes of China and Japan show similar trends, the Price to Earnings ratio of each country shows different market situations. In the 1980s, Japan's PER was much higher than that of the US, but the current Chinese stock market has shown a much smaller volatility and lower PER compared with the PER of the US market. This means that even though the Chinese stock market was once overheated, the market has stabilized after 2008.

In the Japanese housing market, prices started to rise in the 1970s because of rapid growth and urbanization. They declined during the oil crisis in 1974 and again started rising until the bust in the 1990s. In the 1970s, the increase in house prices was more natural because of high growth and hence recovered quickly after the oil crisis was over. In the 1980s, however, urban population grew from 60 percent to 63 percent (from 1982 to 1992). While growth and urbanization slowed down, house prices still kept rising. Hence, the property market could not recover as there was no economic base for growth and thus slumped into a prolonged crisis. On the other hand, in China, urban population grew from 35 percent to 49 percent from 2000 to 2010. The property market cannot be considered overheated since urbanization is still growing rapidly and demand is absorbing the supply.

In China, even though PIR (Price to Income Ratio) in large cities such as Shanghai or Beijing is higher than 20 to 25, PIR for the whole country is around 10 and if we consider only the top 30 percent of households' income as disposable income of PIR, the PIR is further lowered to around 6.

According to the report of National Bureau of Statistics of China released on 18 October, new housing prices in September went down in 17 cities and maintained the same level in 29 cities among 70 large cities. Compared to August, the increase of new housing prices in the remaining cities was merely less than 0.3 percent. The existing housing price had decreased in 25 cities and was maintained at the same level in 21 cities. The increase of the overall existing housing price was less than 0.6 percent compared to the price in August. Overall, property prices have come to a steady state.

4.5. Various issues driving the future of the real estate market in China

The social perspective: The ripple effect of the one-child policy

The one-child policy may have proven to be effective in controlling the growth of the 1.3 billion Chinese population, however, its effects have gone well beyond population control. The 2010 census reported that there are 34 million more men than women, meaning the risk of social instability of men unable to find wives, which translates into a drop in the birth rate. Children now under the age of 14 constitute less than one-sixth of the population. The declining birth rate has also been exacerbated by the growing prosperity. More young couples now prefer not to have children, citing the high cost of child-bearing. The number of infertile couples in China has now reached 50 million. In addition, the census showed that the number of people over 60 has risen to 13.3 percent of the population, compared with just over 10 percent a decade ago. This fact alone categorizes China as an aging society. In big cities, population profiles are far more skewed. For example, a fifth of Shanghai's population is already over 60 and that figure is forecast to rise to 29 percent by 2030. All of these can cause some unforeseen consequences for economic growth. The dwindling birth rate coupled with the aging population could imperil the housing market in the future.

The increase in life expectancy combined with a low birth rate have resulted in a high dependency ratio, where the only-child generation now typically has to support four parents without any sibling help. This may actually mean some will be forced by circumstances to live with their aging parents, which potentially decreases the demand for new homes. At the same time, this generation will bear the double burden of healthcare costs for their own household plus the parents, leaving a smaller share of their wallets for buying new houses, let alone luxury properties.

The political perspective: property-purchasing limitation

Beijing rolled out the new property-purchasing rules limiting the number of houses each family can buy as a rigorous step to rein in the soaring housing prices. However, such a move may not be agreeable to local governments. Unlike the Central Government, local governments have gotten more closely entangled with land development interest groups. Local governments earned RMB 2.3 trillion in 2011 as fees for land transfer, accounting for 55 percent of their annual tax revenues. Many of the local development projects are funded by revenues from land transfer. In a nutshell, they have grown increasingly dependent on land transfer to enrich their coffers. That said, the property-purchasing limitation plan cuts deeply into the interest of the local governments.

Besides, local government officials have immediate control on every land development and receive big benefits or accumulate wealth from the development projects. According to an article on Chinausfocus.com, many local officials are going against the Central Government's rules by loosening the limits in one way or another as long as there is no perceived threat to social and political stability. The question of how long the local governments will go their own ways is unknown at the moment but this will play a significant role in determining the future of the real estate developers.

Is property tax good or bad for China as a whole?

China has not had an established property tax system in place and this is having a big impact on local governments. They account for four-fifths of the country's public spending, but pocket only minimal taxes. To help make up the difference, they rely on expropriating land from farmers and selling it to bullish property developers. But as developers struggle, land sales are dwindling. As a result, local-government revenue is drying up. However, public resentment over the land title debate continues to intensify and is driving social grievances up to the roof. According to an article reported by *The Economist,* aggrieved villagers in the southern province of Guangdong rose up in December against land-grabbing officials, chasing the local party chief away.

It seems that the only logical way to tackle the local spending deficit is to secure additional sources of stable revenue and imposing a property tax could be one of the most viable options. A property tax raises revenue year after year, in contrast to a land lease, which can be sold only once. Apart from that, taxing property allows the local government to capture some of the value invested, such as local amenities. And as property values rise, so do the taxes they are able to collect.

However, taxing property in China can be very difficult. The government has tried imposing a variety of levies on the sale, size and historical cost of property, but none on market value of homes. Chongqing and Shanghai introduced a pilot tax on some upmarket homes a year ago but the tax was largely symbolic, levied at low rates on a few thousand homes in each city.In addition, for such tax to be rolled out nationally, it would require homes to be registered, title to be clear and appraisal of property values to be credible. This is particularly difficult in developing countries when public records are not well managed. Imposing a property tax would make it more expensive to buy or even hold a second or third home as a speculative bet on rising prices. That would have a dramatic influence on the overall profitability of the property market.

Whether there is a bubble in China's property market remains a matter of heated debate but it is undeniable that the Chinese government's prime priority is to curb property speculation. As China is a planned economy, the government could use (i) macro-economic measures, (ii) fiscal policy and (iii) monetary policy to maneuver the real estate market while maintaining social stability and economic growth.

The macro-economic perspective: tightening measures dampening the growth

Growing protests and social grievances in the mainland have been brought to the government's attention since late 2009. Members of the public (including both grass-roots and middle-class) have started complaining about being unable to afford homes in large cities. There is a joke in China that getting a home is a must before marriage.

It is not uncommon to see long queues of people wanting to buy a flat in different parts of China. Since then the government has started tightening macro-economic measures to address the overheated housing market. The effect of tightening macro-economic policies started to appear in 2011 and the property price bubble has started to deflate since then. A number of political and macro-economic measures were exercised:

Prevention of speculative funds

The Central Government has enacted policies to stop the property bubbles from bursting and to prevent new bubbles. It has announced in late 2010 that it would monitor capital flows to stop speculative funds from jeopardizing China's property market as well as the developing China economy. A new nation-wide real estate tax was introduced in 2010 to control speculative investing.

Restriction on home ownership

In order to prevent over-investment by Chinese citizens, the Chinese cabinet has begun requiring Chinese families purchasing a second home to make at least a 40 percent down payment (50 percent in some cities). It has successfully prevented the middle class from over-investing in the property market and controlled the number of vacant residential flats in the state. It also helped to minimize the financial risk of banks when people leverage cheap funding for speculation.

Some major cities, such as Beijing and Shanghai, have actually banned sale of properties to non-local residents. Those who are allowed to purchase a flat in these Tier 1 cities must have resided in the city for more than five years. Even for native Beijing and Shanghai families, they are only allowed to own at the most two flats in the city.

Raising the interest rate

The PBoC has raised the interest rate thrice in 2011, to increase property investors' costs as well as to increase the developers' cost of construction.

There was once a mortgage discount for first-time homeowners; the scheme offered a discount on mortgage payments. However, it has been eliminated in 2011 after the Central Government noticed the overheating of the property market.

Moreover, the PBoC has also raised the Required Reserve Ratio to over 20 percent in late 2011. It has tightened banks' liquidity and enhanced the quality of loans of banks. The majority of the banks immediately lowered the proportion of property developers' loans and other real estate related lending. The banks became more prudent in lending and became more willing to retain more reserve so as to meet the regulatory requirements.

Controlling local governments on land sale

Since the year 2000, local governments in China have taken advantage of the loose regulations from the Central Government. The local governments have sold local land to property developers, in order to raise revenue. This income accounted for about 50 percent of total revenue of some local governments. The result was continued sales and development of local land. In 2010, the Central Government imposed strict restrictions on selling of land for revenue. All land selling activities must be well justified before they can be approved.

The fiscal policy perspective: the role of the Chinese government

Background of fiscal policy

China relies heavily on fiscal policy measures to achieve rebalancing of the economy and also to sustain a harmonious society. An analysis of recent Chinese policies regarding government revenue and expenditure help shed some light on their possible impact on China's real estate market.

Reliance on land sale revenue of government budget

Using data available from CEIC, it is clear how, after the Tax Sharing System (TSS) reform in 1994, government revenue increased significantly. Before the reform, the Central Government set a fixed target tax rate for each province, which meant that local firms only needed to pay the fixed tax regardless of performance, even under normal inflation. This previous system had many imperfections, such as a limited tax base and poor tax collection, resulting in a trough in revenue experienced in 1994–1995, as seen in Figure 4.11:

Before the reform, it was usual for the Central Government to borrow funds from local governments which prompted the saying: "Poor central, Rich local". On the other hand, after the reform, the Central Government started to control the main taxation, known as VAT, with the Central Government receiving 75 percent and local governments enjoying only 25 percent. Subsequently, the positive effect brought on by the TSS reform to government revenue, especially Central Government, was obvious. Furthermore, one could argue that it was in part thanks to this high level of growth in revenue that government expenditure increased accordingly and GDP ultimately grew so fast after the mid-1990s.

However, looking at Figure 4.11, one can see that some additional changes took place in government revenue later on, after this reform. First, the growth of tax revenue became slower in recent years, especially after 2008. China presents an issue called "Rich country, Poor citizens", which means the income, particularly the disposable income of most citizens, is low while the government has large amounts of funds, and one of the rooted reasons for this is taxation. Consequently some revisions were made in 2008. For example the personal income tax exemption limit was raised, in order to boost individual disposable incomes. Additionally, another change that was established was to allow the cost of fixed assets to be deducted from output tax which in turn encourages firms to innovate. The target of this 2008 revision was to lighten the burden of individuals and enterprises.

As of now, there is a debate going on about how the financial crisis might push the Chinese government to use tax policy to correct the unreasonable syndrome "Rich country, Poor citizens" and also to stimulate consumption. This is also due to the fact that China's GDP growth has been on account of high investment, high exports and low consumption, a pattern that has badly suffered from the decline in export demand. Another main change being proposed is that the government's non-tax revenue should increase dramatically. The major part of this

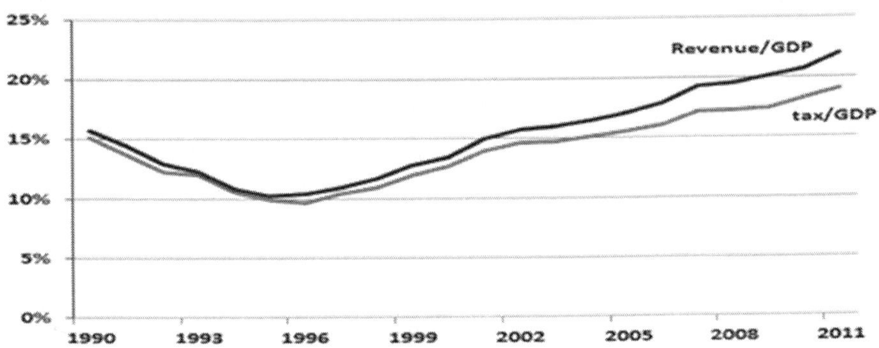

Figure 4.11 Evolution of government revenue as a percent of GDP

Source: CEIC data

non-tax revenue is "land-revenue". Due to the TSS reform, tax revenue of local governments cannot cover their expenditure; on the other hand, revenue from land does not need to be shared with the Central Government. This explains the issue of "Di Wang 地王" which means the "most expensive land". A non-tax revenue reform can increase the revenue, especially of local governments. However, there are some disadvantages. The most significant one is that non-tax revenue has discretionary areas, i.e. it is difficult to control non-tax revenue by related laws. For example, in the case of real estate, which is our main concern here, "land revenue" issues have led to higher prices of land-use rights and the price of real estate is also rising quickly and the burden on citizens has become heavier which contradicts the target of tax revision. However, the government cannot use existing laws to solve this essential problem immediately. In other words, it has hysteresis quality on controlling non-tax revenue.

Government expenditure

The explosive growth experienced in China over the last 20 years can be largely attributed to the vast amount of expenditure incurred for upgrading infrastructure, education, health and social security and welfare. The increased level of government spending, which soared from RMB 339 billion in 1991 to RMB 10,893 billion in 2011 (this is equivalent to a 32.1 times increase over the last two decades), was fundamental in sustaining the level of growth observed over this period as seen in Figure 4.12.

Arguably, an increase in government spending (G) results in an increase in interest rates and an increase in demand for local currency. Fiscal policy was effectively used to stimulate aggregate demand in the case of China. Nevertheless the government should be careful not to boost aggregate demand too much or else inflationary gaps can emerge. Arguably, this issue is what may also be impacting the real estate market; too much aggregate demand for real estate has inflated prices. Additionally, higher interest rates, which have resulted from increased

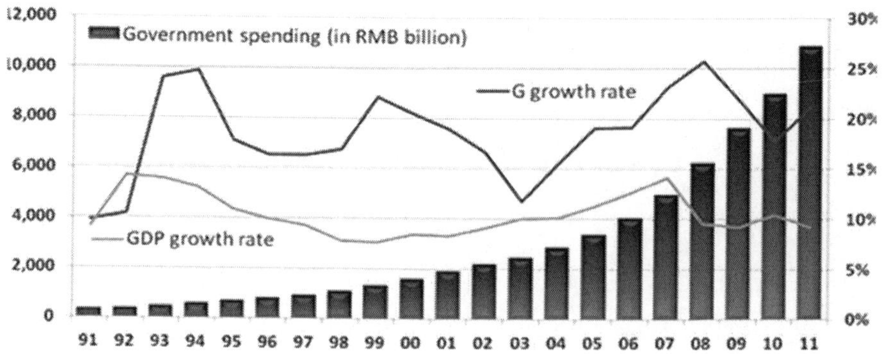

Figure 4.12 Evolution of government spending (G)

Source: CEIC data

government spending as mentioned before, have resulted in more expensive mortgages and hence higher property prices.

The monetary policy perspective: factors determining the housing prices

Background of monetary policies

Fluctuations in China's housing prices can be partly attributed to government control of the economy. The recession starts when the government tries to end speculation in the real estate business by raising mortgage rates and tightening limits on bank lending and mortgage availability. On the other hand, lower interest rates and loosening mortgage down payment requirements tend to accelerate housing price rise. These analyses suggest that Chinese monetary policy actions are the key driving force behind the change of the real estate price rise in China.

The Central Bank of China (i.e. PBoC) monetary policy can affect the real estate price through three major channels:

- PBoC interest rate
- Money supply
- Specific policy on lending to the real estate sector

First, the central bank's adjustment of the long-term benchmark bank loan rate can change the mortgage rate and the rate for real estate development projects, which leads to the change in demand for loans and ultimately decelerates or accelerates rises in real estate prices. Second, expansion or contraction in the growth of money supply can increase or decrease money available with commercial banks for lending, which affects the supply of credit to the real estate sector. It can also change the public's inflationary expectations and demand for realty. Third, the central bank's real estate specific credit policy on mortgage down payment requirements can increase or reduce the supply of mortgage credit, which contributes to change in real estate prices. Mortgage loans play an essential role in most homeowners' lives as the residential home price in major cities in China is around 30 times the average household annual income. At the same time, real estate developers also rely heavily on bank loans to support their project development. The macro control of China's real estate sector through the general monetary policy and specific mortgage credit policy has played a pivotal role in the dynamics of the real estate sector.

To exercise such control, the People's Bank of China can make use of three major tools, interest rate policy, reserve requirements and credit policy through window guidance to control the growth of the real estate market.

Interest rate policy

Bank rates in China are still guided by the People's Bank of China. Interest rates offered by banks can fluctuate only within a range around the benchmark rates. Unlike the US, adjustment of the benchmark interest rate in China is infrequent and is heavily controlled by the central bank. It is not market driven. Mortgage rates are generally according to the long-term (over 5 years) benchmark bank loan rate set by the People's Bank of China and, therefore, it is an important monetary policy tool that affects the real estate prices.

Reserve requirements

A reserve requirement is a frequently used monetary tool in China. It can be used to change the aggregate credit and money supply, as well as to adjust the credit structure through different reserve ratios. For instance, in order to give more support to small and medium-sized enterprises and rural areas, the required reserve ratio for small and medium financial institutions and rural financial institutions is lower than that for the major financial institutions. Generally, a higher required ratio reduces money supply while a lower reserve ratio increases money supply.

Credit policy and window guidance

Most banks in China are state-owned, which means asset prices are highly affected by monetary policy. Therefore, the central bank's monetary policy is expected to have a stronger impact on real estate prices in China than other more deregulated markets. Since commoditization in 1998, the real estate sector has been identified as a strategic focus in China's economic development. For the past 14 years (1998–2012), the Chinese real estate market has gone through many phases of development.

In the initial phase (1998 to the first half of 2003), real estate prices rose steadily under the expansionary monetary policy. During those years, commercial banks were encouraged to provide mortgage loans to individuals under the central bank's guidance. Moreover, there was a significant drop in mortgage rate from 10.53 percent to 5.76 percent and the minimum down payment requirement was only 20 percent.

The central bank began to tighten its monetary policy in June 2003 to prevent price speculation in the real estate market. In addition to applying the traditional monetary policy tools such as setting higher reserve requirements and higher benchmark loan rates, the People's Bank of China also pressured commercial banks to tighten control on real estate loans by increasing the minimum down payment requirement. However, there was still a dramatic rise in real estate prices despite tightening of the monetary policy.

Real estate price rises finally began to decelerate during the global financial crisis in the third quarter of 2008. In order to combat the decrease in exports and economic growth due to the global financial crisis, the People's Bank of China implemented an expansionary monetary policy which resulted in tremendous expansion of money supply and bank loans. Moreover, towards the end of the credit crisis, many global investors shifted their investment focus to China to seek long-term growth on their investments, which leads to enormous amounts of hot money flowing into China. As a result, the national home price index rebounded swiftly from –1.1 percent in the first quarter of 2009 to 5.8 percent in the fourth quarter of the same year.

At the beginning of 2010, the Chinese government once again tightened its monetary policy to try to control the overheating housing market. Nearly two years of tightening policies have cooled down China's once hot real estate market. Volume of transactions in commodity housing in major cities started to drop significantly since early 2011, and by the second half of that year, housing prices in mid- and large-sized cities stopped rising, signaling the beginning of a downward trend. Even though China's commodity housing market has existed for less than two decades, it has quickly developed into a vast industry with close connections to the overall macro-economy.

4.6. What does the future hold for China's real estate market?

The Chinese real estate market has experienced headwinds and many investors, along with the Central Government, are concerned about its growth pattern.

Real estate investment growth has remained very high until early 2012 because private development activity was still brisk, though China's social housing program has begun to make a more substantial contribution to the industry. With officials resolving to maintain strict controls over the property market, the slowdown in real estate investment is not surprising and is likely to persist in the second half of 2012. Property developers have shown a willingness to discount property prices to boost sales and improve cash flow as well as liquidity, thereby strengthening their balance sheet and ability to meet debt obligations.

It is beyond doubt that China's leaders have pledged to continue curbing speculation in the housing market. They are also trying to prevent the property market from having a "hard landing", the Central Government has put in place a series of measures (higher down payments, stricter reserves requirement and higher interest rates to name a few) to prevent the market from hitting a bubble.

Market status after a series of austerity measures

According to the National Bureau of Statistics, prices in more than 70 major cities and growth in sales have decelerated after the austerity measures have taken effect. In particular, since the peak prices in April 2010, there has been a steady deceleration of price increases to just 4 percent as of May 2011 (compared with a price rise of 13 percent year on year in April 2010). Meanwhile, transactions volume has also declined (Figure 4.13), both in terms of land transaction and residential land transaction.

Mid-term market outlook

With officials resolve to maintain property controls, the slowdown in real estate investment is not surprising, and persisted in the second quarter of 2012. However, these measures have forced developers to lower properties in order to boost sales, thereby strengthening balance sheets and improving their ability to meet debt obligations. What is happening now is that buyers are attracted to projects with at least a discount of 15–30 percent, whereas undiscounted projects have drawn little interest. In April, new house prices fell in 46 out of 70 cities monitored by the National Bureau of Statistics (compared to 38 cities a month earlier), with 16 cities recording flat prices and only 8 registering price increases.

Figure 4.13 Land and residential land transaction volume, July 2012

Source: National Bureau of Statistics of China

The tightening measures since 2011 have had the strongest impact on primary market transactions volume and it strained developers' cash flow, bringing in a correction to both primary and secondary market residential prices. It was reported that the Chinese government has pledged to continue curbing speculation in the housing market – essentially banning investment purchases, while cutting some slack for legitimate first-time home buyers. As mentioned in the earlier sections, some easing was identified at the local level, where local governments have been subsidizing purchases of renovated homes, or relaxing the criterion defining first-time homebuyers.

Meanwhile, the social housing program initiated by the Chinese government could potentially cushion the real estate market against the slowdown. According to the Ministry of Housing and Urban-Rural Development (MoHURD), nearly RMB 1.3 trillion was invested in social housing projects last year, with funding from central and local government budgets, bank loans and private sources. This amount equals approximately 29.3 percent of total residential real estate investment in 2011. The official report is that MoHURD has budgeted 7 million new projects in 2012 (from 10.4 million units in 2011), which can bring the total number of units under construction to 17–18 million, with 5 million units planned for completion (compared to 4.3 million units last year). From January to April, 2.28 million social housing units were started, while 1.5 million units were completed. MoHURD estimated that the total investment in social housing could amount to RMB 247 billion.

To secure a steady stream of funding, the Ministry of Finance required all local governments to prioritize social housing projects with proceeds from the issuance of municipal bonds since February (Figure 4.14). The Shanghai and Chongqing governments have also been requested to channel revenues from property tax towards social housing construction. The chart above shows that new property development loans have been skewed towards social housing in recent quarters, whereas commercial (i.e. private sector) development loans have seen a decline.

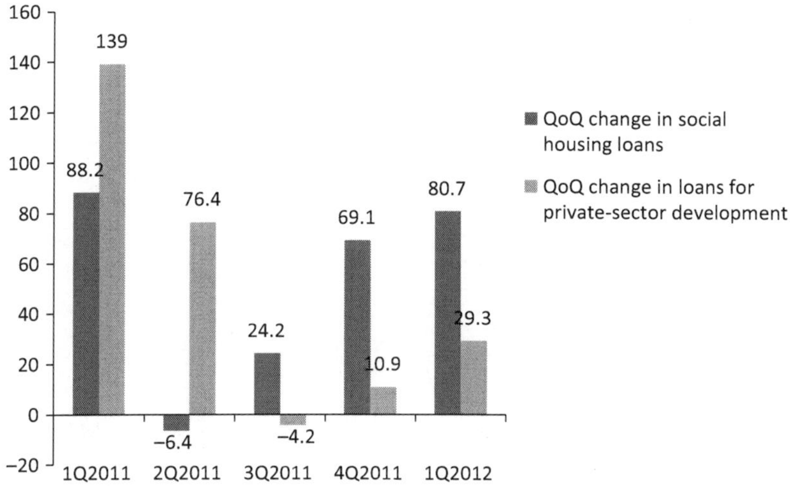

Figure 4.14 Change in China's stock of property development loans from 2011–2012

Source: CEIC

These social housing developments, along with a reasonable level of price discounting, have brought an improvement in residential volumes. According to Soufun, Centaline Property has reported a 28 percent YoY increase in floor space sold in primary markets.

The rapid urbanization in China is another positive factor for the housing market. China's urbanization rate in 1998 was 34 percent and it had climbed sharply to 52 percent by 2011. Though the majority of housing prices remain out of reach for the rural migrants who relocate for work, they have generated a massive rental demand. Many urban families in turn seek to capitalize on this opportunity by renting out their apartments and then moving to a new home of higher quality. Coupled with the effects of inflation, housing prices have climbed in 35 major Chinese cities from 2008 to early 2010. Given that China's economy is forecast to grow at least 8 percent for the next five years or so, the urbanization rate is predicted to rise with economic expansion to about 70 percent in the next 20 years. The rising urban population and growing household income will no doubt produce huge demand for housing.

Another positive factor that is likely to prevent the real estate market from crashing is the low average household leverage. China is well known for its high savings rate relative to other nations in Asia. In 2011, the home mortgage to total bank loans in China was roughly 13 percent only and the percentage of housing debt to GDP was reported to be 32 percent. The down payment requirement in China is typically no less than 30 percent and sometimes can be as high as 60 percent for the second home. With the current household savings rate standing at almost 40 percent, it is very unlikely that the Chinese homeowners will be forced to sell their homes or default on their loans due to a drop in housing prices.

Despite concerns about the oversupply in housing markets in some regions, some luxury property developers believe the China market is not even close to saturation. There is still plenty of room for "five-star" developments, catering to retail tenants with higher brand equity and the ability to pay higher rent. Currently, the lack of know-how in high-end retail property development in China's housing market provides an edge to experienced Hong Kong developers. Some experienced luxury developers, such as Hung Lung, have pointed out that the development of satellite towns in China and expanding public transport linkages create needs for suburban malls and related amenities in these new communities. As the household income continues to rise, so does the demand for high-end property. That said, there is a lucrative housing segment waiting to be exploited, counting on the fact that government policies will increasingly favor developers who cater to first-time homebuyers/owner-occupiers.

References

Ahearne, Alan G., John Ammer, Brian M. Doyle, Linda S. Kole and Robert F. Martin. 2005. House prices and monetary policy: a cross-country study. Board of Governors of the Federal Reserve System, International Finance Discussion Papers. www.federalreserve.gov/pubs/ifdp/2005/841/ifdp841.pdf

BBC. China to control shadow banking and private lending. www.bbc.co.uk/news/business-15380188

Bernanke, B. S. 2010, January. Monetary policy and the housing bubble. Speech at the Annual Meeting of the American Economic Association. *The Economist.* www.economist.com/blogs/graphicdetail/2012/06/focus-1. Retrieved 12 June 2012.

Bloomberg. 2011, 28 January. China approves property tax trials to curb prices. www.bloomberg.com/news/2011-01-28/china-approves-property-tax-trials-in-shanghai-chongqing-to-curb-prices.html

Bloomberg. 2011, 22 September. Chinese developers plunge in Hong Kong trading on trust financing report. www.bloomberg.com/news/2011-09-22/china-developers-fall-on-reports-of-more-lending-restrictions.html

Caijing. 2011, 23 September. Half of developers' new debts are trust loans: Credit Suisse report. http://english.caijing.com.cn/2011-09-23/110871892.html

China 50. 2012. Jones Lang LaSalle. www.joneslanglasalle.com/MediaResources/Global/China50-Research-March-2012.pdf

China Daily. 2011, 14 July. Property loans halted in 2nd and 3rd Tier cities. www.chinadaily.com.cn/2011-07/14/content_12905606.htm

China Residential Market Watch. 中国住宅市场观察 Q3 2011, Knight Frank and Holdways Offices, KnightFrank.com.cn

The Economist. October 23, 2012. A revolution fizzles: Village democracy. http://english.cw.com.tw/article.do?action=show&id=13863

Emerging Trends in Real Estate® Asia Pacific 2013, 2012. www.pwccn.com/home/eng/ap_real_estate_emerging_2013.html

The Free Library. 2011, November 28. China to maintain property curbs. www.thefreelibrary.com/China to maintain property curbs: vice-premier-a01612543272BBC.

Fung, Ester. *The Wall Street Journal.* 2011, 28 November. Latest property move by Beijing might signal concern. http://online.wsj.com/news/articles/SB10001424052970203802204577065790281253290

Geoff Dyer. *Financial Times*. 2011, 27 January. Chinese cities to pilot property tax. www.ft.com/cms/s/0/1fa40714-2a38-11e0-b906-00144feab49a.html

Global Times. 2011, 30 August. China's Second-and-Third-Tier cities expected to impose home purchase restrictions. http://english.cri.cn/6826/2011/08/30/2702s655876.htm

The Guardian. 2011, 5 March. Wen Jiabao makes pledge to China's poor at National People's Congress. www.theguardian.com/world/2011/mar/05/wen-jiabao-pledges-china-poor

Jarocinski, Marek and Frank R. Smets. 2008. House prices and the stance of monetary policy. *Federal Reserve Bank of St. Louis Review* 90 (4): 340–65.

KPMG. 2011, April. China's 12th Five Year Plan: transportation and logistics. www.kpmg.com/CN/en/IssuesAndInsights/ArticlesPublications/Documents/China-12th-Five-Year-Plan-Transportation-Logistics-201104.pdf

Li Ruogu. 2003, October. China's monetary and fiscal policy. Bank for International, Fiscal Issues and Central Banking in Emerging Economies (p. 107). BIS Paper No. 20. Available at SSRN: http://ssrn.com/abstract=1188109.

McMillan, Alex Frew. CNBC. 2011, 7 March. China property boom faces major headwinds in Tier 2 cities. www.cnbc.com/id/41959044

Raymond, Y. C. TSE. 2000. China's real estate market and the Asian financial crisis. Hong Kong Institute of Real Estate. www.hkir.com/Emerging%20Market%20Quarterly.pdf

The Wall Street Journal. 2011, 9 June. A taxonomy of China housing market bad guys. http://blogs.wsj.com/chinarealtime/2011/06/09/a-taxonomy-of-china-housing-market-bad-guys/

WantChina Times. 2011, 12 November. Chinese property developers find themselves in the red. www.wantchinatimes.com/news-subclass-cnt.aspx?id=20111112000006&cid=1202

White, Thomas. 2010, April. China real estate – a boom or a bubble? www.thomaswhite.com/global-perspectives/china-real-estate-a-boom-or-a-bubble/

Xinhuanet. 2011, 26 June. Chinese developers shun construction of affordable housing. http://news.xinhuanet.com/english2010/china/2011-06/26/c_13951033.htm

Yantao Li. 2010, 30 April. Overview: China real estate market. www.chinavestor.com/knowledge-base/economy/71687-overview-china-real-estate-market.html

Zhang, Xiaoling. 2010. Competitiveness for real estate developers: a China study. The Hong Kong Polytechnic University

Zhang, G., and Fung, H. G. 2006. On the imbalance between the real estate market and the stock markets in China. Chinese economy, 39(2), 26-39. Jia You, Hao Wu and Sun Sheng Han. 2011, January. Origin and diversity? the Chinese property developer in the Nanjing affordable housing market. Pacific Rim Real Estate Society Conference, PRRES 2011

Websites

Centaline property, hk.centanet.com
The China Banking Regulatory Commission, www.cbrc.gov.cn
China Trust Association, www.xtxh.net
Ministry of Industry and Information Technology, www.miit.gov.cn
National Bureau of Statistics of China, www.stats.gov.cn
Organisation for Economic Co-operation and Development, www.oecd.org
The People's Bank of China, www.pbc.gov.cn
Soufun, www.soufun.com
The State Administration of Taxation, www.chinatax.gov.cn
World Business Council for Sustainable Development, www.wbcsd.org

5 The insurance market in China

5.1. Brief historical development of the Chinese insurance market

First phase – initial development from the 19th century

Modern insurance practices were introduced in China during the middle of the 19th century. Shanghai was the main city where all the relevant companies set up their offices. Historically the first giants included two British and two domestic insurance companies which merged to form Yong Fu and Da Dong Fang there in 1846. Ren Ji He, a pure Chinese insurance company, was later founded in Shanghai in 1887, providing shipping and marine insurance. Following that in 1911, the first domestic Chinese life insurance company, Hua An He Quan, was founded there. Until 1919, the global giant insurers, including American Insurance Group (AIG) of the United States, set up their establishments again in Shanghai.

In 1949 when the People's Republic of China was founded, Chinese society entered a new era of development. The new Chinese government enacted several measures regarding the insurance market. The first state-owned national insurance company, the People's Insurance Company of China (PICC), was formed on 20 October 1949. The government started to restrict foreign insurance companies and many either left China entirely or relocated to Hong Kong by 1952. Later, PICC became the sole provider of insurance in mainland China, providing all sorts of insurance services. Up until 1976 the insurance industry had almost ceased operations and companies were either state-owned or "self-insured."

Second phase – development after China's Open Door Policy in the late 1970s

In 1980, when the insurance market was first reopened as part of Deng Xiaoping's economic reforms and open door policies, People's Insurance Company of China (PICC) was re-established on 1 January 1984, with its main business being property insurance, agricultural, marine and export credit insurance, in addition to reinsurance. PICC was supervised by the People's Bank of China as an independent insurance company.

Since its economic reform, China has begun to gradually decrease direct social security protection. Insurance has become a necessary protection for many citizens. Due to the desperate demand, the Chinese government allowed new players to join the local insurance market.

In 1987, the Bank of Communications of China set up an insurance department, the predecessor of the China Pacific Insurance Company later established in Shanghai. In 1988, the Ping An Insurance Company was established in the Shenzhen Special Economic Zone, the first joint stock insurance company in China, which was later developed into the China Ping An Insurance Company in 1992.

Third phase – insurance development in China after the 1990s

Both domestic players and foreign insurers were eager to tap China in the early 1990s. In 1992, AIA, a life insurance company of AIG, got the first insurance license from the Chinese government to set up a branch in Shanghai. It offered life insurance and introduced the individual agent marketing method, which further stimulated the development of Chinese life insurance. Three national insurers were major players competing in the Chinese market, PICC, China Pacific and China Ping An, which was also named as the three-pillar stage.

The Insurance Law of the People's Republic of China, the first specialized law for insurance, was issued on 30 June 1995, and took effect on October 1. This set the basic standards of the insurance industry, its policy and regulations, as well as the principle of business separation.

In 1996, according to the principle of business separation under the Insurance Law of China, PICC was restructured into a group company with three subsidiaries, later named PICC Property, PICC Life and PICC Re, which were all independent entities. Later in 1998, the PICC group was disbanded and these companies were renamed accordingly as China Life Insurance, China Property Insurance (PICC) and China Reinsurance.

Three new nationwide insurance companies were set up in 1996, namely, Hua Tai Property Insurance Co. Ltd., Tai Kang Life Insurance Company and New China Life Insurance Company. Two regional domestic property insurance companies were also granted licenses. At the same time, China extended the scope of the life insurance market in 1996. Manulife also obtained a license to set up the first Sino–foreign joint venture in life insurance, the Zhong Hong Company, in Shanghai.

At the end of 1996, there were eight nationwide insurance companies and 13 regional companies (five Chinese companies, one Chinese–foreign joint venture and seven branch companies of foreign insurers) competing fiercely in the market. At that time, the Chinese per capita spending on insurance was USD 7.64 as compared to USD 1.7 in India.

In 1998, the specialized insurance regulatory ministry, the China Insurance Regulatory Commission (CIRC), was set up to take over regulation from the People's Bank of China (PBoC). This was also a milestone in the Chinese insurance regulation that accelerated the development of the insurance industry.

When the insurance industry resumed operations in 1980, insurance premiums totaled roughly RMB 640 million (USD 77.4 million) whereas the market was growing at an average rate of 26 percent at that time and reached RMB 159 billion (USD 19.2 billion) by the year 2000.

Recent development – insurance industry development after 2000

China formally joined the WTO in 2001 and started opening the market for life insurance, non-life insurance, reinsurance and insurance brokerage gradually. Almost all limitations on admittance and business scope were removed in the following three to five years. The Chinese insurance market became part of the world insurance market and more international players entered the market.

The restructuring of state-owned insurance companies in 2003 was a remarkable achievement, a great leap forward to raise the competitiveness of the Chinese national insurance companies. PICC, China Life and China Re also completed their reorganization with PICC as the holding company, holding PICC property; China Life was reformed as China Life (Group) Company and China Life Insurance Stock Limited Company; and China Re was renamed as China Reinsurance (Group) Company, with three subsidiaries, China P&C Reinsurance, China Life Reinsurance and China Continent Property Insurance Company Ltd. In addition, PICC (Holding) and China Life (Group) established their own asset management companies; this was a special milestone for the China insurance asset and investment management system development.

Ping An Insurance (Group) Company also purchased a Chinese regional bank in 2004. This restructuring diversified international development of China's insurance market. Furthermore, PICC Property was the first mainland Chinese insurance company listed on the Hong Kong Stock Exchange (HKSE) in 2003, with a market value of HK$4,226 million. On 17 December 2003, another company, China Life Insurance Company Ltd. got listed on the New York Stock Exchange and traded on the HKSE. The overseas financing scope of China life insurance reached a record high USD 3.5 billion, marking it the highest fund-raising exercise in the global capital market in 2003. Following this, Ping An Insurance (Group) Company Ltd. also listed on the HKSE in 2004 successfully. Chinese insurance companies are clearly moving towards global markets and are seeking a major role in the global financial platform.

5.2. Overview of the Chinese insurance market

The global insurance market is a multi-billion dollar industry. It is estimated that the global premium written is USD 4.3 trillion. In China, however, the market is still in its early growth phase with the gross insurance premium for China being closer to USD 210 billion (circa 5 percent of the global market). This might be small but the market has experienced extremely rapid growth in the past 10 years and has grown almost sevenfold during that time. Insurance penetration in China is a mere 3 percent and this was most vividly illustrated during the devastating

Sichuan earthquake in 2008. Aggregate damages were estimated at RMB 150 billion while assets worth only about RMB 1 billion were insured. This discrepancy caused significant losses for the uninsured and also highlighted the massive opportunity for Chinese insurance companies to take a more aggressive role in the market. As the standard of living in China increases over the next 20 or 30 years due to increased wealth and consumption, Chinese insurance regulations are evolving and China is opening up to more foreign businesses and investors, the insurance market landscape in China will inevitably see equally material changes.

The insurance industry is a tough industry to break into as it takes years to develop a successful business and establish a local presence. Similar to banks, insurance companies' downfalls can come almost suddenly because of one bad decision or risk taken – one only needs to look at AIG as an example. AIG dates back to 1919 when it was founded in Shanghai. The firm grew into the strongest insurance company in the world, but was brought down in one year when the firm took too much risk insuring complex financial derivatives linked to the US housing market (CDOs, MBs, etc.). The difficulties of this industry and the companies which compete in it will also apply to the Chinese insurance companies despite the significant market opportunity they have.

In China there are two main types of insurance – life insurance and property and casualty (P&C) insurance. Life insurance is by far the more dominant of the two and constitutes about 70 percent of all insurance premiums written in China. This breakdown of the market and overweight of life insurance is different from the composition of the global insurance market which is distributed more evenly between these two insurance types. Also missing in China is the global reinsurance market. The following sections examine the Chinese life insurance market, the property and casualty market, and then finally some of the largest domestic players in these two markets. Although not surprising, it is domestic insurance companies that dominate about 95 percent of the market in China.

Life insurance in China

Life insurance was traditionally designed to protect families in situations when the breadwinner passes away. Insurance allowed those left behind to pay for the funeral, the mortgage and other life expenses. However, both the concept and market have evolved into a much more sophisticated service and financial instrument and the proverb of living poor and dying rich no longer applies. Policyholders today can draw down the benefits that would have been previously set aside for their loved ones. Individuals and companies can now use life insurance for asset accumulation and as a wealth management tool.

Within the life insurance market in China, there are four main types of products and insurance policies which place emphasis on savings. This enables future benefits to become more variable and policies are increasingly being classified according to the profit-sharing mechanism.

Traditional: Traditional products do not have any profit-sharing mechanism. Examples of this type of product are term, life, accident and health policies.

As they have a pre-determined liability, the cost is known and underwriters can retain surplus profit. These types are less popular in China, as customers understand that they cannot share investment gains.

Participating: Participating policies developed from the preference for participation in the Chinese market. The premiums are consolidated in a pool and invested, which allows policyholders to share the operating profit. It is not a transparent product as customers are uncertain of its true profitability. Furthermore underwriters have the authority to decide how much they should release. They rarely distribute all of the investment profit in a single year. Even during good years, underwriters are known to use the excess surplus to smooth over the poor years and give the investors / policyholders more stable returns.

Universal life: Universal life policies allow a greater degree of sharing in investment gains. After subtracting the risk charge and expenses from premiums paid by policyholders, the remainder goes into a pool and is invested. This transparency usually leads to lower margins for insurance companies, particularly as the monthly disclosure has led to some insurers maintaining a fairly generous payout even when performance is weak. Similar to participating policies, underwriters are able to hold surplus reserve in good years to provide a cushion for harder times.

Units linked: Units linked policies is the fourth form of insurance policy in China. They act in a manner similar to mutual funds. Insurers charge a management fee and a risk premium, while policyholders can choose their funds and have to bear the related investment risks. It is the most transparent of the insurance products available as the NAV is updated daily. It is a low-risk business for insurance firms and the margins therefore trail other segments.

In China about 80 percent of life insurance products are investment related. Participating policies make up about 51 percent of the market, 23 percent is traditional, universal life makes up about 20 percent and unit linked only 6 percent of the market. It is important to note that both participating and universal products may have an element of guaranteed return in them – thus the insurance firm bears the risk.

Another common way to classify products in China is based on the payment terms “single” and “regular”. Policies involving only one upfront payment are called single premium products. Those that bring recurring premium payments are called regular premiums. This classification also distinguishes the margins. Single premium products are structured as an investment fund with limited protection. The premium size is much bigger than for regular, as it is one-off. The coverage duration is usually shorter and margins are typically in the low single digits. Single premium products make up about 50 percent of the market because of the dominance of bank distribution.

Distribution of insurance products is a key element in the market and integral to the industry’s profitability. Plans tend to be executed via agents or via bancassurance. Agency refers to tied agents, who sell exclusively for one insurer. This channel is the most expensive to develop as an insurer has to provide offices, training and marketing support. The large workforce also poses management challenges, as turnover is high and productivity can vary tremendously. The second distribution platform – bancassurance – is growing very rapidly. Bancassurance constitutes about 50 percent of the life market distribution and refers to distribution through bank branches. It is generally not an exclusive agreement and thus insurance companies can use a diverse set of banks to distribute their products. Banks view the distribution of third-party financial products as a major revenue booster because of the large fee income generated. Insurance firms provide training to bank employees and often even have their own representatives based in local branches. Banks have the widest customer reach in China, and that is why they have become the primary platform for distribution.

Commissions are positively correlated with profitability. The more profitable a product, the more generous the underwriter is with commissions for distributors. The commission rate for a single premium bancassurance product is usually around 3–4 percent. However, it is not unusual for some insurers to pay out more than 5 percent. Lack of control over distribution can cause commissions to rise and is also more risky for the insurer as the banks can remove them from their products overnight – this can be a significant problem.

The property and casualty market

While the life market only targets individuals, P&C involves much wider coverage, providing protection to both individuals and corporations and their assets, casualties and liabilities. The most popular type of product in China is auto insurance, accounting for 69 percent of total P&C premiums, followed by commercial property which accounts for about 10 percent of the business. The remainder of the market comprises agriculture, liability, accident, cargo, construction and others. With automobiles being such a large percentage of the market, the risks generally lack diversity – a direct result of underdevelopment of China's social and economic systems. In the US, coverage of senior directors and officers in large companies through professional indemnity constitutes big business for insurance companies. This segment is almost non-existent in China as the legal system is not mature enough and business owners do not see any need to take liability coverage for their key personnel. Besides workers compensation is not mandatory and a push by regulators is necessary to accelerate the development of this area. As foreign businesses move into China in the future with international compliance requirements, it is fair to expect that this part of the Chinese insurance market will develop further.

The P&C business, unlike the life market, is a short tail business and most policies are paid and renewed every year. Commissions and prices are adjusted annually, according to operational results. However, renewal is not guaranteed and insurers may refuse coverage after a bad claims experience, or if the risk quality and appetite decreases.

Distribution of P&C insurance policies occurs through third-party distributors – car dealers and independent agencies – for more than half of the business. Since auto insurance generates 70 percent of total premiums, car dealers have a significant role to play within the overall P&C insurance market. Insurance companies are then forced to pay them high commissions, leading to very low profitability. Because of the spread paid to car dealers and other third-party dealers, the P&C insurance market has begun to adopt direct marketing. It is a more cost efficient way to sell commoditized products, such as insurance policies. By taking back control from the distributors, insurance companies are better able to control the cost ratio. The incentives also change – third-party distributors take a commission from every policy sold and therefore they are not concerned with the quality of the business or policyholders. Some of the control is ceded to distributors to better manage the cost ratio. The commission rate should reflect the quality of the business underwritten. An insurer is more willing to offer a higher commission to get business with a low loss ratio. The auto business does not follow this principle. It has a disproportionately high commission rate, sometimes more than 30 percent. Quite often, underwriters find themselves not having enough say in deciding the commissions. Although there are regulatory guidelines, the craving for volume tends to shift the balance towards distributors.

Margins are very important in the P&C market. The underwriting profit is measured by the combined ratio, which is the sum of the expense ratio and the loss ratio. It depends on prices charged, commissions paid out, operating expenses incurred and claims expenses. The margin paid out in the P&C business is much more transparent than in the life business. The short duration means profitability is more visible. Companies do not generally share profits with customers and the investment return comes as a bonus to underwriting profit. Nonetheless margins are not particularly attractive in China. Inappropriate pricing is a major problem. Auto is a regulated product and the price category is set in accordance with the CIRC. The industry follows the price guidelines but it plays around with discounts which can sometimes be more that 30 percent, not only in auto but in large-scale commercial risks also. The latter is especially risky because it is not as well modeled as auto. The lack of underwriting discipline puts a lot of expectation and burden on the investment results to turn things around and keep the company adrift. This has driven some managements to overload on equities, impairing risk profiles. The reality can be poor underwriting and poor investment, hurting both earnings and capital.

Maintaining adequate capital is a key to fulfilling promises to policyholders and regulatory requirements. The capital required depends on risks undertaken. It works the same way as a life insurer. A solvency margin of 100 percent means an insurer has enough to meet the minimum required. The comfort level is 150 percent in China.

P&C insurers have to set up loss reserves to pay for future claims. The reserve is established based on actuarial estimates and assumptions, similar to life reserves. It is possible to have insufficient reserves as not all policyholders file a claim at the same time. By cutting down on sales with a high combined ratio, they may improve profitability and gradually get out of a hole. However, it is dangerous to have a shortfall as this can result in regulatory action and natural catastrophes can deal a critical blow. Life insurers enjoy more flexibility with their reserves as their liabilities are locked in the long term. P&C insurers have a tougher job as they need to maintain more liquidity and they may not have enough time to fill up a deficiency.

Domestic company profiles

China has 53 life companies (28 foreign and 25 local) and 51 P&C operators (18 foreign and 33 local). Each listed company has a distinct market positioning and each uses different strategies, stemming from the different backgrounds. China Life, China Pacific and PICC are a restructuring story as they seek to break away from an inefficient state-owned structure. China Taiping and Ping An are positioned for growth. In this section we are going to look at two of these companies – China Life and Ping An.

China Life is the largest life insurance company in the country, with a 30 percent market share. It is an offshoot of the People's Insurance Company of China, the former industry monopoly. It took on its present form after a few reorganizations. It is 68 percent held by the government through the China Life Group and is under direct supervision of the Central Government. China Life does pure life business. It does not have any burden of negative spread policies as it left its book with the state-owned parent before its 2003 dual listing in Hong Kong and New York. The firm also listed in Shanghai in 2007 and was 45 times over-subscribed. China Life is by far the dominant life player but fundamentals are currently weakening because of the intensifying market competition. New business growth remains challenging for the firm. China Life's recent results highlight the challenges that the company faces in getting new business, with both its agency and bancassurance business coming under pressure. The key risk for the company in the near term is volatility in the A-share market that affects the firm's overall profitability. The interest rate cycle is also a cause for concern as a high interest rate environment can affect insurance sales as policyholders seek other higher return savings vehicles.

Ping An is one of the insurance companies that are very well positioned for growth in China. Ping An began as a P&C insurance company in Shenzhen in 1988, backed by capital from ICBC and China Merchants Group. It started underwriting life in 1994, the same year Goldman Sachs and Morgan Stanley were brought in as strategic investors. HSBC came in 2002 and gradually took over the GS and MS stakes. With the exit of the founding shareholders, Ping An is no longer a state-owned enterprise and management is the largest shareholder. The company was listed in Hong Kong in 2004 and in 2007 in Shanghai. While the business is driven by life insurance, its management has a vision to become a financial conglomerate, based on insurance, banking and asset management. Ping An receives 70 percent of its revenue from life insurance and its new business margin is the best within the listed universe – a testament to its underwriting control. However, it is somewhat burdened with negative spread policies. Unlike China Life, being a privately held company, it cannot shift the costs to the government. Ping An has therefore been broadening its revenue base and targeting younger and better-educated consumers. This has seemed to pay off as growth has been much stronger than its competitors. It believes in synergies that emerge from an integrated platform – sharing customer resources and cross-selling of products. Ping An's largest risk lies in the execution of this strategy, as all subsidiaries are expanding and expenses are high, stretching capital and management attention.

5.3. Market entry as a foreign company

Market share of foreign insurance companies in China

There are both domestic-funded insurance companies and foreign-funded companies in China. In April 2010, the China Insurance Regulatory commission (CIRC) listed 27 foreign life companies and 18 foreign property and casualty companies in China. In 2010, the market share of foreign life companies and foreign property and casualty companies was around 5 percent and 1 percent, respectively (CIRC).

Based on the premium income for the first half of 2010, the top 10 foreign life and property and casualty insurers are listed as follows:

Top 10 foreign life insurance companies

Ranking	*Company Name*	*Premium income Jan – Jun 2010 (RMB million)*
1	Generali China Life	4,051.56
2	AIA	3,865.59
3	Huatai Life	3,741.10
4	Sun Life Everbright Life	2,949.60
5	Aviva-COFO Life	2,791.14
6	CITIC-Prudential Life	2,691.32
7	CIGNA & CMC Life	1,281.83
8	Sino-US MetLife	1,090.94
9	AEGON-CNOOC Life	956.39
10	Manulife-Sinochem Life	871.31

Source: China Insurance Regulatory Commission

Top 10 foreign property and casualty insurance companies

Ranking	*Company Name*	*Premium income Jan – Jun 2010 (RMB million)*
1	Chartis (AIG)	514.67
2	Mitsui Sumitomo	224.33
3	Tokio Marine & Nichido Fire	212.62
4	Samsung Fire & Marine	175.04
5	Liberty Mutual Chongqing	159.54
6	Allianz Life	155.59
7	Zurich	123.05
8	Winterthur	91.35
9	Generali China	90.54
10	Royal & Sun Alliance	85.90

Source: China Insurance Regulatory Commission

Market shares of foreign insurance companies have remained stagnant in the past few years. As foreign players consider China as a highly regulated environment, many foreign insurance companies have struggled to try and gain traction and increase market share. Foreign insurers see their domestic counterparts as their major competitors. The larger domestic insurers are a major force, while the new smaller domestic insurers have been aggressive in their geographic expansion, and have increased their efforts to gain a critical mass at a faster pace than the foreign joint ventures (JVs). In view of this threat, some foreign insurance companies have started diluting their shareholdings and are following the path to domestication.

Products and services offered by foreign insurance companies

Foreign insurance companies offer a variety of insurance products and services in China, for instance:

1. life insurance (e.g. endowment insurance, juvenile insurance)
2. health insurance
3. property insurance (e.g. car insurance, home insurance, accident insurance, injury insurance)
4. casualty insurance (e.g. marine insurance, terrorism insurance)
5. export and credit insurance
6. savings-oriented endowment insurance policies
7. reinsurance brokerage
8. asset management
9. pension management
10. financial planning

In additional to traditional products and services listed above, foreign insurance companies have brought many new products and innovations into the Chinese market. Major innovations provided by life insurers include:

- The agency system

It was first introduced by AIA, which has a well-established agency force and provides a full line of life, accident and medical insurance products to customers through a multi-channel distribution system.

- Telemarketing and direct marketing to consumers

This is a method of direct marketing in which an insurance agent solicits prospective customers to buy insurance products or services, either over the phone or through a subsequent face-to-face appointment scheduled during the call.

- Universal life products

This product is intended to combine permanent insurance coverage with greater flexibility in premium payment, along with the potential for greater growth of cash values. This kind of insurance policy includes a cash value. Premium increases the cash values, but the cost of insurance (along with any charges assessed by the insurance company) reduces cash values. Interest is paid at a rate specified by the company, further increasing cash values. Universal life insurance policy addresses the perceived disadvantages of whole life – namely, that premium and death benefits are fixed.

- Unit linked products

It is a type of life insurance where the cash value of a policy varies according to the current net asset value of the underlying investment assets. The premium paid is used to purchase units in investment assets chosen by the policyholders.

- Variable annuities

It is an insurance contract in which, at the end of the accumulation stage, the insurance company guarantees a minimum payment. The remaining income payments can vary depending on the performance of the managed portfolios.

- Risk management

SMEs in China have low risk awareness and insurance companies can thus utilize their broad experience and risk management expertise.

- Dynamic solvency testing (DST)

It examines the effect of various plausible adverse scenarios on the insurer's forecasted capital adequacy. It is the actuary's primary tool for investigation of an insurer's financial condition.

Major innovations provided by property and casualty insurers

- Director and officer insurance

A liability insurance is payable to the directors and officers of a company, or to the organization itself, to cover damages or defense costs in the event they suffer losses as a result of a lawsuit for alleged wrongful acts while acting in their capacity as directors and officers for the organization.

- Environmental liability

It is an obligation based on the principle that a polluting party should pay for the damages caused to the environment by its activities.

- Product liability

Manufacturers, distributors, suppliers, retailers and others who make products available to the public are held responsible for any injuries these products might cause to users. Generally, it is traditionally limited to products in the form of tangible personal property.

- IPO insurance

It covers companies and their directors from the risks involved with capital raising.

- Professional indemnity

It helps to protect professional advice- and service-providing individuals and companies from bearing the full cost of defending against a negligence claim made by a client, and damages awarded in such a civil lawsuit.

- Financial kidnap and extortion insurance

This is to reimburse clients for property or other consideration surrendered as a kidnapping ransom payment, or if the clients make an extortion payment to mitigate or remove a threat.

Distribution channels

Major distribution channels used by foreign insurance companies include:

- Bancassurance channel
- Direct sales
- Telemarketing
- Insurance agents (tied)
- Independent financial advisors
- Brokers
- Internet
- Affinity schemes
- Post office

Based on a survey conducted by PricewaterhouseCoopers of China's insurance market in 2010, most of the foreign life insurers are inclined to move towards telemarketing and direct sales, while the influence of insurance agents and bancassurance is expected to decrease.

On the other hand, major property and casualty insurers are inclined to move towards telemarketing and bancassurance and Internet, while the impact of direct sales and insurance agents is expected to decrease.

Challenges in doing insurance business in China

Foreign players consider China as a highly regulated market and have been struggling to increase their market share. It is difficult to do business in China due to the fact that there are some challenges in entering the China market. This can be divided two aspects. One is the regulatory challenges and the other is non-regulatory challenges.

Regulatory challenges

Foreign insurers need to have relevant licenses in China. It means that the China Insurance Regulatory Commission (CIRC) requires foreign insurers to meet the requirements to apply for insurance license in China:

- Minimum registered capital: RMB 200 million
- At least 30 years of continuous experience in running an insurance business
- Joint venture life insurance business of a foreign insurance company and a Chinese company. The proportion of foreign investment shall not exceed 50 percent of the company's total share capital.

The wholly foreign owned enterprise (WFOE) is a limited liability company wholly owned by foreign investors and the requirements are:

- Minimum registered capital: 100K
- Investors or shareholders must open a bank account with the Bank of China or with a bank designed by the state agency exercising foreign exchange control.
- The amount of share capital deposited should be audited by a firm of certified public accounts.

To briefly summarize, there are some types of companies doing life insurance business in China.

Joint venture is the normal practice and the most favored way for foreign insures. Capital injection can be the shortcut for well-funded financial institutions to enter China, but in an unusual way. Setting up a wholly foreign owned enterprise (WFOE) is a very special case and there has been only one case, AIA. That is because AIA was established before the regulation on share interest took effect.

Major foreign firms currently doing life insurance business in China can be categorized by types.

The current major foreign firms are listed in the table below.

Non-regulatory challenges

There are four key non-regulatory challenges involved in entering the China market.

1. Relationship (Guan-xi): Like doing other business in China, entering the life insurance business needs a relationship, in Chinese, *Guanxi.* It means that building on-going personal relationships is needed. There must be trusted relationships with any potential business partners, customers and, if it is possible, government officials.

Current major foreign insurance firms

Types	*Firms*	*Life Insurance*
Special Case	AIA	Wholly foreign enterprise (WFOE) licensed to operate life insurance business in China
Joint Venture	HSBC	HSBC Life Insurance (50%) Partner : National Trust(50%) HSBC has an insurance broker JV : Beijing HSBC Insurance Brokers (24.9%), partnered with Shanghai Hua Yu Asset Management and Beijing Zhong Engineering to offer full insurance brokering and risk consulting services in China.
	ING	Shanghai JV : with Pacific Antai Life Insurance Guangzhou JV : with China Pacific Insurance (50%) Dalian JV : with Beijing Capital Group
	Prudential	CITIC Prudential with CITIC (50%)
Capital Injection (Investment)	HSBC	Investment on Ping An Insurance (16.8%)

Source: China Insurance Regulatory Commission

2. KICK-BACKS

Kick-backs imply high expectations of the extra expenses in the business. The expectation when doing business in China is frequently that there will be perks for individuals involved in negotiations.

3. RECIPROCITY

Give and take mind is taken for granted in China. A high degree of reciprocity is expected when major negotiations are held in China. Therefore foreign firms which want to invest in the insurance industry need to consider what benefits they can bring to domestic companies before they can think about what benefits they will get from China's domestic companies.

4. MEDIA

Media is considered a social good in China. It is the government's vehicle to provide information and for propaganda, and as such the government retains tight control over the media. Thus, foreign firms should understand the attributes that selectively open up parts of the industry.

References

China insurance market review: major changes, rapid growth. 2006. www.asiaing.com/china-insurance-market-review-major-changes-rapid-growth.html

China insurance market outlook to 2015. 2011. www.researchandmarkets.com/research/30ddae/china_insurance_ma

Foreign insurance companies in China. 2011, December. www.pwc.com.au/asia-practice/china/assets/publications/Foreign-Insurance-China-2011.pdf

Keum Yi, Lee. 2008. The study on entry strategy in China insurance market from Korean insurers' perspectives. Mokpo University.

Market Research Reports: China Insurance Market. 2012. China Knowledge Online Pte Ltd. ISBN: 978-981-4163-40-8.

Wenli Yuan. July 26, 2011. China insurance market and Technology Trends. www.celent.com/reports/china-insurance-market-and-technology-trends-2011

Websites

China-Insurance, www.china-insurance.com
中保網, www.sinoins.com
中國保險資訊網, www.chinabx.com
中國養老金網, www.cnpension.net

6 Private equity in China

6.1. Introduction to private equity

What is private equity?

Private equity (PE) represents nothing more than stakes in companies not listed on a stock exchange, whether it is at the stage of seed, start-up, expansion or maturity. PE consists of investors and funds that make investments directly into private companies or conduct buyouts of public companies that result in delisting of public equity (private investment in public equity, PIPE).

Capital is raised from retail and institutional investors for a target company to nurture expansion, new product development, operations restructuring or balance sheet strengthening. As PE funds are not approved by the Chinese government, with financial investors having no industry background, it is different from industry investment funds and strategic buyouts.

Business model and structure

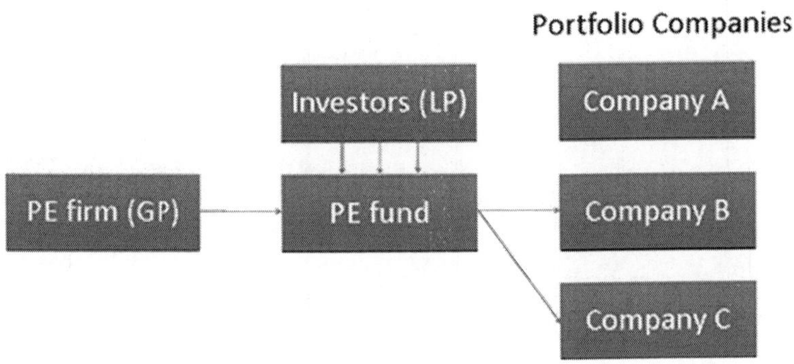

Institutional investors provide private equity capital with a view to receiving risk-adjusted returns which are higher than public equity markets. Most institutional investors do not invest directly in privately held companies because they do not have sufficient expertise and resources to structure and monitor the investment.

Rather, they prefer to invest indirectly through PE funds (closed-end fund) raised by PE firms, known as general partners (GP) which manage the fund and receive management fee plus typically 20 percent of profits (carried interest). Top five GPs in 2011 are TPG Capital, Goldman Sachs Capital Partners, the Carlyle Group, Kohlberg Kravis Roberts and the Blackstone Group. Institutional investors, known as limited partners (LP), provide the capital and receive the remaining profits. They can be corporate and public pension funds, endowments, insurance companies or wealthy individuals.

The model of operation can be company-based or trust-based.

In a company-based model, the fund takes the legal form of a corporation, which operates under sufficient legal protection by prevailing laws and regulations in China. The clear ownership structure is appealing to investors who have high risk control requirements. However, the disadvantages are that investors face the potential risk of double taxation (withholding tax, plus CIT or IIT) and that specific requirements set out in Chinese Company Law may adversely impact efficient utilization of the fund's capital. In addition, conflicts may arise where the fund manager finds investors to be over-involved in their decision-making activities.

In a trust-based model, the fund is jointly set up by the fund management institution and the trust company. They form a decision-making committee to implement operational activities and make decisions as a clear division of work can minimize the conflict between the fund manager and the investors. Risk of double taxation is also eliminated in this model.

Types of PE investment

There are many types of PE investments: leveraged buyouts, venture capital, growth capital, distressed securities, mezzanine capital, real estate, secondary investments, energy and power and merchant banking. The first five investment strategies are the most common types of PE investments.

Leveraged buyouts (LBOs)

LBO (or bootstrap transaction) refers to acquisition of a controlling interest in a company with a substantial portion of the purchase price financed through leverage. The debt raised for acquisition is ultimately secured upon, and looks to, cash flows of the acquisition target for interest and principal payments. Hence, it is often non-recourse to the financial sponsor and other investments managed by the sponsor. Historically, the acquisition debt portion ranges from 50 percent to 85 percent. This kind of leverage structure allows a financial sponsor to provide a minimal fraction of the capital, while the returns to the investor are enhanced (as long as the return on assets exceeds the cost of debt). Debt holders are predominantly locked into a fixed return, while equity holders receive all the benefits from any capital gains. Hence, LBOs can be lucrative to equity holders. The target companies are typically mature.

Venture capital

Venture capital is equity investments made in less mature companies to fund a new launch, early development or expansion of business. It is often applied in new technology, marketing concepts and products that are yet to be proven. Although venture capital is often most closely associated with fast-growing technology and biotechnology, it has been used for other traditional businesses as well. It is most suitable for businesses with large up-front capital requirements, which cannot be financed by cheaper alternatives such as debt due to their limited operating history. High returns are delivered to venture capitalists to compensate for high risk. Venture capitalists usually get a say in company decisions, in addition to a portion of the equity.

Growth capital

Companies seek growth capital to finance a transformational event in their life cycle, e.g. to expand or to restructure operations, to enter new markets or to finance a major acquisition without a change of control of the business. These companies are likely to be more mature than venture capital funded companies, but are unable to generate sufficient cash to fund major expansions, acquisitions or other investment needs. Often, companies that seek growth capital investments are not good candidates for additional debt, either because of the stability of the company's earnings or because of its existing debt levels. The capital obtained can therefore help to effectively restructure a company's balance sheet.

Investment patterns

PE calls for a long-term investment horizon of at least 10 to 15 years, to allow for a turnaround of a distressed company or a liquidity event such as an IPO or sale to a public company. The life cycle generally involves organization and formation of fund, fund-raising (6–18 months), investment period (Year 1–5), portfolio management (Year 2–7) and exit investments (Year 4–10). The average holding period is therefore 6–7 years. Quick flips account for only 12 percent of deals.

The exit strategies include sale to the general public such as IPO, sale to a strategic buyer, another PE fund (secondary buyout), management (management buyout), or bankruptcy/write-off.

6.2. History and development of the PE industry in China

China's initial economic reforms

The "early years" from 1978 to the early 1990s

The concept of private equity was first introduced to China after the country opened up its economy in 1978 under Deng Xiaoping. In the 1990s PE started from Hong Kong's economic growth as China was moving from labor-intensive agrarian and manufacturing environments to technology-oriented undertakings. By then the need for venture capital had become obvious. The first broad-based private equity that appeared in China was during the early 1990s when the Chinese State Council introduced venture capital into the planning of high-tech industrial parks and funded several technology-based ventures in China. The Chinese government set up the first few venture capital firms.

In the early 1990s there were no domestic private equity or venture capital firms as this investment concept was not well developed or understood in China. There were no foreign private equity or venture capital firms in early 1990s as the regulatory environment in China was not yet certain for the foreign investors.

The boom years, from the middle to late 1990s

Professor Chen Siwei, Vice Chairman of the Chinese People's Political and Consultative Conference, made a proposal at the 9th CPPCC National Committee meeting to "promote and develop the Chinese venture capital industry". As a result the number of venture capital firms increased significantly from 50 to more than 200.

During the dot-com boom era in the United States, the venture capital industry gained great popularity and understanding. In the mid-1990s during the peak of the dot-com boom, the younger Chinese generation was increasingly exposed to the Internet and many Internet portals were set up. There was great potential in the absolute size of the Internet economy and high growth rates. Foreign venture capital firms began to pay more attention to the booming Internet industry in China, and invested in several of China's top Internet portals.

Consolidating and developing years, after 2000

After the burst of the dot-com bubble in 2000, the industry was in a period of IT market consolidation and elimination of the weaker players. A selected few of the IT firms remained and became the market leaders in their domains. These VC firms have reaped good rewards after their IPOs.

Private equity penetration in China as a percentage of GDP is at 0.3 percent as compared to North America's 0.8 percent and Europe's 0.5 percent. China received USD 1.7 billion as private equity investment in mid-year 2008 and USD 1.6 billion in the same period in 2007. (See figure 6.1)

Private equity investments in China have attracted a wide spectrum of private equity players, including global buyout firms, regional players and local players. The industries covered by the private equity investment have expanded from IT to retail food chains, healthcare / biotechnology, new materials, construction, high-end manufacturing, renewable energy and retail.

Special Economic Zones

China's economic growth was fuelled by constant economic reforms. One of the main reforms was the implementation of Special Economic Zones. Special

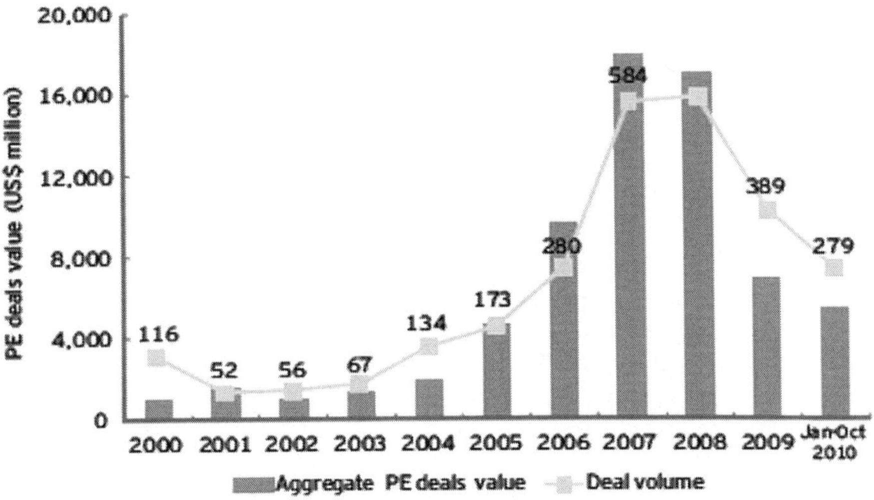

Figure 6.1 PE transactions in China, 2000–2010

Source: Thomson Reuters

Economic Zones are cities / regions / provinces that have special economic policies that are more market oriented, such as:

1. special tax incentives for foreign investments;
2. greater independence on international trading activities;
3. special economic characteristics – focused on utilizing and attracting foreign investment; fostering of Sino–foreign joint ventures; export-oriented production; market-driven philosophy.

The first Special Economic Zone was set up in Shenzhen, which is seen as a model of economic development in China. Located an MTR ride away from Hong Kong, Shenzhen is now one of the richest cities in China after it turned its 126 square miles of stores known for selling knockoffs into an important business metropolis that holds some of the most important and fastest-growing Chinese companies, such as Lenovo, Huawei and ZTC.

Shenzhen's critical location is not only perfect to attract foreign investment but also to welcome back billions of Yuan that have been sitting offshore and that have been finding it hard to come back to China. The looser controls will help money flow back to at least the Shenzhen area as the controls between Shenzhen and the remaining mainland should remain stricter.

Nowadays, there are 5 special economic zones, Shenzhen, Zhuhai, Shantou, Xiamen and Kashgar plus the Hainan Province. Also, China opened 14 other coastal cities to foreign investments and 15 other free-trade zones, 32 state-level technological development zones and 53 new and high-tech development areas. Special Economic Zones have special national planning and have more local independence in respect of economic administration.

The institution of the Special Economic Zones opened up China to Foreign Direct Investment and was a step towards China opening up to external markets and to its development as a free market economy. All these measures led to higher privatization and facilitated the flourishing of domestic and foreign private equity funds in China.

Private equity vs venture capital

Private equity and venture capital are both strong and growing in China, however, they do not mean the same and it is important to distinguish between them to understand what we are indeed talking about.

Private equity are funds or investors that make investments directly in private enterprises or that conduct buyouts of public companies that result in delisting. Mostly PE firms consist of wealthy investors that have large sums of money to invest or PE firms that pool together funds to buy out public companies.

PE firms or investors usually seek undervalued or underperforming companies to unlock value by improving its management, improving its business strategy, improving its operational efficiency or injecting technical expertise.

Venture capital is then technically part of private equity, though it is mainly focused on early-stage ventures, while PE funds / investors are mainly focused on mature companies.

This main difference reflects in everything else. PE investments are not industry focused while VCs tend to be more focused on high-tech firms. PE firms usually buy 100 percent of a company while a VC only contributes to part, sometimes less than 50 percent of the company and therefore PE firms also usually make bigger investments compared to seed investments made by venture capitalists.

Accordingly, the risk associated with VC investments is usually higher and therefore the VC model expects a lot of its investments to default hoping that some of its investments will compensate for all the lost money. Therefore, private equity returns are expected to be lower, with lower risk but more certain as usually before the buyout PE investors / firms already have an idea of how to make money through that investment.

Although VC investment is growing in China, the main growth, with all the privatization and liberalization especially in the Special Economic Zones, is mainly in the private equity sector. Indeed private equity funds and investors are highly regarded by the Chinese economic community and market, as China looks at private equity as a source of expertise, skill sets and contacts that cannot be easily accessed through any other means.

First investments in private equity in China

The private equity market in China is big and growing and with a GDP growth of 9 percent in 2011, though slightly lower than the previous year, China's economy is growing way above other markets – US or European Union – fuelling the need for private equity funds and investors.

Private equity first entered China through Hong Kong in the 1970s; at that time most deals were small and mostly controlled by banks or insurance companies. After the Asian crisis in 1997, the banking reform was not enough to respond to companies' need for capital and private equity started to flourish. However, the big foreign investments from private equity firms only took off in the 21st century when the government started to welcome more foreign investment.

Accordingly, in 2010 China saw the number of private equity deals triple, mostly due to expansion deals. One of the main important deals done at that time was the USD 1.6 billion investment in the Alibaba Group undertaken by a consortium including Silver Lake. However, recently even though the number of deals is increasing exponentially the value growth is not as steep, indicating a slowdown in the value of each deal.

Milestone private equity deals in China

The Newbridge Capital and Shenzhen Development Bank Deal – the first deal in which a foreign investor took control of a Chinese state-owned bank

The whole process of the deal lasted for almost 32 months. The public was concerned that TPG Capital (parent company of Newbridge) had bought Chinese state assets at a bargain and the Chinese government was criticized for selling Shenzhen Development Bank at a discount. The deal was made in 2004. Newbridge Capital invested USD 150 million to own about an 18 percent stake in SDB. The Chinese government was willing to accept the foreign private equity investor mainly for its experience and expertise of dealing with non-performing loans. Newbridge Capital had past experience in reconstructing the Korean First Bank. After the deal was made, Newbridge selected the new management team for Shenzhen Development Bank and successfully reduced NPLs from 11.4 percent to 0.61 percent and tripled its assets. In 2009, Ping An Insurance announced a buyout of Newbridge Capital's stake in SDB for USD 1.68 billion to build itself a financial conglomerate.

The Carlyle Group's bid for Xugong Group Construction Machinery – the failed result of the highest-profile private equity investment deal

Carlyle had agreed to pay USD 375 million for an 85 percent stake, making it the largest-ever announced private equity deal in China at the time. State-owned Xugong Group Construction Machinery makers is one of the country's leading construction machinery makers as well as China's largest manufacturer and distributor of construction equipment and machinery. Xugong was in need of foreign PE investment to expand overseas and to restructure. However, the government ministries were under pressure from the media and competing companies for sale of strategic assets at knockdown prices. Manufacturing was regarded as a national strategic industry. After nearly three years' waiting, the deal was finally rejected by the government even when Carlyle agreed to a minority stake of 45 percent. Carlyle has learned a lesson from this experience that one can never announce a deal unless one is completely sure of government approval.

The Bain Capital and Gome Deal – the first high-profile corporate boardroom battle for control

In June 2009, Bain Capital invested in electronics retailer Gome Electrical Appliances, China's largest retail chain for electrical appliances. Bain invested USD 233 million in the form of convertible bonds for a roughly 10 percent stake in the company when the company was in a leadership crisis: the founder Huang Guangyu was facing charges of bribery, corruption and insider trading. Bain worked with Gome to make significant operational improvements, including expense reductions, improvements in customer service and increasing the retailer's footprint in underserved markets. This is also one of the examples where PE firms invested in privately owned enterprises (POE) and the retail consuming industry, among which there are also others investing in Little Sheep, Hopu investing in China Mengniu Dairy and Warburg Pincus investing in Red Star Furniture Group.

China Investment Corporation's investment in Blackstone – the first overseas investment

In 2007, China Investment Corporation, a sovereign wealth fund, made a USD 3 billion investment in Blackstone for a 10 percent stake. China has a large amount of foreign reserves. The Blackstone move shows China's continued willingness to re-invest its export dollars in the US to earn better returns from its reserves. The Chinese government is confident about private equity investment business, although the loss from the investment due to the financial crisis showed that it will be worthwhile for China Investment Corporation to make a change.

6.3. Current private equity landscape in China

Key facts in the PE industry in China

Since 2012, China's PE / VC market has been cooling down and investment activities have continuously stayed at a low level. China Venture's latest data show 261 PE investments in the first 11 months of 2012 and the total amount equals USD 17.662 billion, a decrease of growth rate from 35.4 percent to 39.1 percent in 2001. In terms of industry focus, manufacturing, energy and other traditional industries are still the most active investment areas while the healthcare industry attracts investors' attention because of its non-cyclical characteristics.

However, the China PE market activity has been downward since the 4th quarter of 2011. As the macroeconomy and capital market remain in the doldrums, PE investments are at relatively low levels. (See figure 6.2)

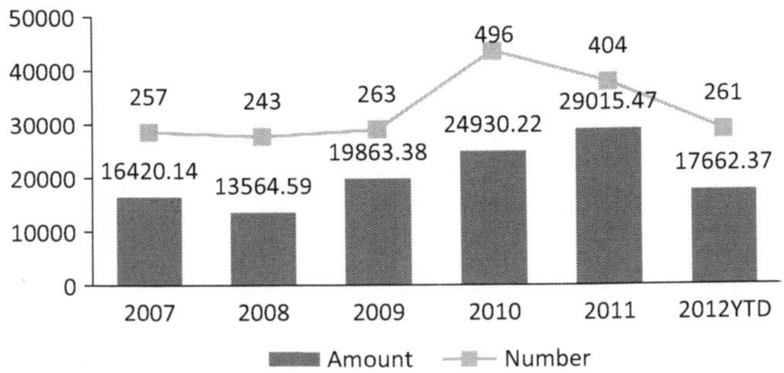

Figure 6.2 PE investments in China

Source: Thomson Reuters

Private equity in China cooled down in 2012 for several reasons:

1. The stock market cooled down in 2012 with fewer IPOs and lower initial PE ratio than before.
2. Economic growth in China is slowing with overcapacity in most industries. Fund-raising has become more and more difficult.
3. Chinese company and business models are not accepted by overseas investors due to financial shenanigans. Chances for exit through overseas IPOs are much less than before.

In 2012, the average number of investments per month was 25 with a range between 10 and 15, except for September when Alibaba Group repurchased shares from Yahoo involving PE investors. The amount of this single transaction was up to USD 2 billion and the total value for that month is USD 4.03 billion, reaching the highest level during the past year. (See Figure 6.3.)

PE investments have been spread over 20 industry segments since 2012. Manufacturing is most active with 43 disclosed investments, accounting for 16.5 percent, which is followed by energy and healthcare with 29 and 24 disclosed investments, respectively. The number for other industries is all below 20. (See Figure 6.4.)

Among different sectors, the financial industry ranks at the top with the total disclosed amount of USD 3.334 billion, followed by the Internet industry with USD 2.921 billion. However, we should notice that the special case with the large investment scale in these two sectors makes this a fact while the number of deals in these two sectors is below 20. (See Figure 6.5.)

Overall, industrywide distribution of PE investments in 2012 was very similar to the year 2011. Manufacturing, energy, chemical industry, agriculture, forestry, animal husbandry, fishery industry and other traditional industries are still the popular sectors. It should be noticed that the proportion of the healthcare industry has increased from last year. This shows that non-cyclical industries are likely to receive more investment under slack macro-economic conditions.

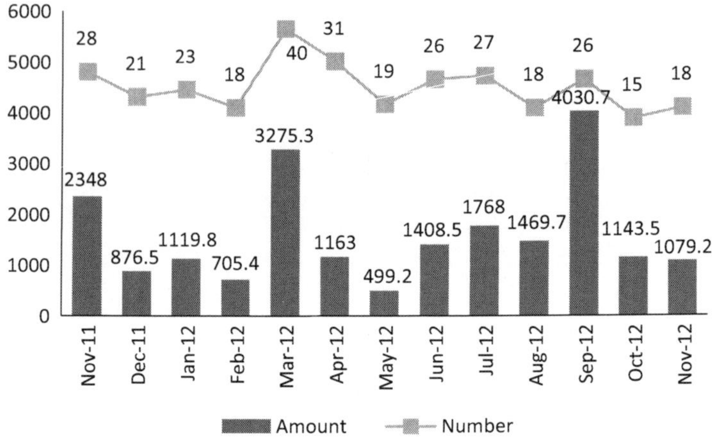

Figure 6.3 PE investments in China in 2012

Source: Thomson Reuters

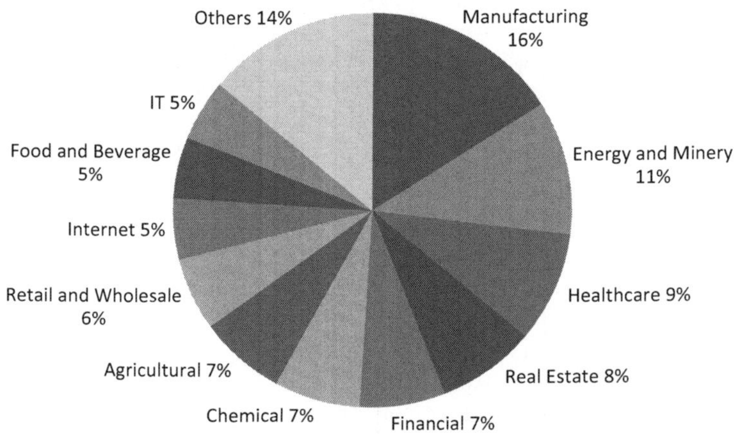

Figure 6.4 PE investments by sector by volume

Source: Thomson Reuters

Domestic versus foreign PE firms in China

According to PE daily's statistics and analysis, there are almost 6,000 PE / VC institutions active in the mainland market including local and foreign firms. Table 6.1 shows the top 10 PE firms, local PE firms and foreign PE firms active in years 2011 and 2012. Kunwu Jiuding Capital Co., Ltd ranks 1 and is also the winner of Active PE firm. Among the top 10 firms, more than half are local firms

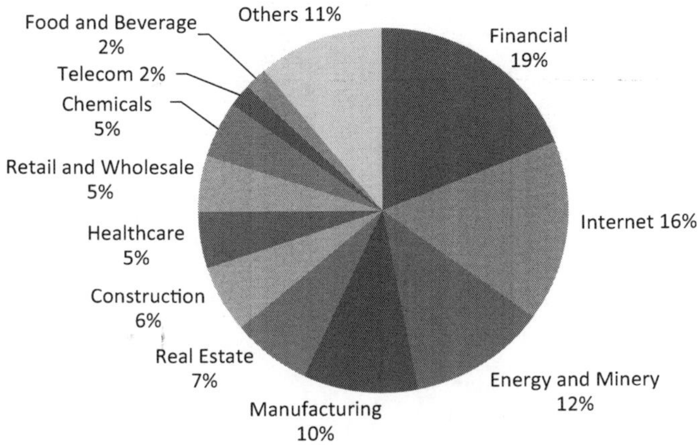

Figure 6.5 PE investments by sector by value

Source: Thomson Reuters

Table 6.1 The rank of China PE firms

Total	*2012*	*2011*
1	Kunwu Jiuding Capital Co., Ltd.	Kunwu Jiuding Capital Co., Ltd.
2	CITIC Private Equity Funds Management Co., Ltd.	CCBI
3	Fosun Capital Group	Hony Capital (Beijing) Co., Ltd.
4	GoldStone Investment Co., Ltd.	Kohlberg Kravis, Roberts & Co.
5	Hony Capital (Beijing) Co., Ltd.	New Horizon Capital
6	CCBI	CDH Investments
7	CITIC Capital Holdings Ltd.	GoldStone Investment Co., Ltd.
8	The Carlyle Group LLC	Fosun Capital Group
9	Kohlberg Kravis, Roberts & Co.	Morgan Stanley Private Equity Asia
10	GF Xinde Investment Management Co., Ltd	Ping An Caizhi Investment Management Co., Ltd
Local	*2012*	*2011*
1	Kunwu Jiuding Capital Co., Ltd.	Kunwu Jiuding Capital Co., Ltd.
2	CITIC Private Equity Funds Management Co., Ltd.	CCBI

(Continued)

Table 6.1 (Continued)

Local	*2012*	*2011*
3	Fosun Capital Group	Hony Capital (Beijing) Co., Ltd.
4	GoldStone Investment Co., Ltd.	New Horizon Capital
5	Hony Capital (Beijing) Co., Ltd.	GoldStone Investment Co., Ltd.
6	CCBI	Fosun Capital Group
7	GF Xinde Investment Management Co., Ltd.	Ping An Caizhi Investment Management Co., Ltd
8	Cypress Capital Group	GF Xinde Investment Management Co., Ltd.
9	China Development Bank Capital Co., Ltd.	CITIC Private Equity Funds Management Co., Ltd.
10	Shanghai Leading Capital Co., Ltd.	Guosen H&S Investment Co., Ltd.
Foreign	*2012*	*2011*
1	CITIC Capital Holdings Ltd.	Kohlberg Kravis, Roberts & Co.
2	The Carlyle Group	CDH Investments
3	Kohlberg Kravis, Roberts & Co.	Morgan Stanley Private Equity Asia
4	CDH Investments	Temasek Holdings (Private) Limited
5	Temasek Holdings (Private) Limited	Trust Bridge Partners
6	Morgan Stanley Private Equity Asia	International Finance Corporation
7	Fountainvest Partners (Asia) Ltd.	Headland Capital Partners Limited
8	PAG	Texas Pacific Group
9	Baring Private Equity Asia	Bain Capital, LLC.
10	Standard Chartered Private Equity Ltd.	Primavera Capital Group

Source: PEdaily.cn

and tend to rank within the first half of the ranking. Only half of the firms appear on the list for both years: Kunwu Jiuding Capital Co., Ltd, Fosun Capital Group, Hony Capital (Beijing) Co., Ltd. (PE fund-raising winner of the year 2012 and 2011), CCBI, Kohlberg Kravis, Roberts & Co.

Table 6.2 shows the contrast between local and foreign PE firms in China in terms of fund source and size, operational mode, investment type, industry, deal diligence and management, exit and policy influence.

Fund source and size: Foreign PE firms have relatively comprehensive sources of funds, including corporate institutions, banks, insurance firms and trusts, VC /

Table 6.2 Comparison of local and foreign PE firms

	Local	*Foreign*
Fund source and size	Corporate bodies, banks, insurance firms and trusts, government funds, initiation funds, VC / PE institutions, asset management companies	Corporate bodies, banks, insurance firms and trusts, VC / PE institutions, pension funds, FOFs, asset management cos., initiation funds and college funds.
Operational mode	Company	Limited partners
Industry	Manufacturing, Energy, Retail & Wholesale	Manufacturing, Energy, Chemicals
Investment type	PIPE	Growth, PIPE
Deal diligence and management	Developing	Mature
Exit	A / H IPO	International IPO, M&A
Policy influence	Relatively low	High

PE institutions, pension funds, FOFs, asset management companies, initiation funds and college funds while local firms have much narrower sources. While most foreign firms tend to have funds running into billions, local firms still count their sources in millions only.

Operational mode: Foreign firms prefer limited partners while local firms prefer joint stock companies. As currently there is no supervisory law for PE firms; they are supervised by separate laws according to their operational modes, which implies different disadvantages like tax burden.

Investment types: As foreign firms pursue higher returns, they emphasize equally on growth type and pre-IPO type. However, local firms are relatively conservative and focus on pre-IPO type.

Industry: Manufacturing and energy are the favorites for PE firms. Foreign firms have their own mature standards for project selection and, therefore, they are less objective investors and explore the opportunities in all industries while local firms only prefer the popular ones or those they are familiar with.

Deal diligence and management: Foreign firms already have well-developed systems and experience for due diligence and post-investment management before entering the China market, which adds to the probability of success. Local firms behave more like speculators. They chase mature projects to reduce the pain of due diligence and management and focus only on the IPO process.

Exit: IPO is the core exit method for PE firms. Foreign firms mainly focus on US exchanges and other international exchanges for exit because of their familiarity with offshore markets while local firms are active only in the onshore market. The Growth Enterprise Market once offered PE firms a great chance to exit with considerable returns. Therefore, there is a great probability that the New Three

Board will be the next opportunity. Moreover, under the long slump of the stock market, overseas M&As are attracting the attention of large foreign PE firms.

Policy influence: Foreign firms are not as familiar with China's onshore market as are local firms, which definitely puts them in a disadvantageous position. Although the advantage of local firms becomes less obvious gradually, it is still hard for foreign firms to lead the China market, especially when the foreign exchange control policy has become tighter and dollar funds are not as popular as before.

The private equity life-cycle process in China

As expected, given the Chinese government's close involvement and intervention in the country's economy and institutions, private equity players are faced with specific issues that they probably do not experience elsewhere. If, for some, these specific characteristics result in barriers and shortcomings, for others, they present opportunities and solutions.

The dynamism common to business initiatives in China gives opportunity for rapid growth, but also sometimes results in sudden failure. Succeeding in this industry requires one not just to observe and learn from precedents but also to properly forecast and plan future actions, as well as to have the ability to move and change course fast.

Setting up the initial fund

Shanghai, Beijing, Chongqing, Tianjin and Shenzhen have been preferred by fund managers as principal hubs for registration of private equity funds in China due to incentives and policies aiming at fostering the local private equity industry.

The recently implemented Qualified Foreign Limited Partners (QFLP) program in Shanghai, for example, encompasses a series of initiatives to allow and facilitate acquisition of equity in local unlisted companies by overseas investors using foreign currency. In December 2011, China promulgated the applicable regulation for the Renminbi Qualified Foreign Institutional Investors (RQFII), permitting foreign investors to invest overseas Renminbi funds in public stocks and bonds, but not in equity of private companies. In October 2012, Shanghai extended the QFLP to allow foreign players to invest in unlisted Chinese companies using Renminbi capital raised offshore. This new initiative, called the Renminbi Qualified Foreign Limited Partner (RQFLP) is part of China's overall effort to bolster the use of Renminbi as a global currency and allow Shanghai to become an onshore Reminbi convertibility hub. A series of Chinese regulatory authorities participated in the design and development of the program, such as the State Administration of Foreign Exchange and the National Development and Reform Commission.

The Hong Kong branch of Haitong Securities will partner with Bank of Shanghai to debut this new initiative by raising USD 100 million in offshore Renminbi from Hong Kong investors. Hony Capital is set to become the first private equity fund to pursue a similar initiative in the Qianhai development zone in southern Shenzhen. Competition between several different cities / regions in China to attract funds has grown, including the Beijing city government's efforts to commit capital for the establishment of fund vehicles to invest in alternative assets such as private equity.

Fund-raising

One of the most peculiar characteristics of fund-raising in China is the differences between dealing with domestic and foreign limited partners (LPs). If, on one hand, foreign LPs are a sophisticated and experienced group of investors that typically do not interfere in the fund's investment strategy and operations, including pension funds, insurance companies, school endowments, fund of funds and even investment banks, the same cannot be said about their Chinese counterparts.

The rapid economic growth observed in China in recent years has led to an increase in the number of funds being managed by inexperienced managers, in an attempt to supply the high demand from Chinese investors that are seeking private equity assets. On top of that, domestic LPs' complete lack of knowledge about these types of investments often results in their interference and constant battle with managers. In order to deal with the frustration of local LPs, managers have to spend a great amount of time and energy educating these investors which often causes delays and complications in the private equity cycle. The points of tension range from an LP's disagreement about certain committed capital decisions to the amount of management fees, to, finally, conflicts of interest in the investment strategy of hybrid funds in allocation of Renminbi and US-dollar funds.

Deal sourcing

Relationships play a key role in deal sourcing in China. The common Western strategy of cold-calling and bluntly approaching investors tends to have little effect in the Chinese private equity environment. Most often, people who represent strong points of contact between the company management and the investors tend to be decisive in the deal selection process.

Local government relationships play an important role in the process of "incentivizing" meetings between investors and potential targets. Also, the existence of a relatively small number of private equity industry professionals in China enhances the relationships among them and facilitates the management–investors relationships that are developed through such means.

Finally, another peculiarity of the private equity industry which is somewhat exacerbated in China is the relatively low sense of rivalry between firms materialized by the existence of a large number of club deals. The cooperation between firms is driven by the firms' necessity to leverage on each other's expertise and, therefore, by the enhancement of the overall investment risk management. Yong (2012) gives an example of this characteristic. The 1999 club deal investment made by TPG, together with Hony Capital and Legend Holdings, in Wumart Stores Inc., whereby previous working relationships at Legend Partners of a certain TPG partner facilitated the cooperation of all parties in the deal.

Execution

When it comes to *guanxi,* or relationship, Renminbi fund managers have a huge advantage over foreign managers in terms of speed of execution as well as easier access to exit opportunities within China. Chinese players have a favored position due to their ability to diligently plug into the right network, at the right time, both within the private sector, as well as within the government level.

Nevertheless, foreign managers planning to improve their *guanxi* management skills in China must be wary of the obstacles that are imposed on foreigners as a result of the one-party structure and the less developed legal system in China.

Valuation

The low sense of rivalry between firms in the Chinese private equity space does not alleviate the fierce competition that exists among too many private equity funds, and consequently, investors competing for too few available deals. This competition has contributed to drive up valuations.

Politically motivated regulatory changes can also directly affect valuation. The initial intent of acquisition of 85 percent of Xugong Group, China's largest construction equipment producer, by the Carlyle Group, was restricted by officials as industry players protested against the sale of vital national assets to foreigners. Consequently, the Carlyle Group ended up being able to purchase only 50 percent of the Xugong's equity and the price was increased by 4 percent.

Exit opportunities

US regulators have been charging Chinese companies listed in the US of violating US securities regulations by issuing misleading financial reports. This so-called recent Accounting Cold War between US and Chinese regulators has been driving down the price of many US-listed Chinese companies and closing the US equity market as an exit door for maturing Chinese private equity and venture capital investments.

The unique and successful case of Kunwu Jiuding Capital

Chinese firm Jiuding Capital has probably been the most successful player in the Chinese private equity industry over the past three years in terms of results and returns for investors, outperforming other players operating elsewhere.

Jiuding Capital is 1 percent to 2 percent the size of its major Westerns counterparts. It is not run by MBAs from top-notch schools and nor does it have modern and sophisticated offices. It is modest when it comes to advertising its business expertise and does not pay exorbitant carried interest to its partners.

In fact, Jiuding's investment strategy is quite simple. It focuses on Chinese companies that it understands are likely to be approved for IPO within a short time frame. Jiuding does not place its bets on complex macro-economic, specific industry or consumer market assumptions, nor does it focus on high growth companies with unproven technology that might be far from hitting the IPO market. As odd as it might seem, its main strategy does not encompass the utilization of complex financial models, but rather it focuses on trying to anticipate the next steps in the IPO approval process carried out by the Chinese Securities Regulatory Commission (CSRC).

Therefore, Jiuding is able to succeed at high-paying multiple arbitrage strategies. Until two years ago, when valuations were higher, the firm exited a certain investment at 80x while it had originally entered at 10x. Recently, entry multiples of 10x have been paying handsome returns, with exit multiples of 25x to 30x.

The strategy encompasses trying as much as legally possible to time the investment with the regulatory approval process. The idea is to try to improve the likelihood of the approval process, by attending meetings at the CSRC and lobbying backstage. In the most successful cases, Jiuding entry to exit period can be as short as three years, including lock-up. Industry benchmark is six to eight years.

Changes in China happened faster than in other places. Thus, Jiuding strategy is to mitigate potential risks arising from regulatory or market changes by shortening as much as possible the investment holding period. Also, it focuses on identifying and monitoring the two major reasons for CSRC's IPO approval or rejection – tax non-compliance and related party transactions. Traditional major private equity players usually perform long and expensive due diligence process aiming at analyzing and predicting, in detail, product and market performance – a process which many times hinders companies from even reaching the stage of applying for an IPO.

Jiuding's so-called PE factory method attempts to systematize as much as possible the investment process. The firm has 10 times fewer employees than other firms in China. Its main job is to collect information to simulate CSRC's approval process and to invite LPs, wealthy Chinese tycoons, to analyze and select deals. This strategy, non-existent among major Western players, as analyzed in the section above, is the key for maintaining a productive and successful relationship with Chinese LPs. Its fee policy, unlike other traditional private equity players that charge 1 percent to 3 percent annual fees, is to charge a one-time 3 percent management fee and small carry on successful deals. This strategy makes Jiuding a unique and successful fund raiser, with over 10 funds raised thus far.

Specific market conditions are now forcing Jiuding to review its formula and to adopt more traditional private equity work analysis, such as day-to-day business monitoring, board member advisory, or providing guidance to target companies for marketing and partnership improvements. These conditions range from difficulty in raising money and finding good targets, increased competition from copycats trying to imitate Jiuding's strategy, to an increasingly slower and bureaucratic IPO approval process.

6.4. Impact of political and economic context

Change in political landscape

In 2013, President Xi Jinping is stepping up as the new leader of the People's Republic of China. The 18th Party Congress, held November 2012, set the new political directions for the world's most populated country and the current second-biggest world economy. The future political and economic landscape in China is, however, still a slight mystery as the views and perspectives on what should be the main focus of Xi Jinping's leadership is still unknown.

A stable power transition seems to be one of the main focuses of the new leadership, in terms of social stability, though social unrest is not really expected, as well as political stability, by trying to reach consensus and manage the differences between the party's two main factions.

Though much is not known about the main focus of the new leadership, experts say that the new government will mainly focus on five main topics: (1) party faction divisions; (2) foreign disputes; (3) demographic changes; (4) environmental sustainability; and (5) push for domestic consumption growth.

In 2012, there were a lot of controversial discussions at the 18th Party Congress about the fine lines that split the two main ideologies and factions in the party. However, this is not a new development; since the 1990s there have been different factions inside the party. The challenge now is to maintain the party's strength and to manage the differences in order to ensure China retains one leading party.

Foreign disputes are also top priorities as China does not seem to be willing to give up or wind down on any of the territorial disputes it is in as there are a lot of natural resources at stake in these territories. One example is the dispute between China and Japan on some island in the East China Sea.

At the same time, demographic changes are starting to worry the PRC as the one-child policy implemented in the 1970s has led to the population profile getting skewed towards a male population. This has had not only social and cultural effects but also economic as this can lead to more men never being able to start a family and therefore not being able to grow economically and contribute to the economy as a family can. Also, a considerably large number of single young men might increase depression, violence and breakdown of law and order as future prospects of such young men become uncertain.

As China transits from a country of cheap and labor-intensive exports to a growing domestic market with educated labor, it leaves a legacy of pollution from unsustainable economic growth. As improving environmental protection is one of the priorities there should be an even higher emphasis on enforcement of environmental laws. Large investments in infrastructures with high risk for the environment have already been stopped, such as the controversial construction of a chemical plant in the eastern city of Ningbo, and this trend is expected to only grow stronger. China is indeed looking for more sustainable and cleaner ways of development and will enforce that on foreign investments, in what seems a priority, experts says, for the new leadership.

As China's economic structure and growth strategy change the focus now is on domestic market growth and policies are being designed to foster domestic consumption. In fact, as China moves to a consumer-based economy, up to today 10 percent of the population holds 57 percent of total income and 85 percent of total assets, meaning that most parts of the population do not have savings to spend in the economy. Income inequality may be one of the reasons why consumer spending still represents a lower part of the GDP nowadays. In this sense, raising the income levels and spending by the poorer segments of the Chinese population is the key to move China towards a more consumption-based economy.

Overall, though these five aspects might be at the center of the new leadership's considerations, the business environment overall should not be affected by major changes. The new leadership is expected to continue to focus on sustainable economic growth and on investment policies that foster foreign business. Indeed, external trade and foreign investments continue to be a major pillar for China's economic development.

Nonetheless, as President Xi Jinping works to move China's economy from being trade led to consumption driven, there will still be strong investment-based stimulus based on infrastructure development. Actually, the government push for economic development to inland areas will probably also create new business opportunities for construction, transportation and retail domestic and foreign companies.

All in all, the trend towards fostering foreign investment and to promote socio-economic development and growth, especially further inland, will continue meaning a continuous growth in the economy and a continuous pipeline of new business that represents a lot of future opportunities for private equity firms and investors in China, especially when Western markets are winding down.

Corruption and unfair trade

The last decade of rapid and slightly uncontrolled economic growth resulted in an uneven economic development across China, and an increase in the wealth gap and inevitability of an increase in corruption.

The issue of corruption in the financial system in China took new importance after the corruption case of the Bank of China in 2001 that went all the way up to the BoC leadership. The economist Hu Angang estimates that in 2000 the known public corruption actually accounted for almost 6 percent of China's GDP; though no recent numbers are known the same statistic is expected not to be lower.

Corruption scandals, like market rigging by fund managers, extortion of company funds, and overuse of government power on state-owned banks to provide loans to local officials have undermined China's financial sector and increased sensitivity for foreign investors.

The current government and the new leadership are, however, focusing on anti-corruption initiatives, as corruption still remains the main threat to the regime and economic stability. Tougher measures are indeed being introduced and several members of the PRC have publicly condemned corruption. Hu Jintao has actually said in a tough statement that "If we fail to handle this issue well, it could prove fatal to the Party, and even cause the collapse of the Party and the fall of the state."

Therefore, though corruption is still a critical issue in China, tougher measures have been implemented to prevent it, fueled by the emergence of social networks that easily expose corruption cases, meaning that China's financial market is moving towards a more open and less risky environment for foreign firms to operate.

6.5. Private equity future in China

The private equity industry in China is strictly related to the national social, economic environment and it presents its own peculiarities.

The steady growth of the economy and the increasing importance of the private sector present many opportunity for private equity funds, in particular in some sectors that we are going to analyze in greater detail. Nonetheless there are still many challenges that it will be important to address to capitalize properly on the many opportunities.

Challenges

Lack of qualified professionals

The lack of qualified and experienced human capital is a constant in China like in any economy experiencing a dramatic development in a short time, where the increasing number of firms raises the demand for talent. The issue is particularly felt in the PE industry for several reasons.

First of all private equity is a very local market and professionals must be fluent in Mandarin and have full understanding of Chinese culture, politics and economic environment. This limits the feasibility of sourcing qualified personnel from the international job market. Second, in private equity companies human capital is always the main if not the only resource, and this makes the competition among funds to attract the best candidates particularly tough. Moreover, PE is a very specialized industry requiring specific knowledge on how to run a RMB fund that the local educational system (including top universities) usually doesn't provide.

In order to overcome the lack of qualified professionals many firms are focusing on quantity, hiring many people and assigning very specific roles to each one. A possible solution to this problem can be represented by the increasing number of Chinese studying abroad. Some of them can get experience in foreign PE funds and then come back to China taking their expertise to the local funds.

Few deals for too many investors

The Chinese economy is still very fragmented and the number of companies competing within a single industry usually vastly exceeds the number of firms that one might expect to find in the same industry in a more developed economy. The venture capital and private equity industry in China is no exception with more than 10,000 venture capital and private equity firms in operation at the end of 2011. In addition to this, as we have seen, more and more foreign funds are looking at China for new opportunities outside of the stagnant Western markets, increasing the capital available for PE investment in the country. The result is too many funds competing for a limited number of deals, and as it always happens when demand overcomes the offers, valuations are driven up. In order to compete for investing in the most attractive target companies PE firms have often to engage in bidding wars that increase the price and affect the potential return. The expected trend in the future is a consolidation process in the PE industry and a consequent adjustment of the offers to the demand.

Disadvantages for foreign firms

The increasing attention foreign private equity firms are paying to the Chinese market hasn't gone unnoticed by the government and some measures to limit the foreign control in this sector, considered strategic for national stability, are being promulgated. In February 2011 the Minister of Commerce announced the introduction of a regulation stating that investments in sensitive industries must be approved by the government. The regulation is applicable to both minority and majority stakes and is applicable to all industries related with defense, economic and social stability and strategic R&D. The main concern is the broad nature of the categories included, that leave huge room for interpretation by the concerned officials. This is not the only structural disadvantage that local foreign private equity funds have to face when operating in China. Local firms know better deal sourcing channels, enjoy shorter deal execution thanks to political connections, and have no restriction in terms of percentage of stakes they can hold and they face no hurdles related to converting the currency. Foreign companies still have some advantages given their longer experience in the industry and by their global footprint, but if these hurdles are not addressed in the near future they are likely to face hard times.

LBOs

Leverage buyouts are not allowed by the Chinese government because of concerns about vulnerability of its financial system. Major changes in this policy are not likely to happen in the near future. Development of an LBO market in China will be the medium-term result of a series of gradual reforms. For the time being the lack of an LBO market seems to have affected more the entity of the deal (more minority than majority stakes) than the number, but for sure in the long term it could constitute a barrier to the further development of a mature PE industry.

Opportunities

Despite the big concerns about the political and macro-economic environment China is still growing at a blistering pace and the trend is not likely to change in the long term, though temporary slowdowns are possible. Some structural changes are taking place in the economy and the government needs to take measures that specifically benefit the private equity sector in the medium term. All this translates into enormous investment opportunities for PE investors in the coming years and the challenges we analyzed can only be partially offset. We will try to analyze better where and why these opportunities are likely to come up in the near future.

Consolidation process

As mentioned before many industries in China still have hugely fragmented capacities with thousands of small companies producing very similar products and having far from optimal scales and efficiencies. In the next few years market dynamics are going to generate a massive consolidation process where only the most efficient companies will survive and these companies would consolidate through acquisitions of smaller firms.

PE firms have enormous opportunity for playing an active role in this process, by investing in top private companies and helping them to define and implement their inorganic growth strategies.

Go West

Until recently private equity firms have concentrated mostly on investments in the more developed coastal provinces. With the 12th Five-Year Plan the Chinese government has adopted a vast strategy to promote investment in the western and less developed sides of the country, with the ultimate goal of gradually reducing regional imbalances. As result of this plan the western part of the country has started to develop dramatically, creating new opportunities for private equity firms to invest in the next few years. The trend has already started and since 2009, more than half of all PE investments have been in companies headquartered in the western region.

Financing demand in the private sector

Demand for financing is growing dramatically in the Chinese private sector, also as a consequence of the recent tightening of bank lending to curb inflation. In response to this many forms of alternative financing are emerging in the markets. As long as private equity firms are able to promote properly the additional benefits they offer, in terms of strategic expertise, they can have the opportunity to intercept a reasonable share of this demand.

Social and environmental development

China's Five-Year Plans consist of a complex collection of government policies, protocols and initiatives addressing the overall economic development of the nation. After the dramatic and generalized growth promoted with the 10th plan, the 12th plan is more focused on making the development more socially and environmentally sustainable. Some industries have been identified by the government as particularly strategic for the next phase of development. Many investments are likely to gravitate around these sectors over the next few years, creating sound opportunities for private equity companies to invest. The industries mentioned in the plan are:

- Energy saving and environmental protection
- Next generation information technology
- Biotechnology

- High-end equipment manufacturers
- Renewable energy
- New materials
- Alternative energy vehicles

Privatization of SOEs

China has gone through a massive process of privatization in the last few decades, where thousands of inefficient SOEs have been transformed into private companies. This process is far from being complete and it is estimated that there are still about 143,000 SOEs in China and the government probably wants only a minor fraction of them to remain state owned. The main reason why the government is taking on the privatization process is to increase profitability and improve the management of these companies. Private equity firms can provide managerial skills, know how, technical knowledge and global networks these companies need to improve their performances and develop and all this can translate into great investment opportunities.

From export to internal market

China is progressively shifting the focus of its economy from exports to the domestic market. In the United States, 75 percent of the GDP is accounted for by consumer spending. In China, that percentage is roughly 30 percent. The Chinese government is trying to get that percentage up and to increase domestic consumption. And as it does so, the Chinese economy will grow differently and provide a lot of opportunities to invest in companies that will produce goods for Chinese consumers.

References

Alvina Yuen. 2012. Shanghai allows offshore RMB to participate in private equity. *Asian Venture Capital Journal*. 25 October. www.avcj.com/avcj/news/2219762/shanghai-allows-offshore-rmb-to-participate-in-private-equity

Chan, Cathy. 2012, May 31. China kicks U.S. private equity aside as local funds rise. *Bloomberg Business Week*. www.bloomberg.com/news/2012-05-14/china-kicks-u-s-private-equity-aside-as-local-funds-rise.html

Chen Siwei. 1998. Proposal for the encouraging development of China's venture capital industry. 9th CPPCC National Committee meeting, Beijing.

Hu Jintao. 2012. Firmly march on the path of socialism with Chinese characteristics and strive to complete the building of a moderately prosperous society in all respects – Report to the Eighteenth National Congress of the Communist Party of China, Beijing.

Lerner, Josh, Ann Leamon, and Abishai Vase. 2011. A note on private equity in developing countries. Harvard Business School Background Note 811-102, May 2011. (Revised May 2011.

Matthews, G., Bye, M., and Howland, J. 2009. Operational improvement: The key to value creation in private equity. *Journal of Applied Corporate Finance*, 21(3), 21–27.

Perkowski, Jack. 2012, August 8. Private equity in China: too much money, too few deals. *Forbes*, www.forbes.com/sites/jackperkowski/2012/08/08/private-equity-in-china-too-much-money-too-few-deals/

Roth Capital Partners Report. 2012, 5 November. *U.S.-listed China – M&A activity, PE investment, and dual-listing*, 20th ed. Beijing, China: Roth Capital Partners.
Yong, Kwek Ping. 2012. *Private equity in China, challenges and opportunities.* Singapore: John Wiley & Sons.

Websites

Center for Strategic & international Studies, www.csis.org
China First Capital Blog: www.chinafirstcapital.com/blog/archives/4499
The Economist, www.theeconomist.com
McKinsey & Company, www.mckinsey.com
Maplecroft, www.maplecroft.com
Thomson Reuters, thomsonreuters.com
Wikipedia, www.wikipedia.com

7 Chinese shadow banking

7.1. Introduction to shadow banking

Shadow banking, due to its depth and breadth across the business environment in China, is viewed as a bottleneck for the financial system. As a result, a critical analysis of the shadow banking environment is carried out in this report.

To quote Pozar, Adrian, Ashcraft and Boesky (2010: 13–14):

> the shadow banking system decomposes the simple process of deposit funded, hold-to-maturity lending conducted by banks into a more complex, wholesale-funded securitization-based lending process that is performed by a variety of non-banking financial intermediaries, or shadow banks. Shadow banking transforms risky, long-term loans into seemingly credit-free, short-term, money-like instruments through a granular set of steps, which in the US includes loan origination, loan warehousing, ABS issuance, ABS warehousing, ABS CDO issuance, ABS intermediation and wholesale funding.

Banks in China include the formal banking system and the informal banking system. Within the formal banking system, banks include deposit-taking commercial banks, which have to observe RRR (Required Reserve Ratio), L / D (Loan to Deposit) ratio and CAR (Capital Adequacy Ratio). However, for the informal banking system, this includes entities and operations such as (a) deposit-taking institutions which are quite unregulated, e.g. underground lenders; (b) non-deposit taking institutions that have the characteristics of a bank, e.g. trust company, pawn shop, guarantors and small lenders; and (c) off-balance-sheet arrangements offered by commercial banks, e.g. wealth management products and LC discounting. These informal operations are called "shadow banks" in our report.

US shadow banking system

Paul J. Cella III (2009) in "The Financial Crisis and the Scientific Mindset" noted that shadow banking can be conceived as "a particular system of debt finance", a technological innovation that "amalgamates computer power and probabilistic modeling to vastly expand the various world markets in debt securities." (p. 31)

As Paul Cella III suggests, without modern technology and assistance of the Wall Street mathematicians or the "quants", the shadow banking system would be an impossibility. The sheer complexity of the whole shadow banking system can be discerned through understanding how the traditional lending and borrowing (which can be performed under a single roof of a traditional bank) are being sliced up and transmuted into multiple steps with a chain of intermediaries involved – namely, originator, aggregator, administrator, underwriter, investor, etc. – just to channel the funds between the consumers and investors of funds. The multiple steps, entities and funding techniques involved in shadow banking credit intermediation can be seen in Figure 7.1.

Since a lot of shadow banks' funding sources rely heavily on asset-backed securities (ABS) or asset-backed commercial paper (ABCP) whose values depend on the underlying assets (mostly payments from home loans and / or even sub-prime mortgages), prior to 2008 the shadow banking system in the US was closely associated with the property market.

Such complexity – consider the granularity of steps and financial instruments involved like ABS, ABCP, repos, swaps, etc. – is worthwhile only if there are handsome payoffs. In "Is Shadow Banking Really Banking?", Noeth and Sengupta (2011) maintained that one of the fundamental reasons that motivates banks and / or other financial institutions to shift their assets off their balance sheets is that it is too costly to keep these assets on the balance sheets. Through the creation of the off-balance-sheet assets, banks and / or other financial institutions can reduce the amounts of capital kept for fulfilling their regulatory capital requirements. Securitization, which is fundamental to shadow banking, allows "risk diversifications

Function	Shadow banks	Shadow banks' funding
Step (1) Loan origination	Finance companies	CP, MTNs, bonds
Step (2) Loan warehousing	Single and multi-seller conduits	ABCP
Step (3) ABS issuance	SPVs, structured by broker-dealers	ABS
Step (4) ABS warehousing	Hybrid, TRS/repo conduits, broker dealers' trading books	ABCP, repo
Step (5) ABS CDO issuance	SPVs, structured by broker-dealers	ABS CDOs, CDO-squareds
Step (6) ABS intermediation	LPFCs, SIVs, securities arbitrage conduits, credit hedge funds	ABCP, MTN, repo
Step (7) Wholesale funding	2(a)-7 MMMFs, enhanced cash funds, securities lenders, etc.	$1 NAV shares (shadow bank "deposits")

Figure 7.1 Illustrative examples in the US of the steps, entities and funding techniques involved in shadow credit intermediation

Source: Pozar et al. (2010)

across borrowers, products and geographic locations."(p. 13) Through securitized banking, capital can be poured into the US real estate market or the shadow banking system from Europe and China and even small-scale funds in remote areas. Through the multiplicity of products with varying risk and maturity, shadow banking enables financial institutions to better manage their portfolios simply by providing the participants greater flexibility, which is often lacking in the traditional banking system. Shadow banking in the US, to a certain extent, represents an ingenious effort on the part of the market participants, empowered by modern technology, to get around regulatory controls.

China's shadow banking system

If shadow banking in the US can be conceived as a creative reaction by the market participants to bypass the regulatory framework, growth of the Chinese shadow banking system is seemingly a logical response to a Communist economy. Despite China's endeavors to open up its economy, the Chinese government has retained a very top-down economic model, encouraging development of the private sector and yet simultaneously exercising stringent control over its fixed income market, interest rates, currency valuation and in particular bank lending lines. Such a paternalistic model implies that when appropriate, the Chinese government is ready to make inordinate or excessive demands on the existing banking system so that the national goals, whether it is to combat inflation or boost the economy, can be fulfilled. The proliferation of shadow banking in China in a way exemplifies the growing difficulties in the government having a strong grip. To take an example, in the face of the rising inflation in 2010, the People's Bank of China (PBoC) increased the bank reserve requirement ratio (RRR) from 17 percent of overall assets to a new high of 21.5 percent. However, the Chinese economy was still growing then and cash was needed to fuel the development; the move by PBoC indirectly dried up funds available to SMEs since they were the less preferred borrowers in comparison with the larger firms or state-owned enterprises. As Vinicy Chan (2011) aptly describes in "The Perils of Shadow Banking's Expansion", "Beijing's credit growth curbs have thrown companies into the arms of unofficial funding resources" (p. 28). Another reason, as suggested by a report prepared by Bank of America Merrill Lynch (2012), is that the desires of local governments to promote local economic growth also lead to local governments' connivance for setting up of these alternative financial institutions, including some shadow banks, to channel local savings into local businesses. (See figure 7.2)

Born of necessity, the Chinese shadow banking system is closely connected with SMEs and comprises mainly informal financial conduits that cater to their capital needs. Perhaps because of these, the shadow banking sector in China is marked by a simplicity of products such as entrusted loans, trust loans, credit guarantees and private lending, entirely diverse from the complex and esoteric products found in the Western shadow banking sector. In the following section of this report, we shall briefly delineate these various products and / or entities in the Chinese shadow banking sector and identify the inherent risk factors.

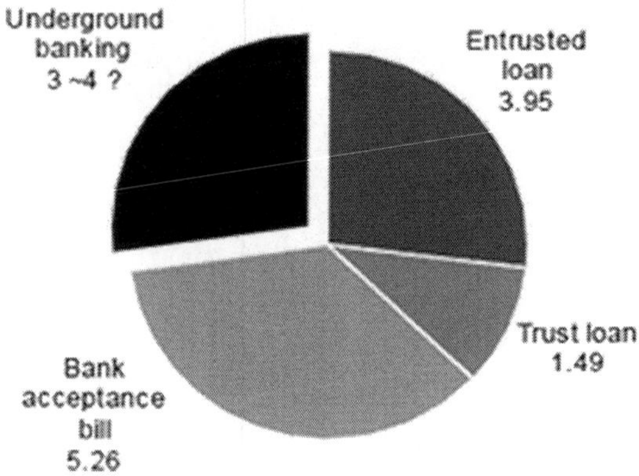

Figure 7.2 Estimated size of China's shadow banking system (June 2011)

Source: PBoC

Trust

The development of the trust industry has accelerated since 2007 after China Banking Regulatory Commission (CBRC) clarified the scope of the trusts' fund-raising activities. In addition, the Chinese government's dear money policy has made trusts an alternative funding source for many companies. Although in theory funding requirements of trusts should be low – after all they just help manage investors' assets – the fact that many trust companies offer guaranteed returns to customers may imply serious trouble when their investments go sour. Most trust funding sources are from wealthy clients and institutional investors and the major investment areas include real estate, industry and commercial enterprises, etc.

The lack of transparency on the part of trusts' returns and the potential failures of certain issuers to repay their loans upon maturity may be the fundamental risk factors associated with trusts. Furthermore, some trust companies may attempt to be "ever-greening" their products in spite of CBRC's ban on such attempts to raise new funds so as to meet old obligations. There may also be liquidity risk amid the repayment peaks.

Pawn shops

Pawn shops are non-financial institutions regulated by Ministry of Commerce (MoC). They are one of the favorite funding sources for the SMEs largely due to their fast loan granting procedures that can take place within one to three days. The major funding sources for pawn shops include trust companies, SOEs, bank loans, private individuals, etc.

Although pawn shops demand high margins (the effective maximum lending rate may be as high as 73.7 percent per annum), the key risk faced by pawn shops is the realization of the collateral value when the customers default. Frequently, the process of realizing the collateral can take very long and the value of the collateral may be highly volatile. Pawn shops can suffer huge losses as a result of these. Where pawn shops use illegal funds, there is also a risk of money laundering.

Guarantors

Guarantors offer repayment guarantees to less credit-worthy borrowers to qualify for bank loans. This market is characterized by many participants and thus low returns. To increase their returns, some guarantors ask for a share of loans that they help get for the borrowers and then relend it to the underground lending market. In theory, guarantors can take funds only by way of equity investment; in reality they may accept individual and corporate deposits.

Where guarantors act like lenders rather than focusing upon their core businesses, banks, rather than getting additional protection through the guarantors, are exposed to a greater probability of bad debts as both borrowers and guarantors can invest badly and default. When a guarantor is regarded as risky, the bank may recall all the loans guaranteed by the guarantor.

Small lenders

Introduced in 2008, small lenders are meant to provide assistance to SMEs and they are largely regulated by local governments. This market is characterized by relatively low returns and funding is often the bottleneck; according to CBRC's guidelines, the funding sources for smaller lenders are limited to bank loans and equity; this may propel the small lenders to take deposits illegally. Closely associated with banks, the small lenders can cooperate with banks in three different ways: (1) a small lender sources a loan for a bank and collects a fee; (2) a small lender can co-lend with a bank; and (3) the agency approach. When small lenders act as agents of banks, the banks can conduct SME loans with better default protection while small lenders can leverage banks for funding to expand their businesses.

Similar to other entities in the shadow banking sectors, the key risk facing small lenders is potential defaults by the key customers, i.e. SMEs.

Underground banks

Probably the most unstable component of the shadow banking sector, underground banks refer to all unregulated agencies which connect lenders and borrowers. Forbidden in the past, underground banks are gradually being recognized as complementing the official lending market. There is a wide spectrum of players in this market and the interest rate is often extremely high. For example, interest rates charged by underground banks in Wenzhou range from 36 percent to 48 percent p.a. for valued customers to 72 percent to 96 percent p.a. for new clients. Borrowers can come from all walks of life – small business people who need a bridge loan to fulfill the registered capital requirement and even SMEs / developers with working capital problems. Listed companies who find bank loans too lengthy a process and even small commercial banks trying to get hold of some cash to meet period end L / D ratio requirements. Funding sources also vary greatly but banks loans surprisingly are the major funding sources of underground banks. To give an example, due to the government's monetary tightening, commodity traders resort to obtain letters of credit (L / Cs) from banks using copper as an anchor to finance their businesses. Because letters of credit are essentially cheaper loans, these traders can lend the money to the underground market so as to arbitrage the rate difference. Similarly, domestic steel traders, established companies and even private individuals relying on bills of lading, group guarantees or mortgages can secure cheaper loans from banks and then relend the borrowed funds to the underground lending market.

The major risks associated with this sector are lack of transparency and regulation. Sudden withdrawals of funds by the lenders are another potential risk.

Bank acceptance bills

Bank acceptance bills accounted for RMB 5.26 trillion of funding in shadow banking, being the largest component of the 15 trillion shadow banking system. Unlike trust, pawn shops, guarantors, small lenders and underground banks being partially regulated or unregulated (in the case of underground banks), the bank acceptance bill is a financing product available in over-the-ground regulated banks, and most often in the stated-owned Big Four banks, namely, BoC, ICBC, CCB and ABC. This kind of shadow funding is provided directly by non-shadow state-owned and privately owned commercial banks.

Although the bank acceptance bill is an official banking product, the booking in financial statement of loan assets under accepted bills (to banks) can be off-balance sheet of a bank, as the loan is booked under bank line against the bank who accepted the bills, but not under the credit limit granted to a borrower (as in the cases in unaccepted bills or bills with discrepancies). Hence, no credit line is needed to be granted to a borrower in order for him to obtain bank financing from accepted bills. This kind of funding does not appear on the bank's balance sheet, does not affect the L / D ratio and RRR of a bank, and hence it is "shadow" in nature. The mechanism is mainly based on issuing export usance letters of credit for the purpose of purchasing goods as a genuine trade, such as commodities like fuel oil, rubber, copper, steel and physical gold. LC issuance, often against a fully cash-secured basis, is usually off-balance sheet as the issuing bank does not provide financing and the LC facility is on uncommitted basis. An exporter letter of credit may call for the beneficiary's drafts to be drawn at a certain number of days after sight, with the following being most popular:

- 90 days USD usance LCs (usually at interest expense of LIBOR + 200 bp p.a. to exporters in Hong Kong)

- 180 days RMB usance LC (usually at interest expense of 3.8 percent p.a. to exporters in Hong Kong)
- 360 days RMB usance LC (usually at interest expense of 4.2 percent p.a. to exporters in Hong Kong)

The issuance of 180 days and 360 days LCs must be supported by genuine third-party documents to provide evidence of genuine trade, such as custom documents (which show specific goods are imported into China). The seller of goods is often a Hong Kong–based company (and in most of the cases, a related party in shareholding or held by relatives of the real "boss" of the LC issuer). Once the buyer's bank has accepted the documents under the letter of credit, the "accepted" LC bills become an (issuing) banker's acceptance. The seller's bank, which provides an exports discounting loan to the exporter based in Hong Kong, is only taking the credit default risk of the issuing bank, but not the default risk of the exporter or the buyer.

Officially, payment of the discounted proceeds to the exporter (in Hong Kong) can be remitted to the supplier only (as required under common practice of banks in Hong Kong). The intended aim of the exporter's bank is to improve the exporter's cash conversion cycle, to let the exporter receive the sales proceeds from the buyer faster. However, through underground banks, the discounted RMB are often being exchanged into China, and in some cases go back to the buyer's bank account (if the buyer and seller are related parties). In this case, the buyer, without actually paying the supplier, can receive the proceeds (to be paid) in advance. The buyer has the potential, though not necessarily the need, to do a simple time deposit or wealth management product to improve deposit yield (for reference, a wealth management product of Bank of China offers 5.4 percent p.a. for a 47-day tenor for a product named "Game-Theory"); or in some extreme cases, the buyer remits the sum of money (which is secretly transferred from the exporter) to another unrelated bank, pledges the deposits and re-issues an LC to purchase the same specific lots of goods. This induces "commercial criminals" for potential double- or triple-financing, so they can use the multiplied sum of borrowed money, to engage in risk-taking activities such as property speculation, or to lend to SMEs and other shadow banks. However, "commercial criminals" are seldom arrested and are even encouraged by buyers' bankers due to the lucrative banking charges they can offer. Hence, the proliferation of professional bankers' acceptance issuers and discounters has created a huge funds flow from Hong Kong to inside China. The fund, with average cost of capital of 4 percent p.a., desperately seeks to have high yield so that the arranger can make a profit. Lending to needy individuals, SMEs and trust companies provide high interest spread and high leverage.

China's government has repeatedly mentioned in publications and meetings its intention to put LC issuance on banks' balance sheets. However, putting the entire RMB 5+ trillion off-balance-sheet loan assets back into banks' balance sheets may result in a huge increase in loan assets of commercial banks. In order to contain these assets, large liabilities such as deposits have to be present in order to meet the RRR and L / D ratio requirements. Hence, China's government has never taken the daring step to slightly formalize LC issuance in China to become on-balance sheet.

7.2. Different manifestations, similar ramifications

While the Chinese shadow banking sector may seem different from its US counterpart both in terms of products / entities involved and reasons for existence, the two share two similar ramifications. For one, the lucrative private lending business / shadow banking has led to a broadening array of players or participants. In the US, big firms such as GE and AIG that previously had little to do with the finance industry had involved themselves in brisk trading in world bond markets prior to 2008. Neither GE nor AIG is a bank in the traditional sense and both suffered calamitous losses amid the 2008 financial crisis, perhaps suggesting that the risks were high when even traditional firms decided to jump on the bandwagon to participate in the shadow banking sector. In China, we are witnessing a similar trend when big firms or SOEs such as China Mobile, China Shenhua Energy or China Railway Construction are starting to involve themselves in private lending. For another, although the Chinese shadow banking sector is related to SME lending, similar to its US counterpart, there seems to be a growing relationship between shadow banking and the Chinese property market. More and more loans and private lending end up with loans made to small property development companies in China. Thus, similar to the US, the risk is that the decline in the property market in China will have a domino effect, leading to the collapse of multiple companies and a spike of bad debts.

Case study 1: Wenzhou financial situation

Wenzhou is a prefecture-level city with a total area of 11,784 square kilometers and a population of 12 million in southeastern Zhejiang Province. It is third in terms of GDP in Zhejiang, after Hangzhou and Ningbo.

Wenzhou has been treated as a test case for a capitalist model relying heavily on small and medium-sized enterprises focused on low-end manufacturing for export. Wenzhou people are well known for their entrepreneurship. This approach was so successful that it became known as the "Wenzhou model" and was adopted throughout the country. The model always represents the dynamics of the private sector, but it also means specifically the development of small-scale manufacturers, often family owned, and distribution networks between producers and consumers all over the country.

Despite this success, the low margin export trade is unsustainable in the long term. Over the past decade, Wenzhou business people have turned to highly speculative activities – real estate investment and financial derivatives – to make a quick buck. The city recently experienced economic devastation and a collapse of its private loans networks. The major exigencies of Wenzhou are the credit crisis, disappearing bosses and underground lending.

- One-fifth of the city's 360,000 SMEs have stopped operations due to lack of funding from the proper banking system.
- Nearly 100 business owners ran away or declared bankruptcy. Those bosses have borrowed hundreds of millions from private creditors.
- Due to the tight monetary policy, state-owned banks are reluctant to offer loans to SMEs, which made them turn to illegal and high-cost private lending.

The private lending industry is estimated to have grown to RMB 4 trillion in value. In the entrepreneurial city of Wenzhou, the size of this industry was about RMB 600 billion to 700 billion with nearly 90 percent of the city's residents involved in gray lending activities.

It has been seen not only as an attempt to legitimize Wenzhou's private finance market, but as a model for cleaning up underground lending in China as a whole, according to a statement released after a State Council executive meeting presided over by Premier Wen Jiabao.

Under the plan, Wenzhou is to have at least 30 rural financial institutions by the end of 2013. Those should include village banks, rural financial cooperatives and 100 micro-credit companies with RMB 40 billion (USD 6.35 billion) in net assets.

Meanwhile, six private asset management companies are to be set up by the end of 2012, and a private equity fund, led by the city government, is to raise RMB 3 billion by 2015.

The new policy allows the government to incorporate those lenders into the formal system to regulate and monitor them. Those private financial institutions can also improve their ability to control risk through the government's guidance.

The legitimate private lenders will be a supplement to the traditional financial system, allowing resources to be fully allocated and improving of efficiency.

Another breakthrough is lowering the barriers to private foreign direct investment. In terms of monetary reform, the new policy will provide deeper involvement of private capital in overseas investment and an increase in cross-border flotation of the Renminbi. This will not only push local financial institutions and regulatory authorities to achieve higher professional competence, but also play a significant role in internationalization of the Renminbi and reform of the exchange and interest rate system in China.

Case study 2: The creation and destruction of Wu Ying

Wu Ying (Chinese: 吴英; born 20 May 1981), at a young age of 31 years, is an entrepreneur from the city of Dongyang in Zhejiang Province; previously she was the sixth richest woman in China. After being convicted of financial fraud, she was at first sentenced to death but the Supreme Court of China overturned the sentence. On 21 May 2012, her sentence was reduced to death with a two-year reprieve, which is usually commuted to a life sentence after two years, partly due to public opinion on the death sentence.

What created and destroyed Wu Ying? It's the shadow banking system. First, the shadow banking story is created by laws and regulations in China. In China, companies are restricted by law to directly lend money to each other. Nevertheless, companies can through banks lend entrusted (by banks usually) loans to specific borrowers. Interest rates of the loan financing can be determined by the party of Trust (usually this role is taken up by a bank). The bank serves as a middleman, but does not take any credit risk of the borrower, and only collects the entrusted loan fee. Market rate of entrusted loan interest is almost 25 percent, which is 4 times the base lending rate (6.31 percent, before the lending rate reduction by 0.31 percent to 6 percent in July 2012).

Second is the social mentality of the "hot money" era in China. As most individuals' investment behavior has become short term, the rise of the "one-day millionaire" has made the people gradually believe that wealth creation is not a prolonged process, but rather a very short-term process. In Zhejiang, where Wu Ying was born and created her fortune, many of Wu Ying's customers were individuals who sold their core manufacturing businesses (mainly driven by poor exports during the 2008 financial crisis) for funding to be invested in real estate developments. As a result, capital gains in multiples of initial investments were realized and so people got into a vicious cycle such that no initial funding and capital gains can be diverted into the manufacturing businesses (real economy). Most long-term investments, real economy investments were done by state-owned enterprises, while private funding mostly went into real estate, stock investment or commodities trading. Wenzhou, which is within Zhejiang Province, was renowned for its property investors who can gather friends and relatives and invest, in some cases even purchase the entire project from large developers. Wu Ying herself also sold her core business in cosmetics retail and retail car services and focused on lending money through investment companies to needy individuals, who are usually private small real estate developers.

Last but not least is the macro-economy in China. Wu Ying, despite earning high interest rates from small borrowers, was also aware that the government's property ownership limit had really impaired the small developers' debt repayment ability in the eyes of the lenders (such as Wu Ying). In the past, small borrowers could always count on fire sales as a last resort, an option that may no longer be available, because genuine demand (vs. investment demand) generally prefers large and more reputable developers. A small commercial banker in Zhejiang has mentioned that by the end of 2010, "black-market" lending rates to small developers had already surged to 250 percent p.a. and had eased back a little to 200 percent to 240 percent p.a. in September 2011. Currently, even the most valued existing customer has to pay 100 percent p.a. for the "wholesale" sector of private lending, i.e. where loans start from RMB 10 million. Wu Ying, who was viewed as a "retailing" shadow banker, served individuals and small companies, and was in a slightly better position to provide loans, irrespective of credit tightening, which resulted in people running to her during emergencies. The rise in interest rates has been much more significant than the official rate of SHIBOR (see Figure 7.6), but the direction of movement was generally the same. Hence, although Wu Ying managed to contain credit default loss by not lending new loans to small borrowers due to increased macro-environment risks, her earlier borrowers (customers) had increased loan delinquency rates and hence her cash flow became tight, making it difficult to borrow from commercial banks as repayment from small borrowers had virtually stopped. Commercial banks which failed to force Wu Ying to settle the loans were forced to chase the money back through litigation. Wu Ying's case may not be isolated and could reflect the huge credit risks taken on by shadow bankers in China, which causes systemic risks in an ineffective shadow banking system. Liquidity had become a major concern for individuals and businesses in 2012, since borrowing from both traditional commercial banks and shadow banking had become difficult. Observing the poor economic indicators from the first quarter of 2012 onwards, the Central Government of China was forced in May–July 2012 to introduce lots of changes in laws and regulations for short-term and long-term liquidity easing, to re-vitalize the financial system in China.

7.3. Forecast on shadow banking with laws and regulations changes

The main reason for the rise of shadow banking in China is that some companies cannot borrow money from banks for their business development. Hence, these companies have to seek help from another channel – shadow banking – which can smooth short-term cash flow. In the above sections, we have discussed some cases of shadow banking practices in China and have observed that the Chinese government has a changing attitude towards companies involved in shadow banking. A question is hence raised from this:

Will the changes in the laws and regulations be a blessing or a curse to the shadow banking system in China?

From the Wenzhou financial reform, the State Council said it would allow private lenders in Wenzhou, whose legal status has been in limbo, to operate as investment companies to augment the financing available to small and medium-size enterprises. This action seems to be a green light for underground banking to be legalized; especially since Wenzhou has been historically the pilot city for China's financial reforms, as seen in the table below.

Moreover, small and medium-sized enterprises (SMEs) in China frequently complain about the discrimination from banks owing to their fewer assets and lack of credit records. According to the *Yearbook of China Small and Medium Enterprises 2010,* the loan coverage for SMEs was only 18.7 percent in 2008

Year	*Event*
1876	Qing Dynasty forced to open Wenzhou to foreign trade
1980	Wenzhou authorities grant China's first private business license to a Wenzhou woman
1984	A Wenzhou boot factory becomes China's first joint-stock company
1988	China formally recognizes the legality of privately owned enterprises
Early 2011	Wenzhou government tries to let locals invest overseas, but lack of consent by the Central Government sinks the move
2011	Premier Wen Jiabao vows support for small businesses cut off from credit
2012	State Council approves financial reform measures in Wenzhou

Source: WSJ Research (2011)

while the SMEs are contributing more than 60 percent of GDP to China. Also, SMEs received only 15.7 percent of the 89.7 billion of new loans issued in 2008. Unlike companies receiving blessings from the government, they have to resort to underground credit paying exorbitant interest rates, sometimes as high as 90 percent, in order to keep their businesses running. With the pilot scheme launched, it is believed that private capital would be encouraged to invest in quality SME companies and hence the interest rates may be lowered, while benefitting the growth of un-blessed companies. The Chinese government is optimistic on this as they are expecting a net growth of non-state sector investment and financial services.

In the meantime, the response received from private capital also reflects that they welcome this pilot scheme. There are some arguments that the shadow banking issue in China is caused by the failure of large banks to provide financing to companies who are in need for development. With the new testing policies, private capital or underground lenders can be registered and establish rural banks. SMEs believe interest rates can be lowered and they too can enjoy most of the "blessing".

We have also interviewed Mr. Calvin Tang, senior project manager in Vantage Capital Shanghai (one of the private equity companies in China) to share his views on whether this would be a great chance for PEs in China. He said: "From the economic prospective, this new policy can help to provide funding efficiently with no doubt. However, I would take risk management in my evaluation as a much higher priority for such kinds of investment projects" (interview conducted by phone on 11 July 2012).

When investing in companies / industries, there are two main factors to be considered for a private capital company: source of funds and client base. There can be different types of funding in a private capital organization, e.g. government funds, personal investments, mutual funds, etc. Different investors may have different appetites. A private equity (PE) has to balance and match the money-lenders to the borrowers in order to prevent "chain reactions". "Let's take development industry as an example. A PE borrowed some money to provide to the developers and the funding sources were personal funding. One day, the investor heard some bad news about the developers and wanted to withdraw the funding. If the developers failed to return the money immediately, the PE would then be forced to find extra financing and that would trigger a chain reaction." Such cases are not rare for private capital. In May 2012, National Australia Bank (NAB) shut down its Integrated Capital Solutions investment arm, just months after the division reportedly lost millions it had invested in collapsed electronics retailer WOW Sight and Sound, which collapsed in February 2012. The failure of WOW to repay its borrowings led to Integrated Capital Solutions shareholders losing USD 30 million on the investment; NAB is understood to have written off USD 25 million in debt. "I would rather take this new policy as an alert on risk management, rather than a very exciting opportunity," commented Calvin.

If the pilot scheme is not necessarily a blessing to the private capital, how about to the money-borrowers, say SMEs?

Calvin explained that money-lending in China is currently based on the "background" of the company. It has been always tough for SMEs to borrow loans from the four large banks as they lack "blessing". "The 4 banks are not following market-trends. For instance, mining is hot for the time being. Some mining companies would like to borrow money to expand their business but the 4 banks may refuse to do so because they are small companies or have no 'referrers' backing them. With more funding sources available, it's true that the SMEs can benefit from it." However, Calvin raised the risk management issue again here. "On one hand, the analysts in PEs have their own specialties. They may only invest in industries they are familiar with as part of the risk control." The opportunities of fund sourcing may be increasing but this is not guaranteeing the SMEs can get investment efficiently, especially for those new, young industries.

On the other hand, although most of the media in China says the new policy can lower the shockingly high interest rates offered by underground borrowers, Calvin took the opposite view, "I think it is unlikely to be lowered by too much, especially when you consider the risk involved." In evaluating investment projects, different cash flow models may be used by different companies. The financing interest rate calculations are mostly based on these models as well as company policies. "The risk calculation for each project should be independent of funding competition and therefore the interest rates would not be affected to a great extent. 90 percent can also be a reasonable rate if it is a risky investment."

To put it in a nutshell, the financial reform in Wenzhou resulted in a new era of financing and banking development in China. The new pilot scheme can help private capital to expand and invest in splendidly growing companies. Also, it can offer more sources for SMEs to borrow money for business growth and maybe enjoy lower interest rates than ever. However, risk management will also be a great challenge for these pilot money-borrowers. Choosing the right companies to invest in and protecting capital investors' profit will be one of them.

7.4. Shadow banking in China from the perspective of a foreign investor

While investment opportunities for Chinese investors are significantly limited by regulation, lack of maturity in the investment life cycle and a high degree of political risk, foreign investors still see China as offering a favorable level of risk versus reward. It is given this fact that we must examine what positive or negative impact the shadow banking system in China may have on the foreign investor.

Using US shadow banking risks as a benchmark

In an October 2011 investment insight titled "Shedding Light on China's Shadow Banks", JP Morgan Asset Management (JPMAM) talks specifically about the risks that foreign investors should think about when they are exposed to shadow banking because of investments in China. The first notable point raised in the article is that shadow banking in China has grown to a sizable mass in only one-sixth the time it took for the US shadow banking to develop (which was about 30 years). Even given this rapid growth, JPMAM still believes that Chinese shadow banking is less of a threat to the financial stability of China and is far better monitored when compared to shadow banking in the West. There are three primary reasons for this.

First, nearly all shadow banking firms are large state-owned trust companies. The size of the trust industry in terms of assets has now reached over RMB five trillion. These trust companies offer a much higher rate for deposits than the banks which sometimes have negative real interest rates. The one benefit to most trust companies being stated owned is that this means they are subject to state control and regulation.

These large firms typically represent the lender and small to medium enterprises (SMEs) typically represent the borrower. JPMAM argues that in fact the trust companies are more risk averse than the Chinese banks since they issue loans in a more capitalistic fashion, asking for better risk-versus-reward. Second, there is no leverage since this practice is banned in nearly all cases for Chinese trust companies. Leverage is primarily what created the problems in the US shadow banking system causing the "great financial crisis". Last, the relative size of the shadow banking system is smaller than that of the US. In October of 2011, the total assets of all trusts sat at about 5 percent of total deposits in the regulated banking system as opposed to the US shadow banking system which had around USD 20 trillion in March 2008, which far surpasses liabilities of all regulated US banks.

JPMAM argues that the high-risk nature of shadow banking notwithstanding, it is a necessary outlet given the Chinese investors' appetite for high-risk investments in a channel other than the volatile local equity markets. We argue that high interest rates help substantiate this claim. The strong demand for finance from capital-starved SMEs is matched with the high-risk appetite of investors. Do venture capitalists not also require high rates of return on their investments?

A commentary by Barclays Capital in an October 2011 article in *The Wall Street Journal* supported the viewpoint that shadow banking presents certain risks but none that investors should necessarily be worried about. The primary reason is that the trusts have very limited risk exposure to commercial banks. Even with a sudden and sharp increase in the number of loan defaults, individual investors and corporations would suffer but this would have no effect on the number of non-performing loans of commercial banks. Should defaults increase, this would in turn cause a large number of redemptions and the overall amount of trust lending would decline. Even given this scenario Barclays does not believe this will lead to a systemic economic or financial risk.

What to fear

So what should a foreign investor lose sleep about? JPMAM proposes that the real area of concern is the fast-growing area of "informal lending". Credit Suisse estimates that this lending sector is currently growing at a rate of 50 percent year-on-year. What characterizes this sector is that the lending firms are small and the rates are ridiculously high at around 60 percent to70 percent. The extent to which trust companies are involved in informal lending is difficult to tell.

The reason why such a sector exists is because access to capital for SMEs is so tight. As the government works to open this up more in the future, SMEs will be less likely to use "informal lending" as a source of capital.

To conclude, we posit a favorable forward-looking outlook on shadow banking in China from foreign investors' perspective. We support this claim by drawing a parallel between the recent emergence of the consumer P2P lending in Western economies and that of the shadow banking system in China. The same reasons that have led to P2P lending can be attributed to factors that make shadow banking in China work. In doing so, we are assuming all conclusions reached in our earlier analysis of the shadow banking environment in China. We are also excluding the "informal lending" that takes place at exorbitant interest rates. These reasons are broadly defined as follows.

In a presentation on how to regulate shadow banking, BBVA Research (Garcia Herrero 2011) has said that one of the primary risks posed by shadow banking is that of systemic risk. In issuing many loans to SMEs, the default rate for the lender is diversified since not all borrowers default and this reduces systemic risk. The existence of such systemic risk is primarily what wreaked such havoc in the US shadow banking system.

The disintermediation of shadow banking eliminates the high overheads associated with traditional financial institutions. This may in some cases result in better rates for borrowers or in some cases loans which may not have been given by Chinese banks. This risk is accompanied by a suitable reward of higher interest rates.

The loan application and transfer of funds can take place much quicker and both the borrower and the lender can access funds much more quickly.

Given the above, we believe the shadow banking system does not appear to be carrying any worrisome systemic risk and perhaps provides a much needed capital lubrication in which high risk is offset by high reward.

7.5. Appendix: Main business data

A) Main Business Data of Trust Companies (1st Quarter 2012)

RMB 10,000, %

1. Income statement of trust company						
1.1 Non-trust assets	**186.735 billion**			**1.3 Total revenue**	**10.617 billion**	
Cash and deposits with banks	Amount	3,712,391		Interest income	Amount	106,429
	Composition	19.88%			Composition	10.02%
Loans	Amount	2,778,391		Commission income from trust business	Amount	524,238
	Composition	14.88%			Composition	49.38%
Investments	Amount	10,499,794		Investment income	Amount	146,194
	Composition	56.23%			Composition	13.77%
1.2 Shareholders' equity	**169.81 billion**			**1.4 Total profit**	**7.718 billion**	
Paid-in capital	Amount	8,734,964		**1.5 Profits per capita**	**62**	
	Composition	51.44%				
Trust compensation provision	Amount	50,2360				
	Composition	2.96%				
Retained profits	Amount	4,446,133				
	Composition	26.18%				

2. Trust assets		**5301.607 billion**				
2.1 Divided by categories of trust property :				**2.2 Divided by trustee duty**		
Collective pecuniary trust	Amount	149,955,995		Financing *	Amount	263,232,600
	Composition	28.29%			Composition	49.65%
Single pecuniary trust	Amount	360,256,841		Investment *	Amount	200,659,311
	Composition	67.95%			Composition	37.85%
Non-cash property trust	Amount	19,947,843		Non-discretionary *	Amount	66,268,768
	Composition	3.76%			Composition	12.50%
3. Pecuniary trusts				**5102.130 billion**		
3.1 Divided by forms of funds application				**3.2 Divided by categories of target market**		
Loan	Amount	190,568,920		Infrastructure	Amount	111,500,348
	Composition	37.35%			Composition	21.85%
Short-term investment	Amount	38,629,603		Real estate	Amount	68,657,013
	Composition	7.57%			Composition	13.46%
Long-term bonds investment	Amount	89,486,788		Securities (stocks)	Amount	18,348,525
	Composition	17.54%			Composition	3.60%
Long-term equity investment	Amount	67,321,157		Securities (public offering funds)	Amount	2,482,696
	Composition	13.19%			Composition	0.49%
Leasing	Amount	883,266		Securities (bonds)	Amount	25,131,894
	Composition	0.17%			Composition	4.93%

(Continued)

Purchase-and-sellback	Amount	9,151,961		Financial institutions	Amount	70,815,212
	Composition	1.79%			Composition	13.88%
Due from banks	Amount	58,959,933		Industrial and commercial enterprises	Amount	11,012,3496
	Composition	11.56%			Composition	21.58%
Others	Amount	55,211,207		Others	Amount	103,153,653
	Composition	10.82%			Composition	20.22%
4. Securities investment trust		**583.163 billion**				
Primary market	Amount	554,819		Cooperation with bank	Amount	41,331,598
	Composition	0.95%			Composition	70.87%
Secondary market	Amount	14,113,768		Cooperation with privately offered funds	Amount	15,698,572
	Composition	24.20%			Composition	26.92%
Fund investment	Amount	312,592		Others	Amount	42,528,179
	Composition	0.54%			Composition	72.93%
Mixed investment	Amount	43,335,110				
	Composition	74.31%				
5. Schemes liquidated last month						
Total liquidated schemes (No.)		502		Companies involved(no.)		60
Paid-up capital of Trust		26,117,970		Annual average fee rate for trustee %		0.46%
Accumulated delivered profit		1,309,155		Actual annual return to beneficiary %		5.67%

Source: China Trustee Association: www.xtxh.net/Trust_Statistics/10457.html

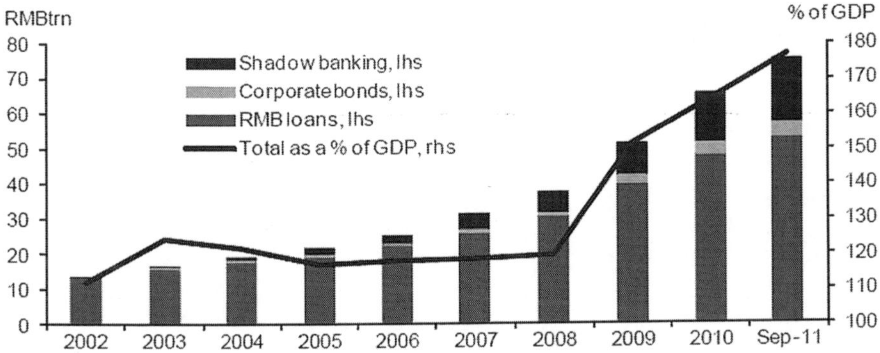

Figure 7.3 Total banking and shadow banking funds outstanding

Source: CEIC and Nomura Global Economics

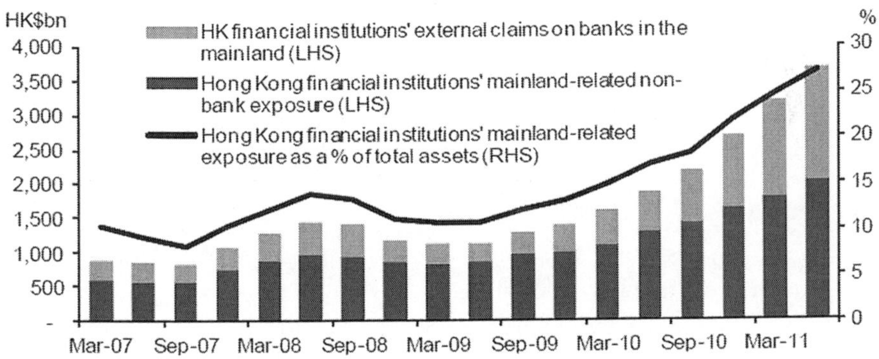

Figure 7.4 Hong Kong financial institutions' exposure to the mainland

Source: Hong Kong Monetary Authority and Nomura Global Economics

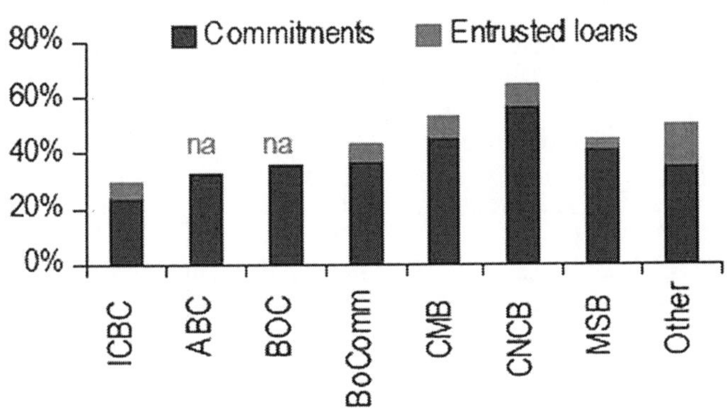

Figure 7.5 Off-balance-sheet exposure comparison

Source: Bank of America AML Global Research, company reports

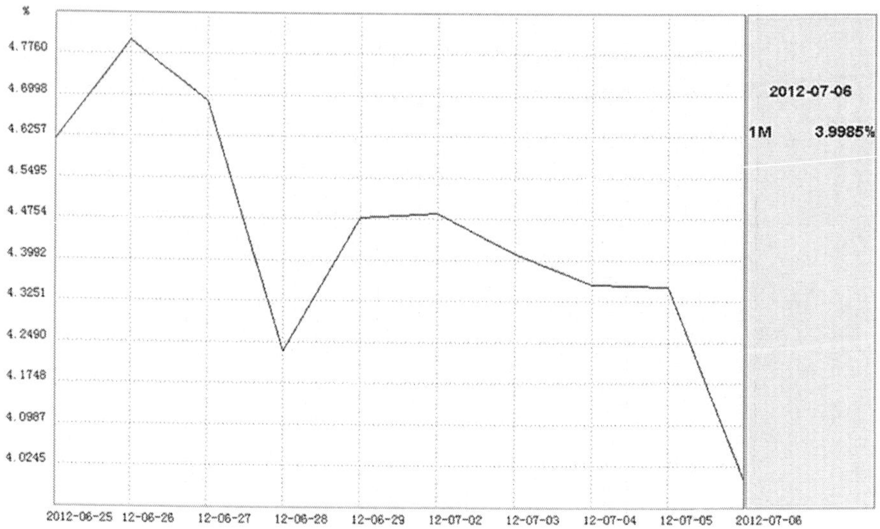

Figure 7.6 1-year chart of 1-month SHIBOR movement

Source: Shanghai Interbank Offered Rate: www.shibor.org

References

Cella III, P. J. 2009. The financial crisis and the scientific mindset. *New Atlantis: A Journal of Technology & Society* 26 (Fall): 31–38.

Chalk, Nigel. 2011, November. Lurking in the shadows – the risks from nonbank intermediation in China. The IMF Blog. http://blog-imfdirect.imf.org/2011/11/03/the-risks-from-nonbank-intermediation-in-china/

Chan, Vinicy. 2011, November. The perils of shadow banking's expansion. *Asiamoney* 22 (10): 24–27.

Cui, D., Tian, T., & Wei, Z. 2012: Shadow banking: risky business, Merrill Lynch, Equity StrategyChina's shadow-banking system. *The Economist.* www.economist.com/node/18118975.

Dong Tao, Weishen Deng. 2013, 2 February. "China: Shadow banking – Road to heightened risks" Credit Suisse.

Garcia Herrero, Alicia. 2011. How to regulate shadow banking: thoughts from the world to China. BBVA Research, 5th Annual China Bankers Forum.

Gongloff, Mark. 2011. China's shadow banking system: the next subprime? *The Wall Street Journal,* 25 October. http://blogs.wsj.com/marketbeat/2011/10/25/chinas-shadow-banking-system-the-next-subprime/

JP Morgan Asset Management. 2011, October. Shedding light on China's shadow banks. www.jpmorganam.com.sg/JFAsset/newsFile/IS_China%20Shadow%20Banking_Oct11.pdf

Left, Andrew. 2012, June. Evergrande Real Estate Research. Citron Research. www.citronresearch.com/wp-content/uploads/2012/06/Evergrande-Real-Estate-Research.pdf

Noeth, B. J., & Sengupta, R. 2011, October. Is Shadow Banking Really Banking?, *Regional Economist* 19 (4): 8–13.

Papadakos, John. 2011. Nomura Asia Special: China economy. Nomura Global Economics. November 10. http://zh.scribd.com/doc/72251949/Nomura-China-Anchor-Nov-2011

Pozar, Z., T. Adrian, A. Ashcraft and H. Boesky. 2010, July. Shadow banking. Federal Reserve Bank of New York Staff Report No. 458.

Rabinovitch, Simon. 2012, 22 March. Beijing reforms: China's lending laboratory. *The Financial Times*. www.ft.com/intl/cms/s/0/90e7f67a-a41b-11e1-a701-00144feabdc0.html#axzz2rVDTGc2c

Stafford, Patrick. 2012, 29 May. NAB shuts down private equity arm after disastrous WOW Sight and Sound investment. www.smartcompany.com.au/finance/26089-nab-shuts-down-private-equity-arm-after-disastrous-wow-sight-and-sound-investment.html.

Tian, Zhong. 2012. Analysis of China's top 10 listed banks for 2011. Pricewaterhouse-Cooper, May 2012.

Wei, Lingling, Dinny McMahon and Tom Orlik. 2012, 28 March. China tests financial relaxation in Wenzhou. *The Wall Street Journal,* http://online.wsj.com/news/articles/SB10001424052702303404704577309051957346004

Winnie, W., Alistair S., Michael L. 2011, May Off B/S exposure: hidden risks and potential tightening. Bank of America Merrill Lynch.

Wong, Edward. Chinese Court Overturns a Young Tycoon's Death Sentence. April 21, 2012. *New York Times,* page A7.

Xinhuanet. 2012, May 21. Death-sentenced businesswoman receives lighter penalty following heated debates. http://news.xinhuanet.com/english/china/2012-05/21/c_131601890.htm

Zhang Dan. 2012. Private financing welcomes "sunlight". CNTV.CN, 13 March. http://english.cntv.cn/program/china24/20120313/121996.shtml

Zhang Dan. 2012. Entrepreneurs welcome financial reforms in Wenzhou. CNTV.CN, 31 March. http://english.cntv.cn/program/china24/20120331/106528.shtml

Zhang Pengfei. 2012. Wenzhou to pilot private investment overseas. *China Daily,* 29 March. www.chinadaily.com.cn/china/2012-03/29/content_14935672.htm

Zheng Xin, Qin Zhihui. 2010. YEARBOOK OF CHINA SMALL AND MEDIUM ENTERPRISES, Beijing: Economic Science Press. ISBN:978-7-5141-0168-3

8 Development of RMB as an international currency

8.1. Background information

Introduction

As the value of the US dollar continues its downward slide after the 2008 financial crisis, the Chinese currency, RMB, has been widely speculated to be a new global currency in the making. While macro-economic conditions are also favorable for the RMB to play a bigger role in the global currency regime, Beijing has yet to set any goal for converting RMB into an international currency because it lacks an essential prerequisite to become a global currency – full convertibility on the capital account.

In this chapter, we analyze the development of RMB as an international currency from a multi-dimensional perspective, from its history to recent market developments, from the Chinese government's policy to international trading disputes and from investors' speculation on RMB appreciation to countries using it as their foreign currency reserves, etc.

Internationalization of the RMB was not previously an eye-catching issue, partially because it is closely related to the issue of RMB convertibility, which in turn was assumed to be conditional on full liberalization of the capital account. Hardly anyone seriously thought that China should, and will, fully liberalize its capital account in the foreseeable future, and hence the discussion on RMB liberalization has taken a back seat in the policy debate.

However, interest in RMB's internationalization process has recently been increasing, partially due to China's fast economic growth and its increasing economic integration with the world, which have led to a significant increase in its influence in the world economy.

Also, more and more people are hoping that internationalization of the RMB could be treated as part of the solution for the problems that China is currently facing. Some others think that internationalization of the RMB seems to be an easy solution to safeguard China's financial interests as well as its stability. All these have made internationalization of the RMB an interesting topic to study.

Advantages and drawbacks of capital account opening

Advantages

Developing countries generally face the problem of limited savings and lack of foreign exchange reserves for rapid economic growth. From a macro-economic view, capital account convertibility can attract foreign capital, which enhances investments and stimulates economic growth. From a micro-economic view, capital account convertibility can improve local financial market efficiency by competition. In the meantime, it enables investors to allocate their assets globally and enjoy the benefits of diversification.

Drawbacks

International capital movement can adversely affect the effectiveness of the central bank's monetary policies. Moreover, once the capital account is open, massive foreign capital can move in and out of the local economy during good / bad periods. This will enlarge the economic cycle and volatility. In addition, when there is a large depreciation expectation in local currency (local inflation is too high), the public may lose faith in the local currency, resulting in currency substitution (people prefer to hold foreign currency instead of local currency), capital outflow and large exchange rate fluctuations.

Principle for China to open its capital account

After China joined the World Trade Organization (WTO) in 2001, there has been an upward pressure for China for further liberalization of capital account transactions. However, the key elements of success for this evolution include: (1) a stable internal and external political environment; (2) an efficient macro-economic management; (3) a broad and deep financial market; (4) a complete legal basis; and (5) a transparent information disclosure system.

At this time, China is not in a position to fulfill all of the above requirements to make its currency fully convertible. After long discussions based on the experience of foreign countries, Chinese scholars suggest China should open its capital account in the following sequence: capital inflows first then capital outflows; direct investment first, followed by portfolio investment and then other investments; long-term investments first, then short-term investments; corporate investors first and then individual investors; debt securities first, then equity securities and derivative products. The whole process of reform must be gradual and smooth. The Chinese government has to consider the risk of a financial crisis after capital account opening.

In the 12th Five-Year Plan, it was clearly stated that "China should further reform its financial system to steadily promote market-oriented interest rate reform and enhance a market-based managed floating exchange rate regime. The country should also improve its foreign exchange reserve management and gradually realize RMB convertibility under capital accounts."

8.2. RMB recent performance as a currency

Over the last 10 years, CNY[1] (a.k.a RMB) has been appreciating gradually and there is a prevailing upward trend. Since China has tweaked the CNY-USD peg in year 2005, it has appreciated by around 30 percent, which means an average of 5 percent over the last six years. (See Figure 8.1)

And if inflation (5 percent–10 percent) is taken into consideration, the real exchange rate has appreciated much higher, 25 percent–40 percent, which is claimed by economists and politicians as the margin by which RMB is undervalued.

Speculation about appreciation of CNY

As illustrated in the previous section, the RMB has been appreciating for the last 10 years and the upward trend is obvious. Investors are betting on revaluation of the RMB for a number of good reasons.

Inflation is a main reason for appreciation of RMB. Currently inflation is at around 5.5 percent (last reported in October 2011). Although it has slowed down, it is still relatively high compared to the three-year high of 6.5 percent in July 2011. And there is strong evidence that PBoC believes allowing RMB to keep appreciating is a good way to control inflation. "To allow the RMB to appreciate would help fight inflation," former Chinese central bank adviser Yu Yongding said in an interview with Bloomberg Television. PBoC has raised the bank's reserve ratio several times but there has been only limited effect. It is reluctant to raise the interest rate as this would attract more inflows of hot money into China, which can further destabilize the banking sector. So it seems that the best solution to fight inflation is to revalue RMB. (See Figure 8.2)

A main reason for China to depress RMB is to boost the competitiveness of its export sector. But China is no longer the favorable choice for setting up factories. According to Credit Suisse, "Salaries for China's estimated 150 million migrant workers will rise 20 to 30 percent a year for the next three to five years. . . . It may take a decade for China to see its export competitiveness erode, but we have seen the

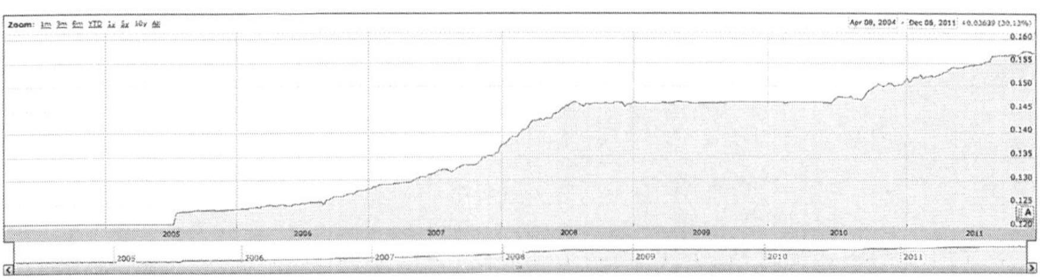

Figure 8.1 Recent performance of RMB

Source: Google Finance www.google.com.hk/finance

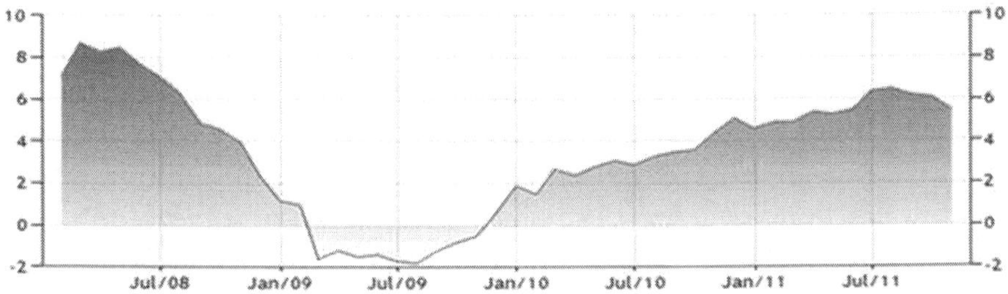

Figure 8.2 Recent inflation rate in China

Source: TradingEconomics.com; China Economic Information Net www.cei.gov.cn/

beginning of this happening." So it is unwise for China to continue pushing the RMB down and steady appreciation of RMB should continue in the coming few years.

Another argument for having a revaluation of RMB is the pressure coming from the international community which continues to blame China for the global economic ills and asks China to stop controlling the direction of RMB. At the 2011 G20 conference, US Treasury Secretary Tim Geithner opposed the request from China about avoiding discussion of its currency policy. "Flexible exchange rates help countries better absorb shocks and that the tension between flexible currencies and those that are 'tightly managed' is 'the most important problem to solve in the international monetary system today.'" Tim said at the conference. Also China is blamed as the first country to not adhere to international rules by controlling its currency. As evidence shows, quite a lot of Asian countries follow what China does and intervene in foreign exchange markets.

Actually some investors even believe that China will quicken the pace of revaluation or even have a one-off appreciation. Because this can reduce further inflows of hot money and also reduce the need to keep piling up foreign exchange reserves, its total value exceeded the all-time record of USD 3 trillion with USD 1.15 trillion in US Treasuries.

Correlations between onshore and offshore RMB trading

After introduction of offshore spot trading in 2010, we now have both onshore and offshore RMB trading. In this section, we would like to examine the trends and performance of CNY, CNH and CNY (NDF) in recent years and the correlations between them.

CNH is more sensitive to the market's condition than CNY is. Also, CNH has consistently traded at a premium to CNY. This is due to the lack of fungibility between CNH and CNY. Also, the large divergence is attributed to capital controls on the CNY market and the allocated RMB supply from the PBoC to Hong Kong. The premium has gradually decreased over time because there are more RMB supplies in Hong Kong and also capital controls have been diluted over time. Recently, the trend has reversed, where USD/CNH has surpassed USD/CNY. (See figure 8.3)

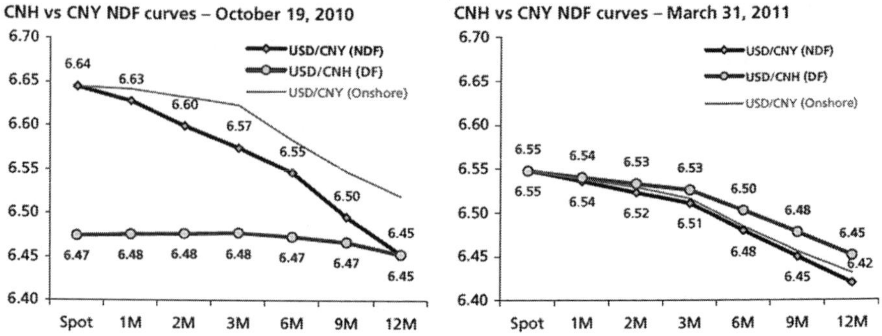

Figure 8.3 CNH vs. CNY (NDF) curves

Source: Google Finance

In the early period for CNH, from August to October 2010, it got a widening premium over NDF. This is due to speculation on appreciation of RMBRMB. It was also more volatile than the NDF. This is suggested by the fact that the NDF market is a more mature market which exhibits participants' expectations about RMBRMB whereas CNH is still a new and "work-in-progress" market which should be more sensitive to the actual changes in the spot RMBRMB exchange rate. After that until the end of 2010, we see that the premium is narrowing and the two are converging. This should be due to the fact that PBoC has started to increase interest rates and the reserve requirement ratio to fight inflation and this has tempered the RMBRMB's appreciation. Also, there was less pressure on RMBRMB's appreciation because the focus switched to other financial issues, e.g., European sovereign debt crisis. And then they continue to converge to each other as the CNH market is becoming more and more mature.

Many people want to find out if there is any price discovery between CNY onshore spot, CNH offshore spot and NDF markets. If there is, then investors can predict the price in one market from the price in another market.

According to the article "The Price Discovery Puzzle in Offshore Yuan Trading: Different Contributions for Different Contracts" (2012), there is no price discovery flow between onshore and offshore spot markets but they do find price discovery between onshore spot and offshore forward prices. And more interestingly, the introduction of offshore spot trading had led to an increase in cross-market price discovery between onshore spot and offshore non-deliverable forward prices. They suggested that this is due to the CNH providing offshore spot rates for the offshore non-deliverable forward contracts and this completes the offshore market.

The article also looks into the relationship between CNY and CNH and that of CNY and NDF. The CNH premium (the percentage difference between CNY and CNH) is more than double the NDF premium (the percentage difference between CNY and NDF). This is suggested by the fact that NDF is more correlated to CNY than CNH is. As NDF is a non-deliverable forward contract, its forward curve acts like a futures curve on onshore RMBRMB spot prices. While CNH is a spot price, its

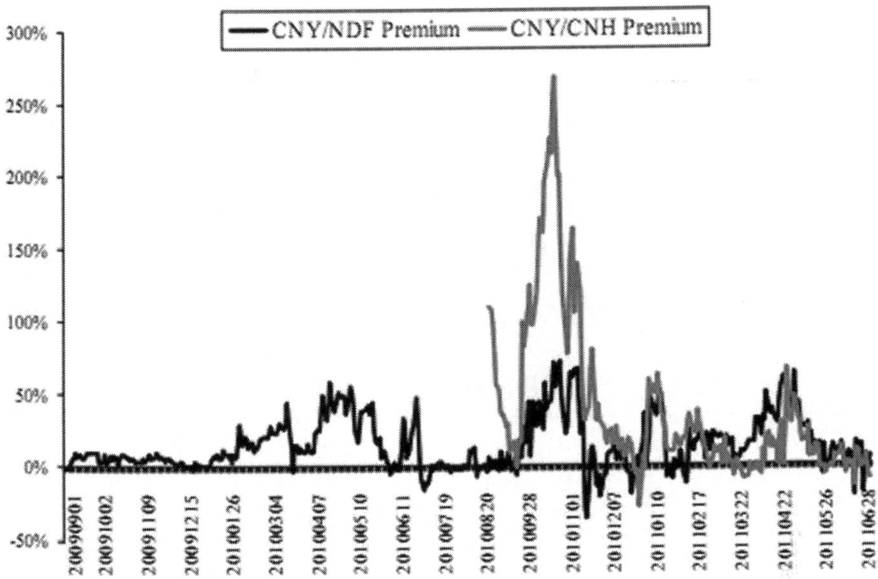

Figure 8.4 Premiums of CNY/NDF and CNY/CNH

Source: Ding, D. K., Tse, Y., and Williams, M. R. 2012. The Price Discovery Puzzle in Offshore Yuan Trading: Different Contributions for Different Contracts. Journal of Futures Markets Volume 34, Issue 2, pp. 103–202.

forward curve acts more like an onshore interest rate curve. This suggests that NDF and CNH track different aspects of the Chinese economy and explains why there is only cross-market price discovery flowing between CNY and NDF. (See Figure 8.4)

8.3. RMB's increasing importance on the international platform

Since the open door policy started in the late 1970s, the fast-growing economy of China has been catching the attention of the world, especially the developed countries in the West. As China begins to take one of the leading roles on the international platform both economically and politically, RMB is also taking an increasingly important position. In this part, we will discuss how the Chinese government is liberalizing RMB with different policies and strengthening RMB's influence over other countries.

According to Chinn and Frankel (2005), an international currency should be capable of playing the role as: (1) a store of value; (2) a medium of value; and (3) a unit of account for both residents and non-residents. It is believed that RMB will likely be internationalized in three steps: (1) use in pricing and trade settlement; (2) use as an international investment vehicle; and (3) use as an international reserve currency. Though currently RMB has not yet achieved the role of an international currency, it has been approaching this gradually.

Imbalance between China's economic activities and the utilization of RMB

China is the world's second-largest economy, the largest exporting country and has the largest foreign exchange reserves which account for about one-third of the world's total amount. However, due to foreign exchange controls in China, use of RMB in global trading settlement, foreign exchange and world reserves remain minimal. Such imbalance increasingly presents risks to China and the global economy. Besides, the recent internal concerns on high inflation in China and external pressures from various countries, especially the US, on the appreciation of RMB and a free exchange rate, forced China's government to pave the way to liberalize RMB. This is also a natural step in the growth and development of the Chinese economy.

Among the countries which frequently criticize that RMB has been undervalued, the US is the most dominant one. It claims that this is how China keeps its exports competitive in overseas markets. "It is undervalued," Obama said of the RMBRMB, speaking to reporters in Seoul after the meeting concluded. "And China spends enormous amounts of money intervening in the market to keep it undervalued" (Bloomberg 2010)

Figure 8.5 shows the total exports to and imports from the US over the past 15 years. The trade deficit of the US increased dramatically in the 21st century.

Besides, given the size of China's economy, the international community is also urging RMB to take on a wider role. "The G20 is to study whether to include the Chinese RMBRMB within the basket of currencies that make up the IMF's Special Drawing Rights." Speaking at the G20 summit in Nanjing, French President

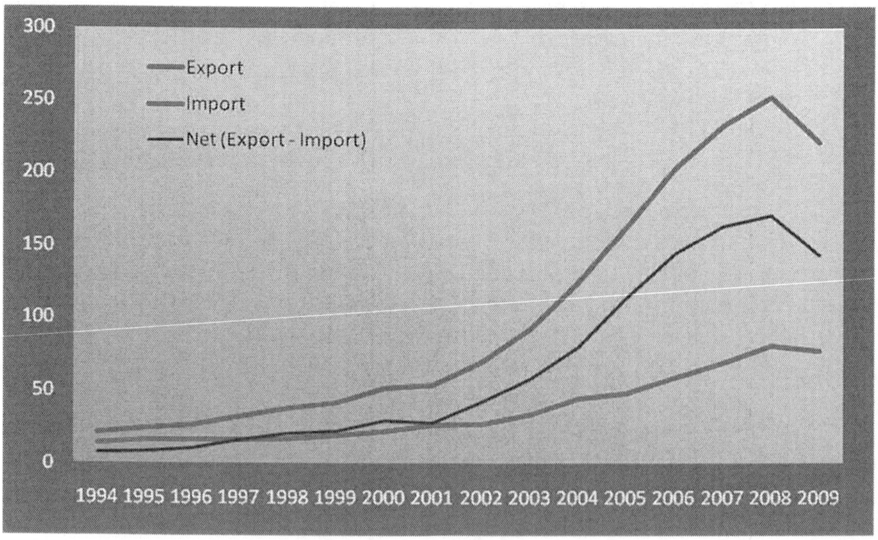

Figure 8.5 China's imports from and exports to the US

Source: National Bureau of Statistics of China

Nicolas Sarkozy suggested that given the importance of emerging economies such as China to global growth, their currencies should be added to the SDR basket. "It is clear that we must evolve toward a more flexible exchange rate system that will allow us to withstand shocks," he added. "Over time, we believe that currencies of large economies heavily used in international trade and financial transactions should become a part of the SDR basket," he said (BBC 2011).

Development of RMB policy and expansion of CNH market

To liberalize RMB usage, the People's Bank of China has introduced various measures. The first step is to allow the "going out" of RMB. Once remitted outside China, the offshore RMB is reclassified as CNH with no restrictions from the Beijing government. Currently CNH is primarily traded in Hong Kong. Back in January 2004, Hong Kong residents were allowed to hold RMB. However, the permitted daily transaction ceiling was set at RMB 20,000. Due to the limited outflow of RMB to this proto-offshore market, the size of the RMB market in Hong Kong at that time was very small, it had little growth and reached just RMB 62.6 billion as of the end of 2009. Shortage of RMB also stunted the innovation of RMB financial products in Hong Kong.

In July 2009, China's government launched a scheme called the Pilot RMB Trade Settlement Scheme. This was an important catalyst that has transitioned the offshore market in Hong Kong from its formation stage to its development stage. Under this scheme, eligible enterprises in five selected pilot coastal cities, namely, Shanghai, Shenzhen, Guangzhou, Zhuhai and Dongguan, were allowed to settle transactions in RMB with their corresponding enterprises in Hong Kong, Macau and in the trade of Yunnan and Guangxi with ASEAN countries. In September 2010, the Scheme was further expanded to 20 provinces in China, with corresponding enterprises in all countries / territories in the world. In August 2011, the Scheme took a further step expanding to the whole of mainland China.

With the introduction of the Pilot RMB Trade Settlement Scheme, the currency risks and conversion costs for domestic export enterprises are reduced, since:

1. Chinese importers can pay RMB to their overseas trading partners;
2. Eligible Chinese exporters can receive RMB from their overseas corresponding enterprises;
3. Overseas trading partners can buy and sell RMB through their own banks outside China; and
4. Banks outside China can buy and sell RMB with the clearing banks and participant banks of the RMB clearing platform in Hong Kong or correspondent banks in China.

As a result, the RMB market in Hong Kong has grown substantially. Transactions settled in RMB through banks in Hong Kong increased from a monthly average of about RMB 5 billion in the first half of 2010 to over RMB 57 billion in the second half of 2010, and further to RMB 134 billion in the first half of 2011. Total RMB trade settlements processed by Hong Kong banks amounted to RMB

369 billion in 2010, which accounted for 73 percent of the total cross-border RMB settlement of mainland China. This percentage further increased to 84 percent in the first half of 2011. (See figure 8.6)

Not only in Hong Kong, the percentage of China's total cross-border trade settled in RMB has also been increasing rapidly, from only 0.7 percent in the first half of 2010 to 4 percent in the second half of 2010, and further to 9 percent in the first half of 2011. It is anticipated that such amounts will further increase given the world's opportunistic view on China's economic growth in the near future, and the recent concern over the US economic outlook and the depreciation of USD.

The Pilot RMB Trade Settlement Scheme not only boosts RMB deposits in Hong Kong (at the end of June 2011, RMB deposits in Hong Kong had exceeded RMB 550 billion), but this sizable and rapidly growing pool of money also encouraged RMB financial products innovation to meet the increasing global demand for RMB financing and investments. This is another crucial step to internationalize the RMB, i.e. as an investment vehicle (this will be further discussed in the later part of this chapter). (See figure 8.7)

Apart from the Pilot RMB Trade Settlement Scheme, China's government has taken various other steps to liberalize RMB. Now, an RMB offshore market has been set up in Singapore. Various RMB-denominated financial products are available in the Singaporean market. In September 2011, China's Vice Premier Wang Qishan held talks with UK officials about developing another RMB offshore hub in London. This could crucially pave the way for RMB to be traded outside Asia and is another important step towards RMB trading around the clock.

In January 2011, the People's Bank of China announced the "Administrative Measures for the Pilot RMB Settlement of Outward Direct Investment". Under this policy, investment flows between China and the rest of the world can also be denominated in RMB. Chinese enterprises can now make overseas direct investments in RMB. Foreign direct investment into China can also be made in RMB upon approval on a case-by-case basis.

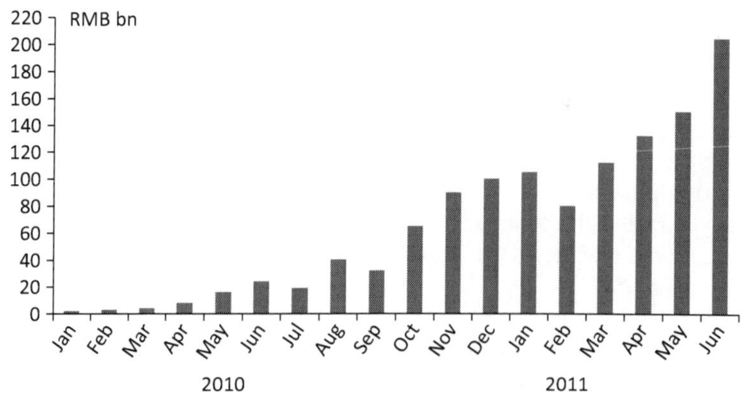

Figure 8.6 RMB trade settlement in Hong Kong

Source: Hong Kong Monetary Authority

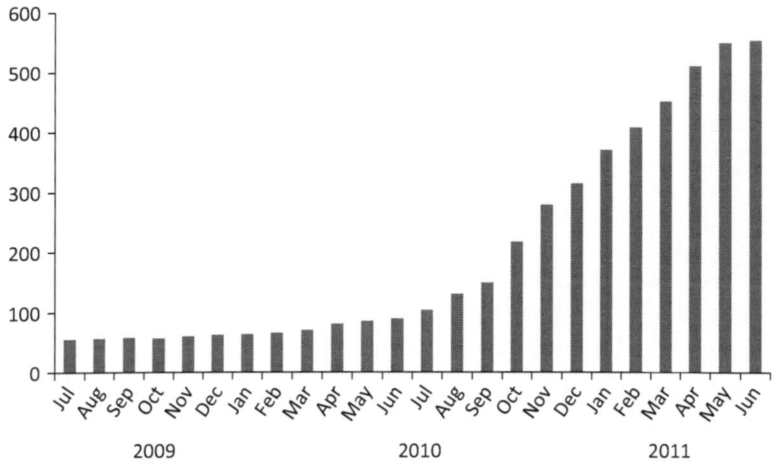

Figure 8.7 RMB deposits in Hong Kong

Source: Hong Kong Monetary Authority

Table 8.1 China's bilateral swap agreements with other countries

BSA	*Total Size*	*Effective Date*	*Expiration Date*
China–Korea	200 bn RMB/38 Tr Won	Dec 2008	Apr 2010
China–Hong Kong	200 bn RMB/227 bn HKD	Jan 2009	Jan 2012
China–Malaysia	80 bn RMB/40 bn Ringgit	Feb 2009	Feb 2012
China–Belarus	20 bn RMB/8 Tr BYB	Mar 2009	Mar 2012
China–Indonesia	100 bn RMB/175 Tr Rupiah	Mar 2009	Mar 2012
China–Argentina	70 bn RMB/Equal Amount Peso	Mar 2009	Mar 2012
China–Iceland	3.5 bn RMB/66 bn ISK	Jun 2010	Jun 2013

Source: PBoC and BBVA Research (2011)

From a country-level perspective, China has been promoting RMB to other trading partner countries. Starting from late 2008 after the global financial crisis, China signed a series of bilateral swap agreements with other countries, including Korea, Malaysia, Indonesia and countries as far away as Argentina, Belarus and Iceland. Participating countries can settle trade with China in RMB instead of in USD. This is another step to help RMB "going out" and to make it play a larger role on the global platform. A stated policy of the People's Bank of China is to sign more bilateral swap agreements in the future. It's expected that there will be more and more RMBs circulating among global markets. (See Table 8.1)

To conclude, the series of deregulation measures that have taken place in the past years will continue to stimulate cross-border flows of RMB and lead to a deeper and broader CNH market, further stimulating internationalization of the RMB. Without disruptions, the policies will kick-start organic growth of the CNH market, as depicted below:

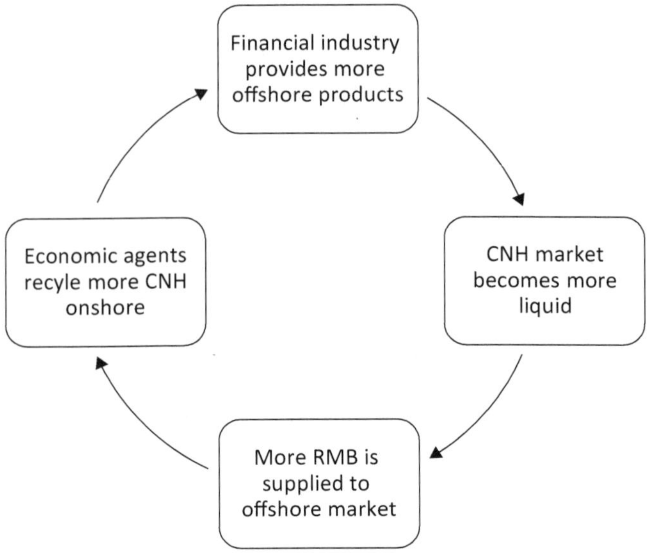

RMB as a foreign reserve currency

The next step toward internationalization of RMB, or to gain a more important role on the global platform, is to promote RMB as a foreign currency reserve. Given the lack of investment vehicles globally and free convertibility, RMB is still playing an insignificant role as a foreign currency reserve at the moment. Figure 8.8 shows the composition of official foreign exchange reserves (in USD billion) from 2000 to 2010. USD is still the most popular foreign currency reserve, followed by Euro. However, the percentage of official foreign exchange reserves denominated in USD has been shrinking over the past decade, from 70 percent in 2000 to 60 percent in 2010.

Given China's increasingly leading role in the international arena, researchers in general believe that RMB is contributing to a larger part of the "other currency" claims from the global foreign exchange reserve, which shows a steady growing trend. Beijing has allowed foreign banks, starting with Malaysia, to hold RMB reserves. More and more countries have expressed their interest in or have already invested in RMB as their foreign currency reserve, e.g., the Chilean central bank reported in 2011 to have USD 91 million worth of RMB in reserves, and the president of the central bank of Venezuela, Nelson Merentes, made statements in favor of the RMB following the announcement of reserve withdrawals from Europe and the US. Nigeria plans to invest 5 percent to 10 percent of its foreign exchange reserves in China's currency, the RMB (RMB) or RMBRMB, the country's central bank governor Lamido Sanusi said. "We will continue with our efforts and are close to . . . taking the RMB as part of Nigeria's foreign exchange reserve currencies," Sanusi said at a press briefing in Beijing (*China Daily* 2011). Another report stated, "Asia's central banks want to diversify their

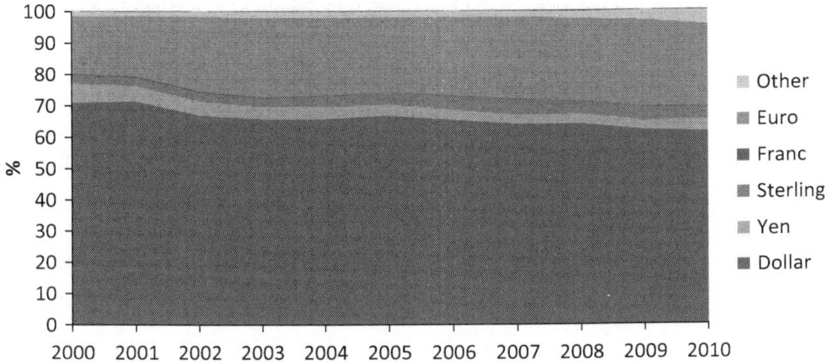

Figure 8.8 Currency composition of official foreign exchange reserve

Source: International Monetary Fund

growing foreign-exchange reserves into RMBRMB-denominated debt issued by China's government, according to Bangko Sentral ng Pilipinas Governor Amando Tetangco" (Bloomberg 2011).

According to the US economist Barry Eichengreen (2011), in 10 years, RMB will account for 15 percent of the global foreign reserves. Given China's commitment to liberalize its capital and current account by end of 2015, it is not so far away that RMB will be fully liberalized and take on a leading role on the global platform.

8.4. RMB-denominated products becoming a trend

We believe that in the process of RMB's internationalization, it is important to have a wide range of RMB-denominated financial products in the market. In fact, RMB-denominated financial markets have developed into a significant sector well ahead of internationalization of the currency, especially after formation of the CNH market, where foreign investors can easily deliver, convert and transfer offshore RMB, which in turn increases their accessibility of offshore RMB products.

There are three different kinds of products covered in this chapter, namely, RMB offshore bonds, RMB-denominated insurance policies and RMB-denominated stocks listed outside China.

RMB offshore bonds

China's offshore RMB-denominated bond market was initiated in Hong Kong in 2007. These bonds are also called "Dim Sum bonds" as they used to have a small scale. The key difference between onshore and offshore RMB bonds is that investors need to obtain Qualified Foreign Institutional Investors (QFII) quota before they can invest in onshore RMB bonds, but there is no such restriction on offshore Dim Sum bonds. In essence, offshore RMB bonds should have a broader investor base.

The offshore RMB bond market has been a booming market, especially after the second half of 2010, when there were active promotions of Dim Sum bonds and relaxation of currency controls. Outstanding offshore RMB bonds currently stand at RMB 75 billion, with more than 125 issuances just in the first half of 2011. (See Figure 8.9)

In terms of bond issuers, the offshore RMB bond market had been dominated by the government and agency issuance but credit has been growing rapidly in recent years given the increasing interest in issuance from both Chinese domestic as well as multinational corporations with significant operations in China. (See Figure 8.10)

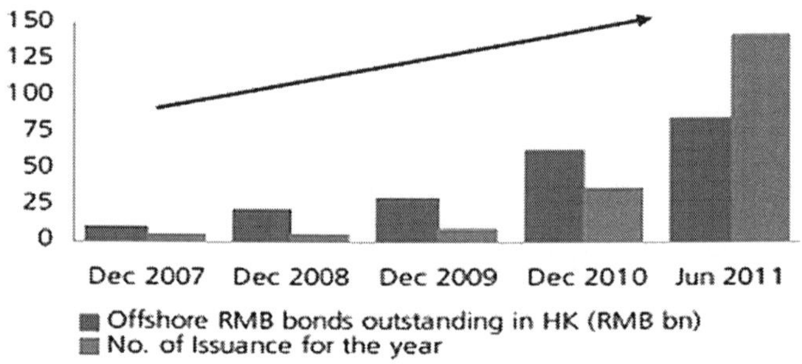

Figure 8.9 Offshore RMB bonds available in the market

Source: Bloomberg, UBS Asset Management (June 2011)

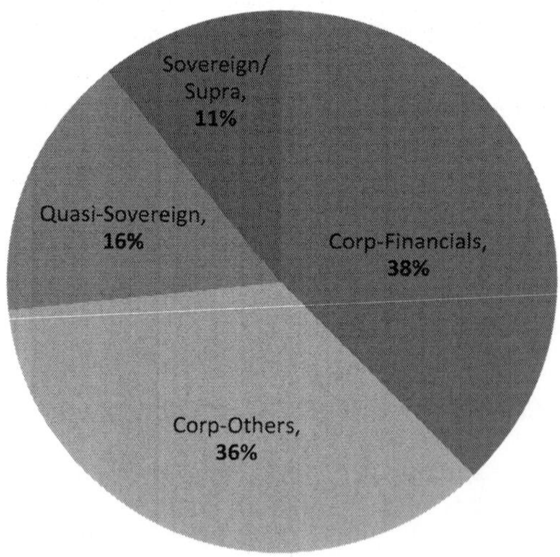

Figure 8.10 Offshore RMB bonds sector allocation

Source: Bloomberg, UBS Asset Management (June 2011)

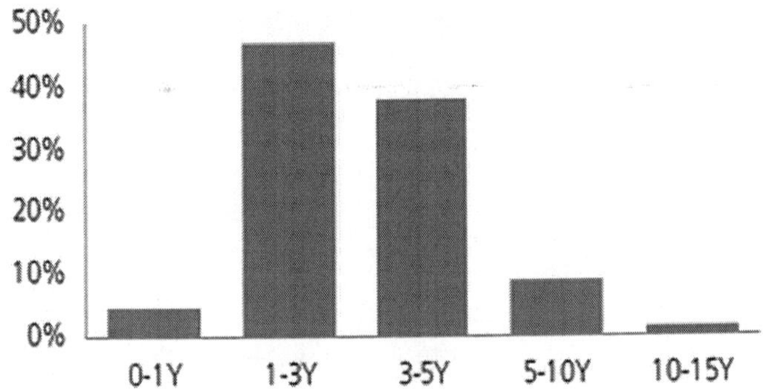

Figure 8.11 Offshore RMB bonds maturity breakdown

Source: Bloomberg, UBS Asset Management (June 2011)

One interesting thing to note is that offshore RMB bonds generally have short durations (average duration only 1.5 years, 80 percent of the total with less than three years maturity), which means that when the corporations need to re-finance themselves when they continue their business in China, it is likely that more Dim Sum bonds will have to be issued, thereby further supporting the offshore RMB bond market. (See Figure 8.11)

In terms of credit quality, offshore RMB bonds generally have high ratings (averaging between single-A and double-A) and the yields are relatively low (normally around 1 percent–2 percent for government bonds and around 4 percent for corporate bonds), showing little correlation with onshore rates as expectations of RMB appreciation are the most important driver.

After all, it is believed that attractive funding costs should invite more supply from both on- and offshore issuers, while growing RMB cross-border trade settlement business will underpin the demand side. HSBC (2010) expects the supply of offshore RMB bonds to rise to RMB 100 billion annually by 2013.

RMB-denominated insurance policies

The increased supply of RMB offshore bonds also enabled the emergence of another RMB offshore product – RMB-denominated insurance policies.

As of December 2011, there were more than 80 RMB insurance policies issued in Hong Kong. While most of these policies are offered by insurance companies with a Chinese background (e.g. China Life, Bank of China Group Life, etc.), foreign insurance companies (e.g. HSBC Life, AXA, Manulife, etc.) have also offered similar products over the past few years.

Generally speaking, the existing RMB insurance policies in Hong Kong offer a guaranteed return (yield) of 1.18 percent to 2 percent, with an investment horizon between 3 to 10 years, while the minimum investment amount ranges from RMB 30,000 to RMB 200,000.

However, due to the lack of variety of RMB investment vehicles in the market, the underlying assets of these RMB-denominated insurance policies are mainly RMB offshore bonds. As a result, only general and life insurance policies are available while Investment-Linked Assurance Scheme (known as ILAS) cannot be offered unless more choices of RMB-denominated stocks, ETFs or unit trusts are available in the market.

RMB-denominated stocks

Among different kinds of offshore RMB-denominated products, the one that attracts most attention from the market would arguably be RMB-denominated stocks. The first offshore RMB-denominated equity was listed in Hong Kong on 29 April 2011. Indeed, it was not a traditional equity but a Real Estate Investment Trust called Hui Xian REIT (87001.HK), controlled by tycoon Li Ka Shing.

The assets of Hui Xian REIT are backed by Oriental Plaza properties, which cover 100,000 square meters (1.1 million square feet) along Changan Avenue in central Beijing. Oriental Plaza consists of eight premium office towers, a shopping mall, a Grand Hyatt Hotel and serviced apartments, according to its website. Since both rents received and dividends of the REIT are in RMB, no foreign exchange risk is involved and the annualized forecast yield is around 4 percent.

Despite market volatility, Hui Xian REIT was still popular among Hong Kong investors and managed to raise RMB 10.5 billion based on an IPO price of RMB 5.24 per unit.

Given the IPO experience of Hui Xian REIT and the policy direction to turn Hong Kong into an offshore RMB centre, it is expected that there will be more listed RMB products in the future. According to the roadmap of the Hong Kong Stock Exchange, following the launch of HKEX trading support facility in October 2011, our market can cater to more RMB-denominated listed products, including RMB equities and other RMB products.

However, there are also uncertainties. The daily turnover of Hui Xian REIT dropped from RMB 350 million on its first day of listing to slightly over RMB 2 million in November 2011. Although we understand that REITs are normally traded less frequently, it still alarmed people that RMB listed stocks may not be as popular as they might have thought.

8.5. China's offshore RMB bond market

Background and key milestones

The offshore RMB bond market has continuously demonstrated rapid development, especially the CNH bond market. The CNH bond market, also nicknamed "Dim Sum", experienced rapid development after 2009. The regulation on the CNH bond market, just like bond markets for other currencies, is very light. Any issuer, including foreign and multinational companies, can issue CNH bonds in Hong Kong, although they will need to get approval from regulators if they want to use their proceeds onshore. There is no restriction in Hong Kong on the use of proceeds of CNH bond issues. Issuers are free to remit the proceeds to places outside Hong Kong or convert them into other currencies.

As of November 2011, the outstanding CNH bonds have reached over RMB 200 billion, a five-fold growth from RMB 46 billion at the end of 2010. The growth of CNH bond market, however, still lags the accumulation of CNH deposits. As of September 2011, RMB deposits in Hong Kong have reached RMB 554 billion, equivalent to 9.23 percent of total deposits (Figure 8.12). Mainland trade settled in RMB has also shown rapid growth, reaching RMB 958 billion in the first half of 2011, compared to RMB 506 billion in 2010 (Figure 8.13). However,

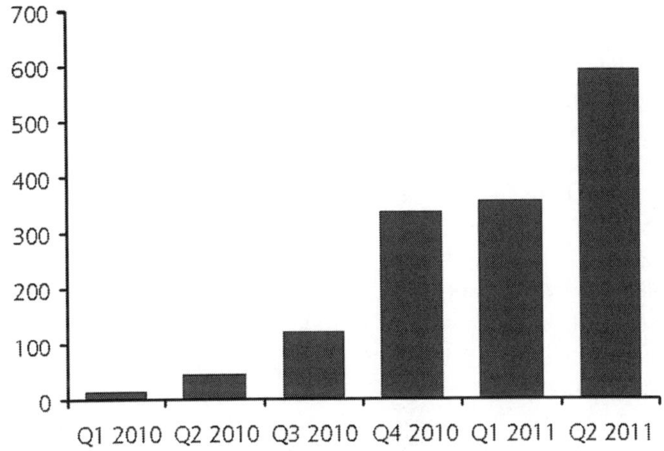

Figure 8.12 RMB cross-border trade settlement (RMB bn)

Source: CEIC, Barclays Capital

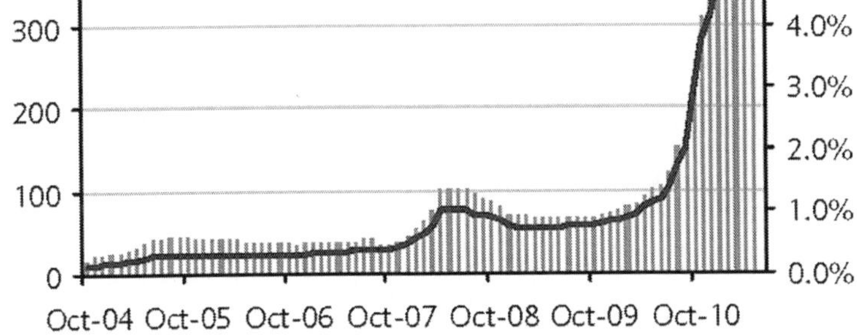

Figure 8.13 RMB deposit accumulation in Hong Kong (RMB bn)

the size of CNH bonds outstanding in CNH market is 1/4000 of the size of the onshore interbank market. Within the offshore RMB bond market, while Dim Sum bonds have grown exponentially, synthetic bonds on the other hand, issuance of which had showed rapid growth in early 2011, slowed down since March 2011 as both demand and supply dried up.

Milestones and development

In this section, we briefly examine some of the important milestones of offshore RMB in Hong Kong. RMB in Hong Kong is also known as CNH as CNH refers to the spot market for deliverable RMB in Hong Kong. Initially, CNH funding started with RMB settlement of border trades in 1997. In recent years, CNH has shown extraordinarily rapid growth due to strong demand and easing of regulatory controls and with imbalanced and insufficient supply (Figure 8.14).

By January 2004, licensed banks were allowed to conduct personal RMB business, such as deposits, exchange, remittances and card business. In 2005, personal RMB business expanded further such that local residents were allowed to make payments in Guangdong by cheque and the door opened up to Designated Business Customers in Hong Kong as well. In 2007, an offshore bond market began and the mainland's financial institutions were allowed to issue RMB bonds in Hong Kong. In 2009, the pilot program for RMB trade settlement began between Hong Kong and five mainland cities and the first RMB sovereign bond was issued by the Ministry of Finance in Hong Kong. Since July 2010, the market has experienced rapid growth of CNH business after the

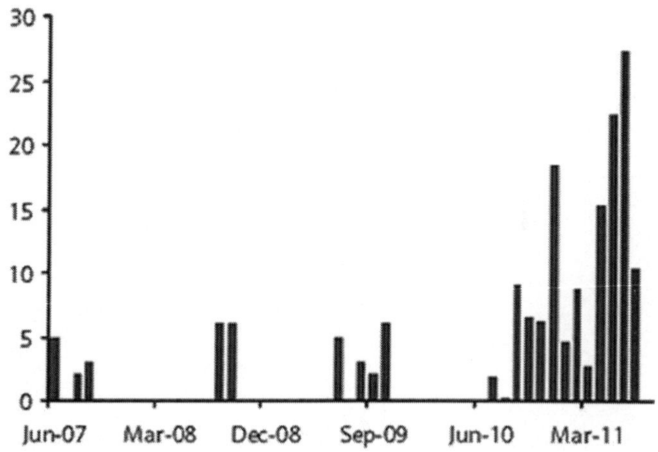

Figure 8.14 Monthly CNH bond issuance, RMB bn

Source: CEIC, Barclays Capital

restrictions were lifted. This deregulation allowed Hong Kong banks to offer RMB accounts and RMB-denominated investment products to corporate customers and individuals. Corporate customers can convert RMB and other currencies without any restrictions and there are no more restrictions on issuers, investors or amount of RMB bond issuance. After the deregulation, all foreign investors became eligible to sell RMB bonds and the volume of CNH bonds issued grew rapidly.

Since late 2010, further regulatory changes occurred reflecting the regulator's view of "firm but measured" RMB internationalization and this resulted in more issuance of offshore RMB bonds. In October 2010, Bank of China Hong Kong (BoCHK) announced that the annual clearing quota of RMB 8 billion had been reached, which increased the concern and worry of the investors that the liquidity of RMB in Hong Kong may be constrained. Later, Hong Kong Monetary Authority (HKMA) announced that it agreed to a RMB 200 billion swap line with the People's Bank of China (PBoC) to maintain liquidity. In December, PBoC approved a RMB 4 billion quota for the first quarter of 2011 and a further quota of 4 billion was approved consequently in the second quarter of 2011. In December 2010, in order to enhance risk management, the HKMA limited Authorized Institutions' RMB net open positions to 10 percent of their RMB assets or liabilities, whichever is higher. In the following year of 2011 January, PBoC announced a pilot scheme to allow RMB settlement of outward direct investment by non-financial enterprises in order to further internationalize RMB and increase potential ODI and lower CNY appreciation pressures. In April 2011, PBoC announced a cut in the interest rate on offshore CNH deposits in Hong Kong from 0.99 percent to 0.72 percent. This cut was intended to further slow down the pace of CNH accumulation and to encourage more CNH investments instead of deposits from investors. Consequently, CNH bonds surged as a reaction to the rate cut. In March and May 2011, the HKMA created an RMB Fiduciary account service to control the Authorized Institutions' (AI) counterparty credit risk with the clearing bank (BoCHK). BoCHK lowered its interest rate for CNY deposits in Hong Kong from 0.865 percent to 0.629 percent. HKMA reiterated with emphasis that AIs were taking counterparty risk with the PBoC and not with BoCHK. Consequently, they were exempted from the large exposure limits.

Here are some of the key milestone issuances since 2010. In July 2010, Hopewell Highway Infrastructure was the first Hong Kong corporate to issue RMB bonds in Hong Kong. In September 2010, McDonald's was the first foreign corporate to issue RMB bonds in Hong Kong. In October 2010, the first CNH bond of 10 years tenor was issued by the Asian Development Bank. In December 2010, the first high-yield bond was issued by Galaxy.

The rapid CNH bond market has thrived recently because there is a lack of CNH investment products. RMB deposits in Hong Kong banks are rapidly increasing whereas net issuance of CNH bonds is still relatively small. There is very strong demand for CNH bonds.

Sources of demand and supply of offshore RMB (CNH)

The sources of demand for CNH are the following:

1. Hong Kong domiciled importers from mainland China who settle their trades in RMB.
2. CNH interbank participants who have access to onshore interbank bond markets.
3. CNH equity issuers who take the issuance proceeds back to mainland China. On the other hand, the supply has not matched the demand yet. This is because there are broader ways for RMB funds to flow out from mainland China to offshore than the other way around and there is still a very long process and multiple layers of approvals required for the issuance of CNH bonds and the remittance of proceeds.

The sources of supply are:

1. The clearing bank (BoCHK), which brings RMB from mainland China to Hong Kong for use by AIs, hedges its trade-related flow.
2. HKMA which has a RMB 200 billion currency swap line with the PBoC. When AIs hedge their open positions and the settlement flow is more than the quota with the clearing bank, the HKMA can use its RMB swap line for AIs.
3. Mainland importers who settle trade in USD. These importers remit RMB to Hong Kong to buy USD for their imported goods.
4. Hong Kong citizens who have accumulated RMB deposits with Hong Kong banks, and investors and tourists from mainland China who bring cash RMB to Hong Kong.

Reasons for growth of the offshore RMB bond market

The first so-called Dim Sum bonds, denominated and settled in China's currency, the RMB, but issued in Hong Kong, appeared in 2007. However, this Dim Sum issuance has risen sharply since July 2010. This section aims to discuss the main driving forces behind the growth of the offshore RMB bond market. Two major reasons are discussed in detail: (1) China's long-term goal of RMB internationalization; and (2) Hong Kong as an offshore platform for building up demand for RMB as currency for international settlement, funding and investment purposes.

Despite numerous regulatory restrictions which should constrain the offshore RMB market development, the offshore RMB market has kept growing. Obviously there are driving forces behind the offshore RMB bond market. Some of the reasons for the exponential growth of this market are further discussed below.

Reasons of high demand for CNH bonds

With a positive outlook for China's economy and potential for appreciation of the RMB, there is a high offshore demand for CNH. However, there is a lack of investment choices for CNH and limited supply of CNH bonds which greatly lags demand.

Despite the restrictions on offshore market such as restrictions on daily purchases of RMB 20,000 per person, CNH still has an obvious advantage for investors as they can buy CNH assets, such as deposits and bonds. The high demand for offshore RMB bonds can be explained by lack of investment options, investors' preference for low volatility, high credit quality of available CNH bonds and the expectation of RMB appreciation.

- Lack of investment options

Due to the restrictions on the CNH market, only a limited number of choices are available to entertain the demand of investors. There has been only one CNH Equity IPO in Hong Kong to date, and most CNH are held in bank deposits. As a result, many CNH investors seek yield enhancement in CNH bonds which is likely to have higher returns.

- Low volatility

Liquidity in the secondary market for CNH bonds is still mediocre, with daily trading volume of about USD 100 million on average. Typical ticket size is about RMB 10 million and bid-off spread is around 10–20 cents for sovereigns, 40–70 cents for IG names and 100–200 cents for HY names. Although offshore RMB bonds are quite illiquid due to the size of the market, it is actually relatively more stable than other bond markets such as offshore USD bonds and as such it attracts longer-term investors with a buy-and-hold strategy.

- High credit quality

Typical issuers of CNH bonds are financial institutions with high credit quality with at least single-A rating by international rating agencies such as S&P and Moody's. According to Table 8.2, until July 2011, around 80 percent of issued CNH bonds had a rating distributed between A– and AA–. Since the global financial crisis in recent years has resulted in heightened concerns of credit risk, investors take credit risk into consideration and will be attracted to existing CNH bonds as they have such high credit quality.

- RMB appreciation

CNH bonds give investors exposure to both credit risk and currency risk and hence its performance is highly correlated with the global risk sentiment and the

RMB appreciation expectation. As such, investors in RMB bonds are expressing an RMB appreciation view. Furthermore, with the recent downgrade of US sovereign credit rating, the Chinese government has to slow down the build up of USD foreign reserves, which reinforce the expectation of RMB appreciation over time.

Reasons for supply of CNH bonds: lower yields than onshore

The Dim Sum bond market offers a unique low-cost funding source. Since there are restrictions on offshore investors (with Qualified Foreign Institutional Investor licenses) to access the onshore bond market, demand for CNH bonds has increased as there are no such restrictions on CNH denominated assets. Therefore CNH bonds trade on average 100–300 bp below comparable onshore bonds in general (Figure 8.15), which gives issuers an incentive to sell bonds in the offshore market instead of the onshore market. The low interest rates in the CNH market have resulted in most CNH bonds trading more frequently than onshore

Table 8.2 Credit rating of RMB bonds in Hong Kong

S&P	*No.*	*Moody's*	*No.*	*Fitch*	*No.*
AAA	2	Aaa	2		
		Aal	1		
AA–	12	Aa3	17		
A+	3	A1	4		
A	3	A2	2		
A–	15	A3	2		
BBB+		Baal	1		
BBB	2				
BBB–	2				
BB–	2	Ba3	1	BB	1

Source: Hong Kong Monetary Authority (July 2011)

Category	*CNH Maturity*	*CNH Yield*	*CNY Yield*	*CNY Maturity*
SINOCHEM	Jan. 2014	3.48	4.86	Nov. 2014
POWINV	Dec. 2015	4.55	4.86	Jun. 2014
SINOTRUK	Oct. 2012	2.68	5.36	Aug. 2012
COFCO	Jun. 2014	3.30	4.87	Jun. 2014
GZRF	Apr. 2014	18.90	6.56	Oct. 2014
EXIMCH	2 Dec. 2013	1.65	3.61	4 Dec. 2013
CDB	11 Nov. 2013	2.25	3.60	22 Nov. 2013

Figure 8.15 Yield comparison between CNH bonds and CNY bonds (onshore) for selective issuers

Source: Bloomberg

bonds, as well as bonds denominated in other currencies. Certainly the expectation for RMB appreciation has also played a part in keeping the yields low.

RMB internationalization

China is taking the initiative to internationalize the RMB and with the end goal of establishing RMB as a primary global reserve currency. A deep and liquid bond market is necessary for an internationalized and reserve currency and, therefore, there is reason to start an offshore bond market in Hong Kong. This initiative for RMB internationalization has facilitated the growth of both Dim Sum bonds and synthetic bonds.

China currently holds the largest amount of foreign exchange reserves in the world. Since the Asian financial crisis in 1997–1998, one of the major policy priorities for China has been internationalization of RMB, which is viewed as a solution for safeguarding China's financial interests as well as stability. China has taken several steps since 2007 to allow the RMB to be used as a medium of exchange. However, given the immaturity of the Chinese domestic bond market, the government has decided to take advantage of the well-developed financial market of Hong Kong. The issuance of offshore bonds in Hong Kong helps set the protocol for both infrastructure and regulation of the future opening of the onshore bond market. In addition, issuance of RMB bonds in Hong Kong is a big step towards internationalization of RMB as it promotes usage of RMB in a bond market outside the mainland.

Strong capability of Hong Kong

Hong Kong has long been recognized as a global financial centre, with the depth and sophistication of its market, and it can help accelerate the development of offshore RMB trading while at the same time boosting its position in international banking. As such it is not surprising that Hong Kong has been selected as an offshore platform for building up demand for RMB as a currency for international settlements, funding and investment purposes.

Hong Kong has many unique features which no other city in China can provide, for example, the long-established international trade linkage with other Asian countries and emerging markets, which is attracting international business to trade in Hong Kong and encourages the acceptance of the RMB in transaction settlements. The value of RMB trade settlement conducted through Hong Kong increased from RMB 23 billion in the second quarter of 2010 to RMB 310.8 billion in the first quarter of 2011. That is a 12.5 times increase and it is still going strong. In addition, as Hong Kong is a part of China, mainland authorities can monitor the offshore RMB development in Hong Kong and play a large role in deciding how this offshore market operates.

Below is a summary of the differences between the onshore bond market and the Hong Kong CNH bond market:

	Onshore bond market	*CNH bond market*
Eligible Issuer	Onshore entities, supranationals	No restriction
Currency	RMB (CNY)	RMB (CNH)
Minimum denomination	RMB 100–1000	RMB 50,000 (institutional tranche)
Tenors	3 month to 50 years	2–10 years
Coupon	Fix, float and zero coupon	Fix and float
Coupon frequency	Annual or semi-annual	semi-annual
Day count	Act/365	Act/365
Amount outstanding	RMB 21tn (Sep 2011)	RMB 211bn (Oct 2011)
Primary market		
Auction style	Mixed, Dutch and book running	book running
Average size	RMB 1bn - 30bn	RMB 200mn - 5bn
Secondary market		
Trading platform	Interbank, Stock Exchange	OTC, Stock exchange
Trading hours	9–12am, 1.30–4.30pm for interbank; 9.30–11.30am and 1–3pm for exchange	n/a
Quoting convention	Yield to 2–4 decimals	Price to 2 decimals
Average bid-offer spread	2–10bps	3–10bps
Average trade size	RMB 30–200mn	RMB 1–5mn
Volume	RMB 5bn per day	RMB 50mn per day
Settlement	T+0/T+1	T+3
Clearing	CDC or CSDCC	CMU, Euroclear
Regulaton for foreign investors		
Restriction on foreign investment	QFII, foreign central banks, offshore RMB clearing bank, participating bank in cross-border RMB trade settlement	None
Custodian	Local custodian required	None
Interest income tax	25% except from treasury bonds	None
Capital gain tax	5% business tax, capital gain/loss will be included in 25% profit tax	None
Entry/Exit	SAFE approval required	None

Analysis of the Dim Sum bond market from issuers' and investors' perspectives

Since 2007, mainland authorities have permitted financial entities incorporated in China to issue RMB-denominated bonds in Hong Kong after obtaining prior government approval, with the stipulation that the issuing entity repatriates all bond proceeds to the mainland.

This section discusses the Dim Sum bond market from both issuer (such as McDonald, Caterpillar) and investor perspective. As a number of issuers seek to tap the Dim Sum bond market, this section presents the key motivation for issuers of such bonds, rather than seeking alternatives such as USD benchmark bonds. This section also presents the driving forces behind investor demand for Dim Sum bonds.

Reasons to issue Dim Sum bonds: issuers' perspectives

CHEAPER THAN FUNDING RMB ONSHORE

Offshore bonds are a cheaper alternative than onshore bonds because of the overhang of demand for RMB assets versus uninvested RMB deposits. For example, the Chinese government issued a 2-year RMB bond in December 2010 at a coupon of 1.6 percent versus the prevailing 3.37 percent yield of the onshore traded 2-year bond then. Despite the uncertain future direction of interest rate hike or cuts by the PBoC, the cost benefit of issuing offshore RMB bonds is quite obvious. We compared the funding costs of recent RMB bond issues with the lending rate and fixed deposit rates set by the PBoC. For example, the RMB 500 million 3-year CD issued by Bank of Communication in January 2011 was at a coupon of only 1.4 percent, much lower than the 3-year fixed deposit rate of 4.15 percent at issuance time, which was recently raised to 4.5 percent–5 percent.

The same rationale applies for non-banking corporates. Against the PBoC's guidance for 1-year to 3-year lending rate of 6.1 percent, a 10 percent discount from the base rate would still cost 5.5 percent for a large corporation. This compares with the 2 percent coupon paid by Caterpillar for its RMB 1 billion 2-year Dim Sum bonds and the 3 percent coupon paid by McDonald's for its RMB 200 million 3-year bonds.

China has raised interest rates five times since October 2010. However, strong demand for offshore RMB products continues to drive yields of bonds down in the secondary market (Figure 8.16). For example, coupon on the 2-year ICBC Asia issued on 8 October 2010 was set at 2.3 percent, coupon on 2-year Agriculture Bank of China (HK) issued on 15 December 2010 was 1.4 percent and a 2-year CD by ICBC Asia issued on 20 February 2011 has only a 1.1 percent coupon.

EASIER THAN FUNDING RMB ONSHORE

Given the continual tightening in China and the continual increase in RMB deposits in Hong Kong, it is easier to find RMB funding offshore.

However, we should note that a majority of existing users of the market have been Chinese companies taking advantage of the arbitrage between offshore and onshore RMB rates. For international issuers, there is one obvious restriction: the ability to deploy the funds. Remitting the money back onshore is problematic at the moment. A number of foreign issuers have been able to do that but it's still an area of great uncertainty and it is restricting the number of deals.

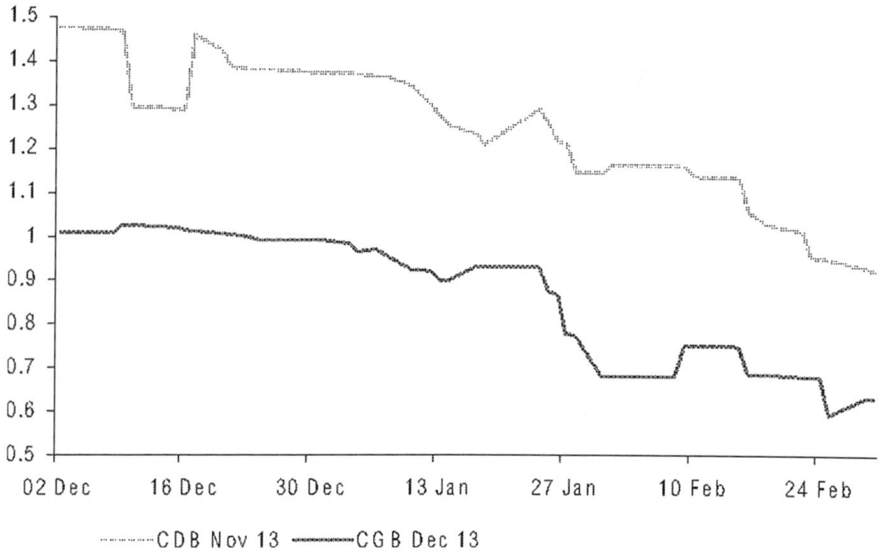

Figure 8.16 Secondary trading of Dim Sum bond issues by China Development Bank (CDB) and China Government Bond (CGB), (YTM, bid %)

Source: Bloomberg

NO REGULATORY APPROVALS REQUIRED FROM MAINLAND CHINA, HONG KONG OR ELSEWHERE

After the HKMA clarified that all Dim Sum bond issuers will be given the same treatment as those issuing bonds in HKD and other currencies, as long as the proceeds are not intended for repatriation to China, it has become very attractive for issuers that do not have strong credit ratings or face difficulties in raising funds onshore to come to the Dim Sum bond market.

Unlike offshore bonds, there are certain strict requirements for issuance of onshore RMB bonds (i.e. Panda bonds):

- Issuers of Panda bonds are required to prepare their financial statements under Chinese accounting standards, unless an exemption is granted by the MoF.
- Issuers' financial statements must be audited by accountants registered in China unless the issuers' home country or region has entered into a "registered auditors public supervision agreement" or a similar treaty with the MoF.
- A local credit rating of AA or more must be provided by at least two rating agencies, one of which must be registered in China.
- Issuers are required to possess an investment track record of more than USD 1 billion.

USE OF RMB ONSHORE OR OFFSHORE

Issuing RMB bonds makes sense only if the issuers have use of RMB, either onshore or offshore. This is because the RMB cross-currency swap market is deeply inverted, implying a substantial cost of as much as 500–600 bp for swapping the RMB proceeds into USD, not to mention that the market lacks liquidity.

ABILITY TO BETTER MATCH RMB ASSETS AND LIABILITIES

Liabilities of companies with operations in China are mainly denominated in RMB and the issuance of Dim Sum bonds provides an opportunity for corporates to raise RMB directly to settle their RMB liabilities and thereby provide a better ability to match RMB assets and liabilities.

SUCCESSFUL PRECEDENTS BY NON-PRC CORPORATES SUCH AS MCDONALDS, CATERPILLAR, UNILEVER

More high-grade Western multinationals are expected to tap into the Dim Sum bond market. In the circular issued in June 2011, the Central Bank provided guidelines for RMB-denominated foreign direct investments into China, going so far as to spell out the nature of such investments, spreading optimism that the process of bringing RMB raised outside China back into the country would soon be streamlined.

Currently, approvals for transferring RMB across the border can take months, with issuers having to lobby government offices to secure the necessary permits.

More repeat issuers will benefit from the secondary market for Dim Sum bonds. The fact that multinational companies usually have investment grade credit ratings and the deals are off their respective medium-term note program – a mechanism which allows them to issue bonds quickly without having to secure approvals – almost guarantees good liquidity in the secondary market.

Reasons to buy Dim Sum bonds: investors' perspectives

Any company or institution in Hong Kong or overseas can invest in CNH bonds. An investor needs an RMB bank account to make subscription payments, trade in bonds and receive interest and principal payments. Currently investors in the CNH bond market include foreign central banks, commercial banks, private banks, insurance companies, mutual funds and hedge funds, etc.

RMB APPRECIATION

This is the key motivation for virtually all Dim Sum bond investors.

YIELD ENHANCEMENT

Although this is a smaller consideration for most investors, yields of Dim Sum bonds are nevertheless more attractive than interest rates of either RMB fixed deposits offered by banks in Hong Kong or implied from the RMB NDF curve. This has helped to keep bond yields of Dim Sum bonds on the low side and in fact, the spreads continue to widen below onshore RMB bond yields as the onshore market undergoes a bear trend.

LIMITED ACCESS TO THE ONSHORE CHINESE MARKET

Even though foreign investors can enter China's onshore bond market with a QFII license, they can invest only in bonds listed on the exchanges, where the magnitude of trading is far smaller than the interbank bond market.

DIVERSIFICATION

The offshore RMB bond market not only offers a new market for global investors' portfolio diversification but also allows QFII investors to diversify onshore risks since regulatory and settlement risks are lower than the onshore market.

Issuers' and investors' risks

Apart from the abovementioned incentives for both issuers and investors, there are some risks also, for both.

EXCHANGE RISK

While RMB appreciation is the key motivating factor for investors in Dim Sum bonds, it is also the biggest risk. First, the offshore RMB currency swap market is still very shallow. Second, the curve is deeply inverted, in line with the existing non-delivery currency swap that extends from the NDF curve. It is therefore expensive for investors to swap the currency risk, but worthwhile to swap to lock in the exchange gain already priced into the curve, which might not be much after subtracting the substantial bid / ask spread. Third, the offshore RMB market theoretically trades on a real-time basis, independent of the onshore RMB market, which gets a daily fixing by the PROC in the morning and trades within a + / –0.5 percent band for the rest of the day.

CREDIT RISK

As the Dim Sum bond market is relatively underdeveloped, issuers face refinancing risk since the average maturity of Dim Sum bonds is only three years. This is also a result of investors' appetite for short durations given that they are mainly interested in the potential exchange gain. On the flip side, this means that investors are underestimating their credit exposure since credit risks are not fully reflected in the exceedingly low yields of Dim Sum bonds.

REGULATORY RISK

There is a significant risk for issuers in that they might not be able to obtain approval for remitting bond proceeds back to China but this risk looks fairly transparent in terms of procedural details. For investors, the risks are more opaque, as the progress of the market is still heavily dictated by Chinese rather than Hong Kong regulators. However, we would rule out the risk that China closes down this market, making all existing Dim Sum bonds non-deliverable and forcing existing RMB deposits offshore to be taken back. China's ambition to internationalize the RMB is very strong, but one that policymakers are careful not to rush into. Hence, we believe we should be prepared for tightening or fine-tuning of regulations of the Dim Sum bond market which thus far has grown too rapidly, in a lopsided fashion.

Case studies on recent offshore RMB bonds

This section presents a few recent cases different from the offshore RMB bond market – specifically, the (1) largest CNY synthetic bond launched to date by Evergrande Real Estate Group; (2) debut issue of Taiwanese company Advanced Semiconductor Engineering in the offshore Dim Sum bond market; and (3) latest "innovation" within the Dim Sum bond world – bank capital securities issued by ICBC Asia. We analyze each case in detail and highlight what we found interesting.

Largest CNY synthetic bond to date: Evergrande Real Estate

WHO IS (ARE) THE ISSUER(S)?

The issuer is Evergrande Real Estate Group Ltd. (Evergrande). Evergrande is one of the largest developers of quality residential property projects and a leader in adopting a standardized operational model to manage various projects in different cities across China. Founded in Guangzhou, Guangdong Province, in 1996, it is a leading national property developer enjoying economies of scale and a widely recognized brand name. The company focuses primarily on provincial capitals and other selected cities that have high-growth potential. Through its standardized operational model, it has been able to simultaneously manage projects in various development and sale stages in 62 cities across China as of 31 December 2010.

WHAT TYPE OF DEAL IS THIS?

This is the largest CNY synthetic bond deal to date (CNY 9.25 billion), where both coupon and final repayment will be in CNY, but payable in USD. Investors bear the full consequences of appreciation or deprecation of the CNY when they receive the interim coupons and principal at maturity. It is the third such debt issue following Shui On Land Ltd. and China SCE Property Holdings Ltd. synthetic CNY bonds, which are meant to offer better pricing to the issuer than comparable dollar debt because it offers the prospects of CNY appreciation to investors. Issuers such as Evergrande had to turn to such types of notes instead of pure Dim Sum bonds because they could have faced trouble getting approval for remittance of any cheap CNY funding raised offshore to onshore, as regulators are trying to control property prices in China.

The bonds are 3-year and 5-year maturity rated bonds with fixed coupon and senior unsecured status with offering format RegS, sold to a global investor base. The notes are listed in the Singapore Stock Exchange. The use of proceeds is to repay existing onshore bank borrowings and to finance existing and new property projects, as well as for general corporate purposes.

The final order book was around CNY 33.1 billion, with over 80 percent of investors from Asia. Private banking clients bought almost half the deal, with fund managers as the next biggest investors. Banks only bought approximately 10 percent of the issue, probably as it is a non-investment grade issue.

Joint lead managers are Bank of America Merrill Lynch, Deutsche Bank, Citigroup and Bank of China International.

Issuer	Evergrande Real Estate Group Limited	
Issue Ratings	Moody's: B2 (Negative) / S&P: BB- (Stable)	
Status	Fixed rate, senior unsecured	
Currency	CNY denominated notes, payable in USD	
Format	REGS	
Maturity	3Y (1/19/2014)	5Y (1/19/2016)
Size	CNY 5,550 million	CNY 3,700 million
Final Pricing	7.50%	9.25%
Coupon / Price	100.00	100.00
Terms	Singapore Stock Exchange Listing, CNY 1 million minimum trading size, 10k denomination. NY law	
Timing	Launched on 13 January 2011 with settlement date 19 January 2011	

IN OUR OPINION, WAS THE DEAL SUCCESSFUL? WHY?

From the issuer's perspective, the deal is successful:

- The issuer successfully raised CNY 9.25 billion (USD 1.4 billion) for property investments, one of the largest raised by a property company in the offshore synthetic bond market. Although coupon interest is going to be repaid in USD, Evergrande will face increasing cost with RMB appreciation expectation, which can be hedged via derivatives such as non-deliverable forwards.
- As Evergrande has already issued a 5-year USD debt in 2010 at 13 percent coupon, it may have exhausted this route to raise funds and hence this synthetic bond is a success as it has been able to raise capital.

From investors' perspective, the deal is a mixed success:

- Evergrande's existing 5-year bond denominated in USD was traded at the prevailing 9.65 percent, the 5-year synthetic bond pays a coupon of 9.25 percent plus potential appreciation of CNY, with CNY appreciation expectation to be approximately 2 percent–3 percent, and investors are earning a higher coupon on a relative value basis.
- However, in the secondary market right after the bonds are free to trade, the bond traded below the 100.00 issue price and went to as low as 98.50, before

it bounced back to close at 99.50. The reason cited for the weak performance was the large issuance size.

- As of 25 November 2011, the 3Y and 5Y tranches of bonds trade with mid-market cash price of around 77.00 and 71.00, respectively, meaning investors in the original trade have lost 23 percent–29 percent of their investment. Although this can be explained by the overall market environment, i.e. Evergrande equity stock (3333.HK) too is down around 25 percent since the bonds' launch date.

From the bookrunners' perspective, the deal is successful:

- The deal size is large, which means the bookrunners earned good underwriting fees and they demonstrated to Evergrande strong placing capabilities for cross-business opportunities.
- Book building was good, with the deal three times oversubscribed.

Taiwan company debuts Dim Sum bond: Advanced Semiconductor Engineering

WHO IS (ARE) THE ISSUER(S)?

The issuer is Advanced Semiconductor Engineering Inc. (ASE). Incorporated 23 March 1984, ASE is one of the world's largest independent providers of semiconductor packaging and testing services, based on 2010 revenues. The company's services include semiconductor packaging, production of interconnect materials, front-end engineering testing, wafer probing and final testing services. As a result of its acquisition of Universal Scientific Industrial Co., Ltd. (USI) in 2010, the company now provides integrated solutions for electronics manufacturing services in relation to computers, peripherals, communications, industrial, automotive and storage and server applications. The company's global base of over 200 customers includes leading semiconductor companies across a wide range of end-use applications.

The company has been listed on the Taiwan Exchange since 1989 and ADSs representing its common shares have been listed on the New York Stock Exchange since September 2000.

For the years ended 31 December 2009 and 2010, the company's consolidated revenue was NT$85,775.3 million and NT$188,742.8 million, respectively. As of 31 December 2009 and 2010, its consolidated total assets were NT$161,974.8 million and NT$208,139.7 million, respectively. For the six months ended 30 June 2011, the company's net revenues increased 9.9 percent to NT$92,259.6 million (USD 3,204.6 million) from consolidated net revenues of NT$83,970.4 million for the same period in 2010.

WHAT TYPE OF DEAL IS THIS?

This was the debut offshore bond issue for ASE, and it is a Dim Sum bond where all coupons and principal are denominated and paid in CNY. To date,

ASE has only issued onshore TWD bonds. There are 2 tranches – 3-years and 5-years maturity, the 3-year is a small private placement deal and the 5-year was a much larger tranche and focus of the issue. It is issued by an SPV with a guarantee by ASE.

These are unrated bonds with fixed coupon and senior unsecured status with offering format RegS. As it is a debut offshore bond issue for ASE, it is not well known to the global investor base, hence the bonds were placed to the Asia investor base. ASE has received approval from Chinese regulators to remit funds onshore for business development, the use of the proceeds is for its onshore working capital use and capital expenditure. This also highlights the Chinese government's policy direction as it is allowing technology companies such as ASE to raise cheap RMB funding offshore, while turning away property companies such as Evergrande.

Final order book was around CNY 800 million, with 100 percent of investors from Asia. The largest investors of the 5-year tranche were fund managers, followed by private banking clients. Corporates and banks also invested. Citigroup is the sole bookrunner for this deal.

What are the main terms and conditions of the deal? What was the pricing?

Issuer	Anstock Limited	
Guarantor	Advanced Semiconductor Engineering Inc.	
Issue Ratings	Unrated	
Status	Fixed rate, senior unsecured	
Currency	RMB	
Format	Offshore CNY denominated guaranteed bonds / REGS	
Maturity	3Y (9/22/2014)	5Y (9/20/2016)
Size	CNY 150 million	CNY 500 million
Final Pricing	3.125%	4.25%
Coupon	100.00	100.00
Price		
Terms	Unlisted. CNY 1 million minimum trading size, 10k denomination. NY law	
Timing	Launched on 9 September 2011 with settlement date 20 September 2011	

IN OUR OPINION, WAS THE DEAL SUCCESSFUL? WHY?

From the issuer's perspective, the deal is successful:

- The issuer successfully raised CNY 650 million, which is the full amount approved by Chinese regulators to remit onshore. With liquidity tightening onshore, ASE is likely to have raised the amount at cheaper costs than if it had relied on onshore borrowing.

From investors' perspective, the deal is a mixed success:

- Investors are presented with a unique opportunity to invest in a rare issuer which is a leader in its sector. In addition, there are only a handful of 5-year maturity Dim Sum bonds available in the market, with very limited supply.
- As the issuance size is relatively small, there is relatively little secondary trading in the market for these bonds, hence price volatility is small.
- As of 25 November 2011, the 5Y tranche trades with mid-market cash price of around 97.00.

From the bookrunner's perspective, the deal is successful:

- Although deal size is relatively small, it only has one bookrunner, hence the bookrunner is able to earn the full fees on this deal. In addition, the bookrunner is able to demonstrate its strength in placing Dim Sum bonds to other potential issuers (especially Taiwan issuers, who have business onshore), for future Dim Sum bond issuance opportunities.

Bank capital securities: ICBC Asia

WHO IS (ARE) THE ISSUER(S)?

The issuer is Industrial and Commercial Bank of China (Asia) Ltd. (ICBC Asia), a licensed bank in Hong Kong, and a wholly owned subsidiary of Industrial and Commercial Bank of China Ltd. (ICBC).

WHAT TYPE OF DEAL IS THIS?

ICBC Asia issued a CNH1.5bn (~USD 225 million) loss-absorbing subordinated debt in 2012 maturity and callable in 2016. This was the first BASEL III complaint security to be priced in Asia. Subordinated bonds rank after loans and senior bonds for repayment in the event of a borrower default. When sold by financial institutions they are regarded as capital designed to meet regulatory requirements. This is an interesting issue as it took place in the Dim Sum bond space, rather than USD which is a much larger market. Reasons can be attributed to the strong technicals and tight valuations in the CNH market versus prohibitive valuations in the USD market. If this bond performs well, other banks from Singapore, Hong Kong and Australia are also likely to be candidates for similar future issues.

The deal adds more depth to the fast-growing Dim Sum bond market, while also introducing a new form of contractual loss absorption feature to the bank capital sector. The bonds will be permanently written down to zero should the regulator Hong Kong Monetary Authority declare ICBC Asia non-viable. Non-viability events include: (1) without the write-off of the notes the issuer would become non-viable; or (2) there is a public sector capital injection without which the issuer would have become non-viable. The structure forces bondholders to shoulder losses and allows the deal to count towards Tier 2 capital under the latest BASEL rules. It is only the fourth issuance of hybrid bonds to include contractual loss absorption since the rules were released in December 2010 and January 2011.

ICBC Asia is rated A2 and A by Moody's and Fitch, respectively, and the bond issue is rated A- by Fitch. Fitch rated the issue one notch below the issuer rating due to the debt seniority and loss-absorption feature.

The final order book was around CNY 5.1 billion, with over 85 percent of investors from Asia. Private banking clients bought over half the deal, with insurance companies as the next biggest investors (probably due to the long tenor).

HSBC and ICBC International were Joint Global Coordinators, together with Bank of China (HK) Ltd., Credit Suisse, DBS Bank and Goldman Sachs, as Joint Lead Managers and Joint Bookrunners.

Issuer	Industrial and Commercial Bank of China (Asia) Limited
Issue Ratings	Fitch: A (Stable)
Status	Fixed rate, subordinated (BASEL III compliant)
Currency	RMB
Format	Offshore CNY denominated subordinated bonds / REGS
Maturity	10Y (11/4/2021) (callable @ 100.00 on 11/4/2016)
Size	CNY 1,500 million
Final Pricing	6.00%
Coupon	100.00
Price	
Terms	Unlisted. CNY 1 million minimum trading size, 10k denomination. NY law
Timing	Launched on 28 October 2011 with settlement date 4 November 2011

IN OUR OPINION, WAS THE DEAL SUCCESSFUL? WHY?

From the issuer's perspective, the deal is successful:

- The issuer successfully raised a large sum of money, CNY 1.5 billion, at 6 percent per annum, which is deemed low by industry analysts, given the lower ranking of the debt, loss-absorption write-down to nil and the likelihood of the bond not being called.

From investors' perspective, the deal is a mixed success:

- As of 25 November 2011, the 5Y tranche trades with mid-market cash price of around 101.75, meaning investors made 1.75 percent on capital appreciation since the bonds were issued 3 weeks earlier.

- Investors might not fully understand the complex structure, especially the loss absorption feature where investors might have been pitched that there is a small likelihood that ICBC Asia will become non-viable. As per the above, investors may not have been fairly compensated for this risk.

From the bookrunners' perspective, the deal is successful:

- The deal was 3.4 times oversubscribed.
- As the banking industry is expected to go through a long period of restructuring of capital securities to comply with new post-crisis requirements, more such deals are expected. As the bookrunners are able to demonstrate success in placing such capital securities via the Dim Sum bond market, this will definitely help bring future opportunities.

Outlook of the Dim Sum bond market

Finally, the last section provides an outlook of the offshore RMB bond market. The future development will focus on opportunities and challenges of the RMB bond market.

We expect the future of offshore RMB bonds to continue to evolve: (1) issuance of longer tenor (> 5–10 years) RMB bonds; (2) increase of bond size that may not be "Dim Sum" anymore; (3) requirement of credit ratings; (4) appreciation of RMB will continue to attract foreign investors; (5) establishment of RMB as a reserve currency in the long run; and (6) development of Panda bonds.

Issuance of longer tenor (> 5–10 years) RMB bonds

In recent years, the average tenor of CNH bonds has been 3 to 5 years and the market has only a small supply of longer tenor CNH bonds. The reasons are: (1) to meet demands of investors less willing to take a longer term view on appreciation of RMB; and (2) lack of a track record of long dated bonds. While investors of the current Dim Sum bonds are generally taking an appreciation view of the RMB, these investors are also likely to have a prudent outlook of the longer term trend as RMB is still a policy-controlled currency. As a result, it is difficult to determine the pricing (i.e. coupon) of longer dated bonds.

Figure 8.17 summaries the maturity profile of Dim Sum bonds issued between the years 2007 and 2010.

The above chart shows that most of the Dim Sum bonds have short maturities and most of the investors may tend to hold the bond up to maturity (provided there are no significant changes in default risk of the bond); this may have an impact on the liquidity or trading volume of the Dim Sum bonds in the secondary market.

We expect CNH bond issues with longer maturities of, say 5 to 10 years, in which the duration will be similar to USD bonds because (1) the CNH bond market will eventually have a track record, i.e. once investors have confidence after making good returns from existing CNH bonds, they will have more appetite for longer tenor bonds; (2) issuers will prefer to issue longer term bonds to better plan

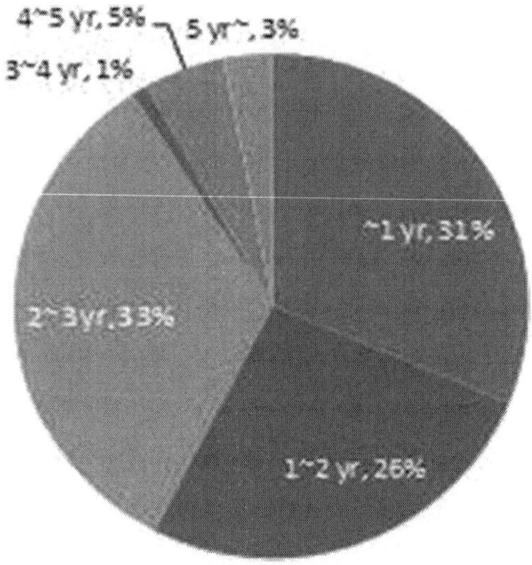

Figure 8.17 Maturity profile of existing Dim Sum bonds

Source: HSBC (2010)

their long-term goals as they can invest the money in projects with longer return periods; and (3) investors may also prefer longer maturity since they can enjoy the appreciation of RMB over a longer period of time.

Increase of bond size that may not be "Dim Sum" anymore

The Dim Sum bond is named as such because most of the issuers are based in China with RMB as their operational currency; in addition, the bonds typically are small in terms of issuance size, i.e. most of them are less than USD 100 million. This compares to the relatively more established USD bond market, where normal issuance sizes are at least USD 500 million or larger. The larger issuance size can boost the liquidity of the bonds in the secondary market; as such, USD bonds have a well-established secondary market and are traded frequently. However, the small issuance size of Dim Sum bonds limits the trading volume of the Dim Sum bond market.

Individual issues of Dim Sum bonds may become larger in the future. From the issuer's point of view, the issuer can enjoy (1) larger capital raising exercises and find better allocation for funds; (2) lower cost, such as one-off professional advisor fees, rating fees and other one-off issuance costs; and (3) an increase in the liquidity of the bond transaction.

From the investor's point of view, investors can invest more money in one transaction to fulfill their demand in RMB investments, and the increased liquidity of the bond will provide a more accurate reflection of the secondary market value.

Requirement of credit ratings

In the current Dim Sum bond market, credit ratings from international agencies such as Moody's, Standard & Poor's and Fitch are not a practice or compulsory requirement for issuance of Dim Sum bonds. Bond investors may not require the issuer to get a credit rating because issuers are still facing overwhelming demand for RMB investment products in order to speculate on the appreciation of RMB. Hence, investors are willing to take the risk of buying a Dim Sum bond which does not have any credit rating, especially high yield bonds (bonds which are below investment grade). In the USD bond market, most issuances of bonds need a credit rating in order to ensure the quality of the issuer and provide some comfort to the investment community.

However, as the Dim Sum bond market matures, more companies are likely to issue Dim Sum bonds and investors will have more choices to invest their RMB holdings, hence they are likely to increase their requirements and demand credit ratings. This may increase the issuance cost and prolong the process.

Appreciation of RMB will continue to attract foreign investors

In the year 2007, USD/CNY was around 7.8 and in December 2011, USD/CNY was around 6.3, implying appreciation of around 20 percent. RMB is growing in importance in the global economic environment. In recent years, other than being used in trade settlements, RMB has also been treated as a speculative currency. Some of the investors believe that after the economic crisis in September 2008, China has become one of the few countries that have maintained positive economic growth and this has fuelled the demand for RMB and it is one of the reasons behind RMB appreciation in recent years.

The development of Dim Sum bonds is closely linked with the valuation of RMB. Investors are interested in Dim Sum bonds because they are willing to earn a relatively lower yield rate in order to speculate on the appreciation of RMB.

The above trend shows that the RMB has room for a further 15 percent appreciation, which is likely to be attractive to global investors. As long as the trend of appreciation is maintained, we feel the Dim Sum bond market will continue to have a fast and stable development since this can provide a good investment opportunity for foreign investors who would like to speculate on the RMB.

Establishment of RMB as a reserve currency in the long run

In the global economic world, USD is regarded as a safe-haven currency, which is the reason why the United States can print money and issue US Treasury bonds to global investors. However, as the demand for RMB continues to rise and China's role in the world economy and politics keeps increasing, RMB may one day be one of the reserve currencies in the world.

However, we acknowledge that before RMB can become a reserve currency, several policy issues need to be resolved. For example, onshore RMB is hard to remit offshore as foreigners are prohibited to remit funds out of China. This remittance out of China requires approval from the Ministry of Finance and People's Bank of China. On the other hand, foreigners can remit money to China mainly through the channel of shareholder's loans and capital injection. These limitations may discourage the growth of RMB as an international reserve currency.

Development of Panda bonds

Since the year 2005, four Panda bonds have been issued by Asian Development Bank and International Finance Corporation, proceeds of which were used for funding various projects in China. One of the criteria for the approval is that the proceeds from Panda bonds must be spent in China.

However, there was a change in September 2010 – the government relaxed one of the thresholds by amending an issuance rule. International development institutions have been allowed to remit proceeds from Panda bonds to offshore accounts with approval of the State Administration of Foreign Exchange. This may have some impact on the Dim Sum bond market as one of the advantages of Dim Sum bonds is that there are no restrictions of location on the use of the proceeds. Some of the foreign issuers can exchange RMB for their own currency and invest the money in their own country.

As a result, if proceeds from Panda bonds are allowed to be invested offshore, this may threaten the attractiveness of Dim Sum bonds. However, to date, no new issue of Panda bonds has taken place after the revision of the regulation and as such its impact on the Dim Sum bond market is still to be observed.

Note

1. Renminbi, or RMB, refers to China's currency. CNY refers to the spot market for deliverable RMB in onshore China. CNH refers to the spot market for deliverable RMB in Hong Kong.

References

Aaron B., Dinny M. and Nathalie B. 2011, April. China meeting highlights currency conflict. *The Wall Street Journal*. http://online.wsj.com/news/articles/SB10001424052748703712504576233931135818222. Retrieved 20 December 2013.

BBC. 2011, 31 March. G20 considers wider role for China's yuan. www.bbc.co.uk. Retrieved 20 December 2013.

BBVA Research. 2011, 9 March. RMB Cross-Border Settlement: Origins, Mechanics, and Opportunities.

China Daily. 2011, 6 September. Nigeria bank chief sees yuan becoming reserve currency. www.chinadaily.com.cn/world/2011-09/06/content_13635209.htm

Chinn, Menzie D. and Frankel, Jeffrey. 2005. Will the euro eventually surpass the dollar as leading international reserve currency? Paper for NBER Conference 'G7 Current Account Imbalances: Sustainability and Adjustment', Newport, RI, 1–2 June.

CNH market primer – Casting a wider net, Barclays Cross asset research, September 2012. http://bg.panlv.net/code.ashx?action=downreport&file=fe2fb9fe5d3a08d0. Retrieved 20 December 2013.

Ding, David Y. T. 2011. The price discovery puzzle in offshore yuan trading: different contributions for different contracts. 8th Conference of Asia-Pacific Association of Derivatives Busan, Korea.

Dong Tao, Amlan Roy, Sonali Punhani, Liyan Shi, Christiaan Tuntono. 2011, January 5. China: The turning point of the labour market. Credit Suisse. https://doc.research-and-analytics.csfb.com/docView?language=ENG&source=emfromsendlink&format=PDF&document_id=803723570&serialid=venp1e1vazGYc6SgpEjWIHFakdFhF1n8H0N%2Bi6HSDsc%3D. Retrieved 20 December 2013.

Eichengreen, B., and Tong, H. (2011). The impact of chinese exchange rate policy on the rest of the world: Evidence from firm-level data. *Global Economic Review*, 40(2), 211–225.

Forsythe, Michael and Julianna Goldman. 2010, 12 November. Obama sharpens yuan criticism after G-20 nations let China off the hook. *Bloomberg*.

HKEX. 2011, 28 July. RMB internationalization and HKEX RMB strategies. www.hkex.com.hk/eng/newsconsul/speech/2011/Documents/sp110728.pdf. Retrieved 20 December 2013.

HKMA. The monetary date for September 2011. www.hkma.gov.hk. Retrieved 20 December 2013.

HKMA. 2013. Hong Kong the premier offshore Renminbi business centre. www.hkma.gov.hk/media/eng/doc/key-functions/monetary-stability/rmb-business-in-hong-kong/hkma-rmb-booklet.pdf. Retrieved 20 December 2013.

HKTDC. 2009. The Pilot RMB Trade Settlement Scheme and RMB internationalization. http://economists-pick-research.hktdc.com/business-news/vp-article/en/1/1X05VOBP.htm. Retrieved 20 December 2013.

Hui, Daniel, and Dominic Bunning. 2010, December 1. The offshore Renminbi, a practical primer on the CNH market. HSBC Global Research. www.chinalux.eu/wp-content/uploads/2012/11/The-offshore-renminbi-A-practical-primer-on-the-CNH-market.pdf. Retrieved 20 December 2013.

Lester, Karl., M. Yap and Fion Li. 2011, April 12. Asia's central banks want to add yuan to foreign reserves, Tetangco says. *Bloomberg*.

Moody's Global Credit Research. 2011, January 19. The current menu for renminbi bonds in Hong Kong Dim Sum or synthetic. www.institutionalinvestorchina.com/arfy/uploads/soft/110209/1_0843072771.pdf. Retrieved 20 December 2013.

Offshore Renminbi roundtable: the bond markets in depth, August 2011. www.emergingmarkets.org/Article/2904840/OFFSHORE-RENMINBI-ROUNDTABLE-The-Bond-Markets-in-Depth.html. Retrieved 20 December 2013.

Newnham, Stewart, and Yee Wai Chong 2010. CNH: The internationalization of the RMB. Morgan Stanley research report. http://linkback.morganstanley.com/web/sendlink/webapp/BMServlet?file=fh1m6qrs-3o3n-g000-868e-002655211000&store=0&user=j64buwyomf6z-0&__gda__=1430787631_67838003920364cd71a9baf8a466411a. Retrieved 20 December 2013.

Trading Economics: www.tradingeconomics.com/china/inflation-cpi

Wang Ziwu, Zhang Yuze, Huo Kan and Tian Lin. 2011, May. China's forex cache: too much of a good thing. Caixin online. www.marketwatch.com/story/chinas-forex-cache-too-much-of-a-good-thing-2011-05-02. Retrieved 20 December 2013.

Wong, Nethelie. 2011, 16 January. Evergrande's massive offshore yuan bond pushes boundaries. Thomson Reuters. www.reuters.com/article/2011/01/17/evergrande-yuan-bond-idUSL3E7CH03G20110117. Retrieved 20 December 2013.

Yu, F.C. 2011, April 12. Former China Central Bank adviser Yu calls for stronger yuan. Bloomberg Television interview.

Zhang, Z. 1999, December. Foreign exchange rate reform, the balance of trade and economic growth: an empirical analysis for China. *Journal of Economic Development* 24, 143–162.

9 Private banking and wealth management in China

9.1. Global wealth management landscape

Since its inception in the late 2000s, China's private banking and wealth management sector has experienced tremendous growth. Driven by the nation's economic growth, the number of HNW (High Net Worth) individuals and households has soared in recent years. With Asia expected to become the second-largest wealth management market in the world by 2015 and China being its main growth engine, Chinese private bankers as a whole still possess ample opportunities for growth and expansion. However, the industry is still in its development stage and many challenges lie ahead as it continues its learning process in the decades to come.

In this chapter we seek to explore the landscape in which the Chinese private banking and wealth management industry is developing. First, we present an overall discussion on the global and Asian wealth management landscape. Then, we take an in-depth look at China's High Net Worth Individuals and their unique characteristics. This is followed by an analysis of private banking strategies and methods of attracting investors, as well as the types of products and services currently available. Next, we discuss the macro factors that will shape the wealth market in the future. Finally we take our research as well as current and relevant trends in the market to generate our own predictions on the direction in which China's wealth management and private banking industry is going as well as some key success factors and strategies that private banks and asset managers should take going forward.

Overview of main global players

While the banking sector showed the first signs of recovery, the global wealth management industry and especially the traditional offshore centers suffered from the increasing complexity of regulatory frameworks.

After the financial crisis, structural changes in the US banking sector have cleared the way for new international large wealth managers. In this highly dynamic market, UBS Wealth Management was able to defend its position as the world's largest private bank. Credit Suisse, which used to rank third, now ranks second. Bank of America Global Wealth and Investment Management gained size through the acquisition of Merrill Lynch in 2009. However, it has downsized again by selling its Asia division to Julius Bar. Morgan Stanley Global Wealth

Management Group ranks number four due to its majority stake in a joint venture with Citigroup. Together the four largest wealth managers jointly manage half the AuM of the top 20 players. However, due to the highly fragmented global wealth management market, none of them has a market share of more than 4 percent.

There are some fundamental differences between strategies of individual banks as well. For example, the predominance of US players can be structurally explained by their large home market (the largest wealth management market in the world), which allows them to pursue a scalable business model in even less favorable environments. Also, there is a country-specific perception of wealth management as well. For instance, US clients are more open to wealth management services than European clients and they are more open to brokerage-oriented relationships in the US.

Different from the US banks, most of the European wealth managers are actively pursuing an offshore or cross-border business, but there is almost no pure player in the "super league" of wealth managers. Most large players have integrated into a financial conglomerate or a universal bank.

Macro-economic instability leads to declines in global wealth

In 2011, the global wealth market was heavily impacted by the euro zone sovereign debt crisis, natural calamities and declines in global markets. Although there are regional differences, at the global level total liquid wealth showed no growth in 2011 compared to 2010. The euro zone was the most affected. The unpredictability of the future of the euro and the worsening of the sovereign debt crisis in Western Europe affected the global wealth market significantly.

As euro zone member states spent most of 2011 to formulate responses to market-driven events, wealth recovery that had begun after the financial crisis was once again put on hold and liquid assets held by Western European affluent individuals declined by 0.05 percent during 2010–2011, which reflects how much wealth creation had stalled.

While mature markets like Western Europe and Japan will show limited growth in the coming years, emerging markets (Middle East and Africa, Central and Eastern Europe, Latin America and Asia Pacific [excluding Japan]), however, will continue to show relatively strong growth.

Increased regulatory focus on selected international banking

In August 2011, the UK and Switzerland reached an agreement to tax undeclared UK assets held in Swiss bank accounts, to come into force on 1 January 2013. As said in the agreement, accounts and assets held on 31 December 2010 will be subject to a one-off levy of between 19 percent and 34 percent, and then subject to withholding taxes with a maximum of 48 percent on interest from 2013. The agreement also allows the UK to request of Swiss banks details of up to 500 UK citizens every year. The increased focus on Switzerland – especially from Germany, the UK and the US – will encourage offshore banking clients to seek services in other global financial centers like Hong Kong and Singapore.

Hong Kong and Singapore have the substantial benefit of being able to learn from experiences of established centers like Switzerland. First, both Hong Kong and Singapore have entered into over 100 double taxation avoidance agreements between them to meet suitable global tax transparency obligations and both have accepted the Organization of Economic Co-operation and Development (OECD) standards on tax. Despite their distance from Europe, both Asian financial centers have legal systems based on British law. By the end of 2012, several prestigious law firms were beginning to establish a presence in Singapore and Hong Kong to serve the increasing demand for private legal advice.

Emerging markets like Asia will challenge the mature markets

As a high-growth region, Asia provides significant opportunities for private banks and the wealth management industry. Because of its high potential, Asia is a fiercely competitive market. To succeed, banks should understand how to serve entrepreneurs and business owners effectively as well as to adopt innovative incentive schemes to attract and retain talent.

APAC remains the region with the highest potential in terms of penetration of affluent individuals, size of the liquid assets pool and total number of affluent individuals. Asia (excluding Japan) had more than USD 8 trillion in HNW personal financial assets (PFA) in 2011, equivalent to about 14 percent of the global total. It is also expected to be the fastest-growing region over the next 5 years, with HNW assets growing at 13 percent–17 percent, more than half of which will be contributed by China alone.

The number of affluent individuals in the overall Asia Pacific is expected to grow from 92 million in 2011 to 118 million in 2015. In terms of the number of HNW Individuals, wealth distribution is quite unbalanced in Asia Pacific, with the number of millionaires in Asia Pacific (excluding Japan) having been higher than the total in Japan alone since 2006. In terms of HNW penetration, APAC ex-Japan is 2.8 percent, which is double the figure of Japan.(See Figure 9.1)

Onshore banking will show more potential in the long run

Due to the increasing customer interest in Asian markets, Asian private banking centers are benefiting from re-allocation of international clients' assets. Although the onshore market generates lower ROA than the offshore model, its potential is much larger over time.

A prime driver of affluent and HNW Individuals to move assets offshore is a specific business need. However, across the globe indebted governments will continue to focus on offshore wealth and uncollected tax revenue of their most affluent citizens. Offshore banking has come to be demonized by many developed countries since the financial crisis. Initiatives to regulate the offshore banking sector will continue to affect the largest offshore centers, including Switzerland, the Channel Islands, Hong Kong and Singapore in 2012. The main drivers of change will be the continuing focus of tax authorities on undeclared offshore

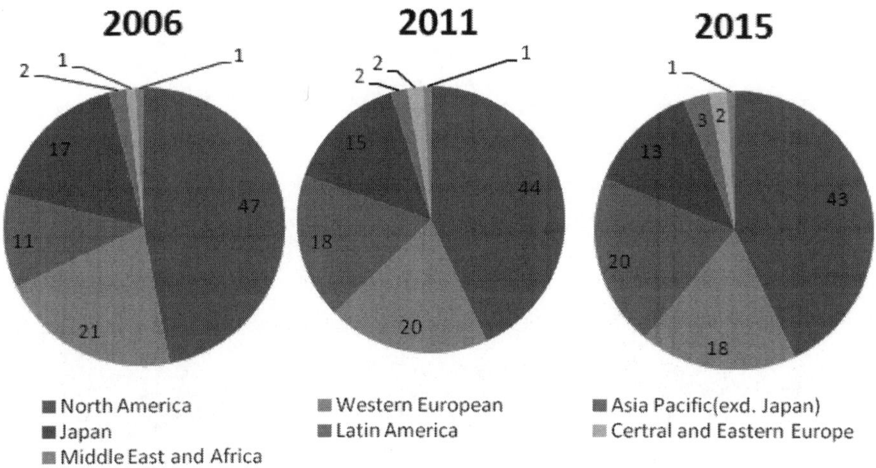

Figure 9.1 Global wealth markets (regional contribution by liquid assets held by affluent individuals 2006, 2011, 2015)

Source: Datamonitor (2012)

assets. Although the tax authorities are restricted to the US and Western Europe, their implications are global. As established offshore banking hubs become less attractive, assets will shift to more attractive financial centers, especially in Asia.

Besides business needs, most Asian HNW customers have more than three wealth management relationships and place increasing importance on having a relationship manager who understands their needs. These factors suggest that banks need to address both personal and business needs more systematically. Many banks have a pool of HNW customers whose wealth they do not fully capture. On the other hand, the cost-to-serve has increased significantly as both RM compensation and compliance costs have risen. Despite these rising costs, RMs are becoming less productive in the face of less-entrenched client relationships, which makes it harder for them to capture client assets. The average AuM per RM in Asia is about 20 percent below the European average.

Banks targeting the fast-growing Asian market need to decide which segments to target, which markets to operate in and how to make the economics work. Trying to be everything to everyone is not a sustainable model. Segments can be divided by wealth band (e.g., UHNW with > USD 30 million or HNW with USD 1 million to 30 million); by origin of flows (e.g., Chinese, Southeast Asian, non-resident Indian or Middle Eastern flows); or by their special requirements (e.g., small business owners, large family offices). Out of all the Asian emerging markets, China is by far the most intriguing and has the biggest potential of growth in the near future. Many of the banks are fighting in order to be in a position to capture the wealth from the country with the largest population in the world. In a market where investors are demanding that wealth managers understand their unique needs, in order to successfully capture the Chinese market, wealth managers must develop a deep understanding of the Chinese clientele.

9.2. China's high net worth individuals (HNWI)

Who are China's high net worth individuals?

Among China's HNW Individuals, entrepreneurs and business owners represent 40 percent of the market. The second-largest category is corporate executives that represent 33 percent of the market. The third segment is made up of other working professionals representing 11 percent of the market. Each individual represented in these groups has more than RMB 5 million of investable assets.

China is driving most of the growth

China is estimated to contribute over 50 percent of the growth in Asia. Revenues from private banking in China are expected to grow from RMB 23.3 billion in 2010 to RMB 46.8 billion by 2015, over half of which will be from Tier 1 and Tier 2 cities. In terms of the number of HNWIs today, 40 percent are located in the Pearl River Delta, 31 percent in the Yangtze River Delta and another 11 are in the Bohai Region.

Beijing has the most HNWIs, followed by Guangdong Province, Shanghai and Zhejiang Province.

Tier 2 cities already represent more than 30 percent of China's HNW wealth, compared to about 20 percent for Tier 1 cities. It is expected that Tier 2 and lower-tier cities will continue to grow in the near future.

Chinese HNWIs are seeking innovative products

The profile of investments of Chinese HNW Individuals is that they have more than 30 percent of their assets in real estate and 60 percent of them have assets offshore.

This is an indication that Chinese HNW Individuals are hungry to invest and grow their wealth; however, they do not find convincing investment avenues in onshore markets and products.

McKinsey survey findings

According to a joint study by MinSheng and McKinsey (2012), many Chinese HNWIs are not satisfied with the current level of private banking services on offer and an even larger number of wealthy individuals are just warming up to the idea of private banking.(See Figure 9.2)

- Nearly 40 percent of those interviewed say they are "not satisfied". In addition, nearly 50 percent of customers allocate 20 percent or less of their investable assets to their primary bank.
- The average Chinese HNWI is still not aware of private banking services. In fact, 45 percent say they have only a basic understanding or less of private banking services.

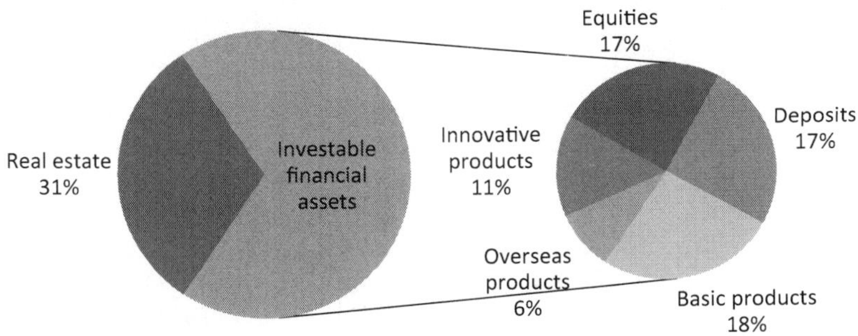

Figure 9.2 China's HNWIs asset allocation

Source: McKinsey Global Research Institute

Several reasons contribute to the survey results: (1) low awareness of private banking services; (2) private banking services are too similar to high-end retail banking services; and (3) low product knowledge.

The survey shows that there are still ample opportunities for new players. While many private banks and wealth management firms have experienced tremendous growth in China, client relationships are not established.

Interest in investments of passion grows among Chinese HNWIs

The growing number of HNWIs has prompted the demand for certain categories of luxury goods: watches, art, jewelry and collectibles. Many Investments of Passion (IoP) have emerged as an important component of the overall investment strategy for Chinese HNWIs.

In 2011, China (including Hong Kong) has overtaken the US as the world's largest market for art and antiques (see Figure 9.3).

The following table shows that China is definitely a booming market (see Table 9.1). The top two auction earners, Zhang Daqian and Qi Baishi, were both Chinese artists. Zhang generated over USD 500 million and is well known for his landscape paintings. Qi is famous for his ink depictions of animals, birds and insects. Andy Warhol and Picasso ranked third and fourth, respectively.

Also, two out of the five highest auction price items were sold in China (see Table 9.2). In total, the country posted 774 auction sales of more than USD 1 million in 2011, compared with 426 in the US and registered a 49 percent growth in art auction revenues.

Again, these trends indicate that Chinese HNWIs are willing to spend heavily on exotic and unique investments.

Outlook for HNWI wealth remains positive

Overall, Chinese HNW Individuals are extremely different from their counterparts in the developed and Western markets. Extensive research and surveys have

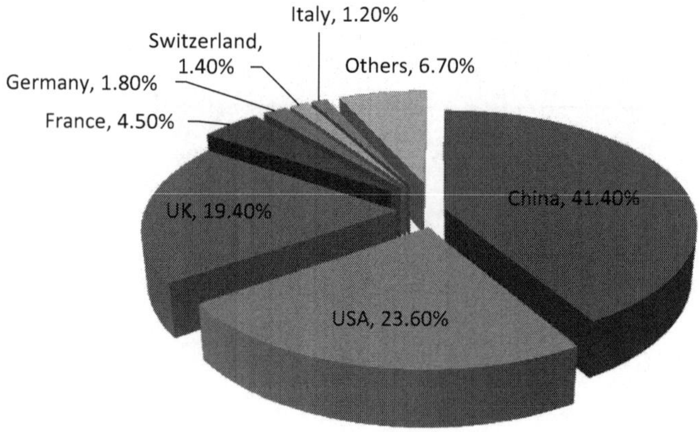

Figure 9.3 2011 fine arts auction sales revenue

Source: "Art Market Trends 2011" from Artprice

Table 9.1 2011 fine arts auction sales revenue

	Artist	*2011 Total Auction Revenue (USD)*
1.	Zhang Daqian	$550 million
2.	Qi Baishi	$510 million
3.	Andy Warhol	$325 million
4.	Pablo Picasso	$315 million
5.	Xu Beihong	$220 million

Table 9.2 Top auction sales of art pieces in 2011

	Artist	*Auction Price (USD)*	*Art Work Name*	*Auction Location*
1.	Qi Baishi	$57.2 million	Eagle Standing on Pine Tree	Beijing
2.	Clyfford Still	$55 million	1959-A-No.1	New York
3.	Wang Meng	$54 million	Zhi Chuan moving to Mountain	Beijing
4.	Roy Lichtenstein	$38.5 million	I Can See The Whole Room	New York
5.	Francesco Guardi	$36.7 million	La lecture (1932)	London

shown that Chinese HNW Individuals are different in two distinct ways that private banks must learn to adjust to and accommodate.

The first is that on average Chinese HNW Individuals are not as educated and well versed in investing. About 45 percent of HNW Individuals have a basic or less than basic understanding of investing and private banking services. Additionally, Chinese HNW Individuals do not necessarily seek a complete set of solutions and services from private banks. Instead they look for a wide and diverse range of products and above average VIP services and privileges. However, there is a small number of very sophisticated HNW Individuals and they are as intelligent and market savvy as they come. Some of these investors are even more sophisticated than the regulators and their investing capabilities and choices are limited only by the availability of investment options in the market due to China's tight regulations on the finance industry.

The second characteristic of Chinese HNW Individuals is that they are much more willing to take on investment risk as compared to their Western HNW counterparts. McKinsey's survey shows that 70 percent of Chinese HNW Individuals prefer products that are high risk and high return versus products that are low risk and low return. Chinese investors are interested in more exotic and alternative investments such as hedge funds and private equity. Given China's recent developments in providing QDLP allocations, it seems that the hedge fund and alternative investment industry has increased potential to expand in terms of capturing number of clients, capturing a higher percent of their wealth and offering a wider product range. These Chinese HNW Individual characteristics are insights into trends in the private banking industry and methods of future expansion.

Going forward, the number of HNWIs and ultra-high-net-worth individuals (UHNWIs) (defined as individuals with investable assets of more than USD 10 million) is expected to grow by about 20 percent per annum in 2012–2015, reaching around 2 million and 130,000 individuals, respectively.

While the financial crisis briefly slowed the growth in the number of millionaires in China, massive stimulus spending by the Chinese government has helped the Chinese economy recover quickly. China, despite its challenges, is likely to remain the fastest-growing economy in the world in the near future.

9.3. Private banking and the wealth management industry in China

Three major themes have recently emerged and dictated the way in which private banking must operate in China and Asia. The first is lower investment opportunities in developed countries causing Western investors to look to Asia and the emerging markets. The second is that the highly uncertain political and economic environments including the euro zone crisis and leadership changes in most major countries in the world have made investors more risk averse. The third is a significant increase in industry regulation and government oversight following the global financial crisis. These themes combined with the increase in China's wealth have transformed Asia and China into the new hub of private banking services and development.

Private banking is a personalized financial and banking service that is offered to individuals who have more than USD 1 million of investable assets. The availability of this type of clientele greatly influences a private bank's ability to grow, let alone generate investment flow and consequently revenue and commissions. These individuals with more than USD 1 million of investable assets are called High Net Worth Individuals (HNWI). While HNWIs in the developed and Western countries remain risk-averse and fearful of the markets, HNWIs in China are growing in numbers. A recent study of the private banking industry by McKinsey(2012) revealed that Asia's private banking industry is growing and will become the second largest in the world, after North America, with an estimated total investable assets of USD 16 trillion by 2015. China is the primary driver of this growth with an estimated 2 million individuals with more than RMB 10 million of investable assets.

Private banking industry trends

While the GDP of Western countries reflects little growth in their economies, Asia, and China in particular, is still showing strong growth.

Additionally China's new focus on becoming a self-dependent consumer-driven economy will only serve to increase China's ability to grow in the future. Asia has also created a small ecosystem of trading within the region wherein each country supports its Asian neighbors with imports and exports. Given these encouraging economic indicators and initiatives, asset managers are seeing increased investor demand to access Asian and Chinese markets.

Chinese HNW Individuals are also allocating their resources to other Asian countries and often see Hong Kong and Singapore as strong markets. However, each of these Chinese HNW Individuals often does not allocate all of his/her wealth with one private bank. Instead they tend to maintain an average of three private banking relationships. As we previously saw, around 40 percent of HNW Individuals source their wealth from being entrepreneurs and business owners, which means that HNW Individuals tend to find one private bank to handle their business and a different private bank to handle their personal finances. In order for a private bank to capture both the personal and professional wealth of the HNW Individual, it must be able to cater to both the personal and business sides of the client. These relationships are slightly more complex and require relationship managers who are able to fully understand and cater to the needs of the individual client.

Another trend that is slowly emerging is that Chinese sovereign wealth funds and an increasingly large number of family offices hope to have financial management in-house. This is so that they are certain that the financial advisor has the intentions aligned with the company. This method also saves on fees and additional costs related to maintaining a private banking relationship. Although this may be bad news for private banks in that they are potentially losing clients or assets to the managers, there is opportunity for larger and more sophisticated private banks. These sovereign wealth funds and family offices are requesting private banks and asset managers to take on their in-house financial advisors as employees in order to train and coach them to be sophisticated investors. They will be able to apply what they learned and advise and invest for the sovereign wealth fund or company. Increasingly, we are seeing private banks and asset managers willing to do this in order to build a relationship with the sovereign wealth fund or family office.

Government regulation of private banks

Like many of China's industries, the finance and banking industry is heavily controlled by the government through various regulatory bodies including the Ministry of Finance, State Administration of Foreign Exchange and the People's Bank of China which serves as China's Central Bank. These regulatory bodies control various aspects of China's finance industry. Additionally, the industry is controlled by the four largest banks, which include the China Construction Bank (CCB), Agriculture Bank of China (ABC), Industrial and Commercial Bank of China (ICBC) and Bank of China (BoC). These banks not only offer retail banking services and VIP services but also private banking services. There is also an increasing number of Qualified Foreign Institutional Investor (QFII) licenses allocated to foreign banks to enable them to invest in China.

Another interesting aspect of China's regulation is that the stringent adherence to BASEL III requirements as well as liquidity ratios and operational standards makes the China market one of the safest in the world. Additionally, regulations offer banks a relatively unexpected degree of freedom in that they are able to do anything with their investable assets. As China seeks to further modify and reform its banking and finance industry, private banks will find increased opportunities to meet domestic HNW Individual demand for money managers as well as increased abilities to help foreign investors invest in the Chinese markets. Finance reform will also bring increased regulation of the stock market providing domestic and foreign investors with more confidence to invest in equities and fixed income products.

Products and services

This is an interesting and complicated topic in that private banks and asset managers based in Asia must cater to both foreign inflows as well as domestic clients. The theme for the near future, however, is to help investors navigate the challenging investment environment that the aftershock of the global financial crisis has created. Currently, the investment environment is plagued with low interest rates and a high amount of political and economic risk (especially in developed markets). Investors are relatively more risk-averse and will be seeking products that provide them adequate risk-weighted returns. Private banks will begin to offer products and services that cater to this, meaning that there will be increased focus on funds that seek to deliver higher yield and dividends. Given this type of environment, private banks also find themselves in a predicament when catering to domestic Chinese investors who seek higher risk and higher return exotic products such as private equity funds and hedge funds and foreign investors that have abandoned the low yield developed markets.

To cater to Chinese investors, private banks will begin to offer funds that have non-China and perhaps even global exposure. There will also be an increase in the number of funds that invest in private equity funds that seek opportunities in relatively new and interesting arenas such as real estate mezzanine debt and the aircraft leasing business.

To cater to foreign investors, private banks will offer funds that invest in China A-share markets as well as general exposure to other growing Asian economies such as Southeast Asia. These essential themes of higher yield and stable dividend income still remain the same.

Increasingly, asset managers and banks are also entering the Exchange Traded Fund (ETF) field where they are able to capture the investable assets of HNW Individuals by providing index-based solutions. These ETFs offer investors the opportunity to pay lower fees while investing in funds that should perform on par with the market. Given the challenging investment environment and the high probability that fund managers will not be able to deliver alpha returns, ETFs offer investors the ability to grow their money while paying lower fees.

The dichotomy in client characteristics may also give way to industry structure changes. Private banks must ask themselves whether they want to provide a complete set of products and solutions that offer access to a broad range of markets, sectors, asset classes and risk or do they want to structure themselves to focus on specific types of markets, segments, asset classes and risk. A case can be made for both structures. Private banks that offer a broad and complete platform may be able to capture a higher proportion of investment flow. However, the concentration and quality of their products may vary. Additionally, this strategy may only work for private banks that have a high amount of support from a parent bank. Private banks that choose to offer more specific products that target fewer market segments may find that their customer base is smaller and will struggle to achieve desired levels of Net New Investment and consequently Net New Revenue.

It is our prediction that private banks will start structuring themselves based on the Barbell Strategy, which is a way of investing where an investor allocates a portion of investable assets to low risk products such as cash, treasury bills or ETFs. At the same time, the investor will allocate the remaining investable assets to higher risk and higher return products such as hedge funds and other exotic financial products. Private banks can follow this investment strategy in structuring themselves. They do not have to offer clients access to every type of market, sector, asset class or risk level. Although currently, many Chinese HNW Individuals seek private banks that offer them a wider choice of products, eventually investors will find meaning in private banks that offer products and solutions that will add value to portfolios rather than diversity for the sake of diversity.

The last trend that we will see emerge in the private banking industry is the need to educate investors. This will not only increase private banks' ability to sell more products, this will also increase client loyalty towards the bank. Investment education is also not limited to clients. It seems that regulators will also need to be educated on investment products in order to reform the banking and finance industry and help the China markets grow and mature. An example of this was seen in 2012 when the government examined increasing Qualified Domestic Limited Partnerships (QDLPs) quotas. This is an excellent opportunity for foreign-based hedge funds increase their fund-raising abilities in Chinese markets. However, it seems that Chinese regulators were not sophisticated enough in their understanding of hedge funds to be able to adequately manage the regulatory changes. Private banks, especially foreign private banks, that believe in creating a long-lasting relationship with the government should jump at the opportunity to host educational seminars that help regulators better understand more complex investment products and solutions.

Previously in this chapter, it was stated that a large proportion of Chinese HNW Individuals have a weak understanding of the art of investing. Although this is a relatively important aspect for private banks and asset managers to tackle, it is not as important as the fact that most of these Chinese HNW Individuals do not fully understand private banking services and are not aware of the difference between premier retail banking status and private banking. It is clear that private bankers face a challenging environment not only in the markets but also in investor education in that they do not know what private banking is. In the near future, we believe we will see private banks increase initiatives in hosting educational seminars for HNW Individuals as well as institutional investors. The type of investment education must, however, be such that it provides what the audience wants.

China holds the key to client base growth and increased net flow for private banks from both foreign and domestic investors. However, China is a very different market compared to the rest of the world in that there is a lot of potential energy stored in HNW Individuals' bank accounts. These HNW Individuals are faced with the challenge of not only not knowing what to do with their money but also finding the best way to manage their wealth. Private banks have the means and the tools to benefit from these investors as well as to help them manage their wealth. An additional layer of complexity comes in through the relatively diverse market in terms of risk appetite and lack of investment education. It is essential for private banks to examine their capabilities and to offer investors the service and products they need instead of what they think they need. Most important, we believe that private banks must structure themselves correctly in order to cater to investors, foreign and domestic. It is true that China holds the key to success for private banks, but it is essential for private banks to find the right way to "unlock" China.

9.4. Future of the wealth management industry in China

The private banking and wealth management industry in China continues to evolve as we head into a new decade under the leadership of President Xi Jinping. Increasing competition and client sophistication will highlight the industry moving forward. Wealth managers will be challenged to find a sustainable strategy to capture growth in this increasingly important sector in China's financial system.

The future prospects of private banking and the wealth management industry will most likely come down to basic economics and where the money is going to be in the future. The amount of wealth and investable assets available in China will drive the success of the industry. We expect that four factors are going to affect the amount of wealth in China: the inflow and outflow of capital, the economy and the ability to create wealth, and finally, the government. We will now review how these factors might influence the industry moving forward before discussing some key success factors and strategies for wealth managers. (See Figure 9.4)

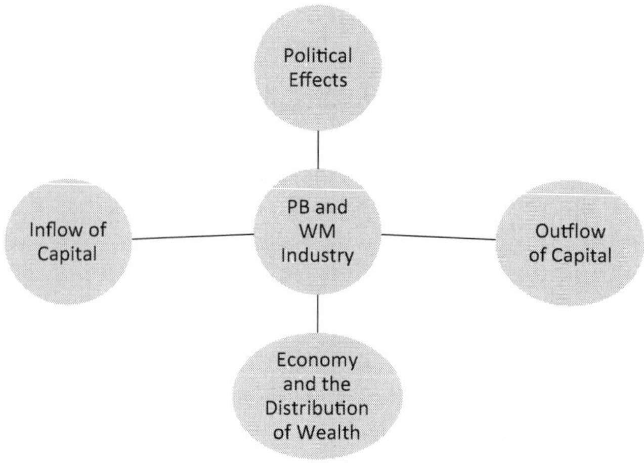

Figure 9.4 Factors affecting private banking and the wealth management industry

The economy and the distribution of wealth

As mentioned earlier in the chapter, many analysts forecast that China will continue to grow at around 7 percent to 8 percent going forward. Although the days of double-digit growth might be over, China still shows very strong growth and should have an economy that has the ability to create a lot of wealth in the future. While the economy is expected to create wealth in the future, where this wealth is going will be a concern for wealth managers and economists alike.

While the economic reform lifted many out of poverty, the wealth gap problem in China is worsening even though the economy is booming. The Gini coefficient, an index used to measure wealth inequality, in China is 0.61 (2010), which is significantly higher than the global average of 0.44. While a high level of Gini coefficient is a normal characteristic for an emerging market, the magnitude of income disparity has gone beyond the warning levels and this can lead to many issues including social unrest. More economists agree that relying on market forces alone cannot narrow the wealth gap and China will need to make some structural changes in fiscal policies in order to keep the wealth gap in control. One of the remedies to the growing wealth gap would be to promote the development of a bigger middle class. We expect that eventually the Chinese government will have to make policy changes that favor a bigger middle class. As China continues its transition from an emerging market to a developed market, the Chinese economy will shift from the current investment- and export-focused economy to a more consumption-based economy. The economic impact of this shift will help the middle class and help redistribute wealth more evenly among the whole population.

A report from McKinsey (2012) has forecast that by 2015, over 60 percent of China's disposable income will be earned by the middle class. By 2025, over half of the income will be earned by the upper middle class. In the future, wealth in China will no longer be held by selected individuals and the demographics of wealth management clients would be significantly different as well. As mentioned earlier, 11 percent of the current HNWIs are working professionals. This number is likely to increase significantly with the rise of the middle class. The middle class will also be significantly younger than the current batch of HNWIs, so their wealth management needs would also be significantly different. Wealth managers must anticipate this growing trend and learn to serve tomorrow's middle class today in order to maintain sustainable growth in the future.(See Figures 9.5 and 9.6)

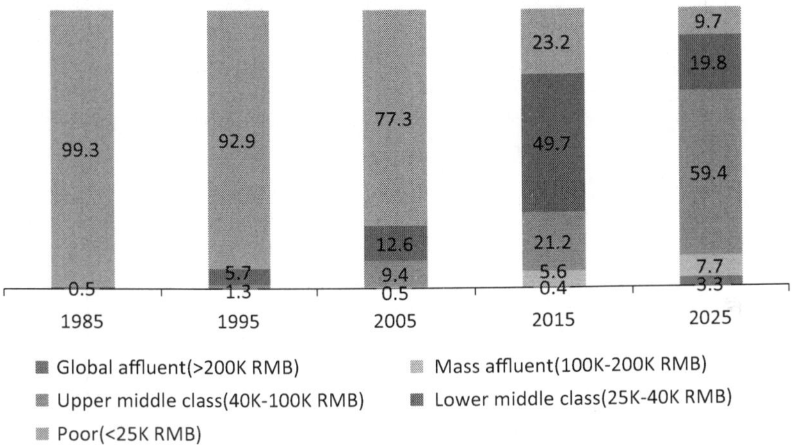

Figure 9.5 Share of Chinese urban households

Source: National Bureau of Statistics of China, McKinsey

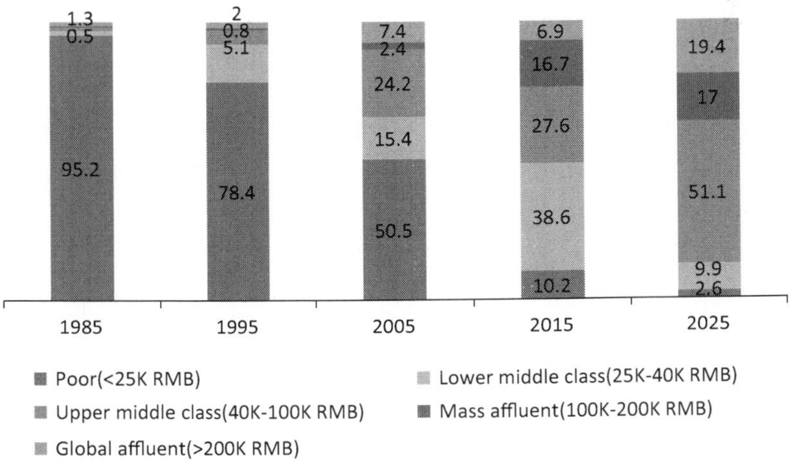

Figure 9.6 Share of total urban deposable income

Source: National Bureau of Statistics of China, McKinsey

Inflow of capital: increase in foreign investments

Since the financial crisis, the private banking industry in developed countries has been going through a mass transformation. Although these private banks are experiencing increased profits, they do not see the same amount of inflows as before the financial crisis. This indicates that in the future, these private banks must end up competing on pricing and fees.

With the complexity of the regulatory system in the developed world continuing to increase, HNW Individuals as well as institutional investors are increasingly looking towards the emerging markets for investment opportunities. In the current low yield environment, emerging markets, especially China, offer higher yields that investors seek. This emerging trend indicates that Western investors will put their investments into China and other surrounding financial centers such as Hong Kong and Singapore. In the future, these countries will experience a high level of inflow from investors who are looking to take advantage of long-term value-oriented investments.

As mentioned earlier, there has been an increase in QFII licenses issued by the Chinese government. According to the CBRC, as of May 2012, there are 170 QFII licenses and we can see from Figure 9.7 that there is an exponential growth trend.

If the new leadership indeed pursues an aggressive economic reform, we can expect further expansion of foreign investments and this trend to continue. As of 15 December 2012, China's foreign exchange regulator has removed the previous 1 billion dollar limit for foreign sovereign wealth funds, central banks and monetary authorities buying Chinese assets through the QFII route. While these developments are a step in the right direction, SAFE remains the authority that oversees the allocation for foreign investments. There is still no existing free market for foreign investors to enter the Chinese financial system, which will remain a big concern going into the future.

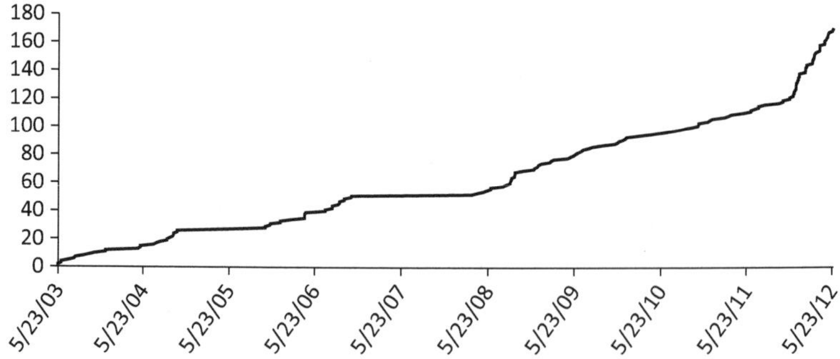

Figure 9.7 Number of Qualified Foreign Institutional Investors

Source: China Banking Regulatory Commission

Outflow of capital: export of HNWIs

The Boston Consulting Group (2012) has shown that the client appetite for offshore wealth managers is positively correlated to the amount of wealth. Out of the clients with more that RMB 50 million in assets, 22 percent are already using offshore products and services and this trend is expected to increase in the future; 60 percent of HNWIs in Tier 1 cities will increase their overseas assets in the future. This is certainly having a negative effect on the development of wealth management services domestically. At the end of 2009, there were RMB 63 billion deposited offshore, but this number increased rapidly and reached RMB 1 trillion by the end of 2011. One must wonder where this massive amount of money is going and why is it leaving the country. There are many factors that might have led to this massive capital outflow from China, but one of the key factors is HNWIs' attitude towards the government, social stability and environmental issues in China.

A report by Bank of China and the Hurun Report (2012) reveal that 60 percent of China's millionaires are either considering or in the process of immigrating to a foreign country.(See Figure 9.8)

The number increases even more with the ultra-high-net-worth individuals. Out of the HNWIs having more than RMB 100 million, the percentage considering or in the process of emigrating is almost 80 percent. It was highlighted that China's wealthy are worried about the quality of life at home, despite the tremendous economic growth. After having earned their riches during the decades of economic boom, the HNWIs in China are now concerned about the social issues such as pollution, corruption and poor education, etc. Both immigration applications and real-estate sales to Chinese people in foreign countries have shown increases in recent years. In another report from BBC (2012), HNWIs expressed concern at

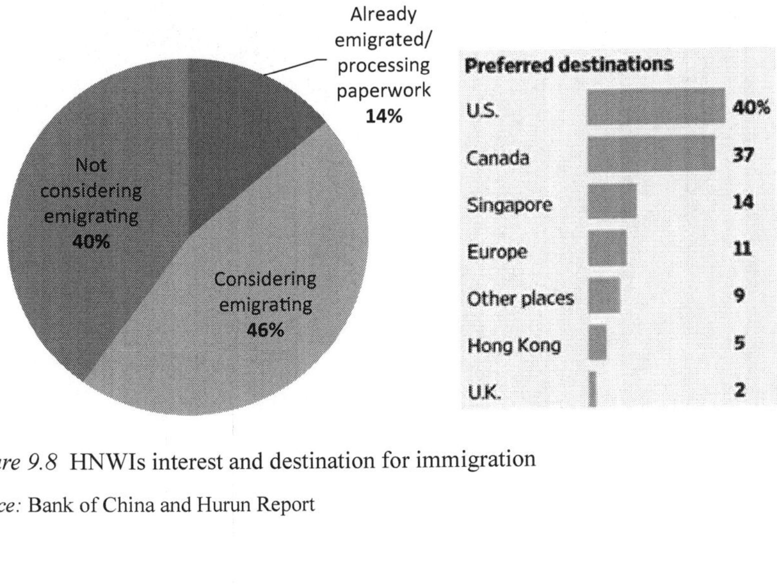

Figure 9.8 HNWIs interest and destination for immigration

Source: Bank of China and Hurun Report

the lack of safety in mainland China. One HNWI was quoted as saying, "Many are thinking, I have so much money now, but maybe one day the government changes policies and takes back everything that I have." In 2006, there were only 63 Chinese applications to the US Immigrant Investors program. By 2011, there were 2,408 and by 2012, as of September, there were over 3,700 applicants. Many of the HNWIs are using investment immigration schemes to move themselves and their assets overseas. According to a report by the *China Daily* (2010) in the US in 2010, in the three years preceding the report, Chinese families had spent more than RMB 17 billion for immigration overseas. This number excludes any other investments that these families make when they arrive in their destinations.

In addition to the physical outflow of HNWIs, another concern is the outflow of future inheritors of the current HNWIs. In a report by Hurun Report and Industrial Bank Co. Ltd. in March 2012, it was shown that children's education is one of the top three areas of spending for HNWIs. For many HNWIs, the educational system in China is an area of concern and in recent years they have been paying more attention to their children's individuality and creativity. Traditionally, China follows a production-line style of education, which is exam-centric and preparing for the university entrance exam (*gaokao*) takes precedence over everything else. HNWIs now prefer the more Westernized, "all-round development" education, where student development is the focus.

With the one-child policy in China, many HNWIs have high hopes for their only child and are willing to invest a lot of time and effort on them. Sending their children overseas to study is now the golden standard for HNWI families: 85 percent of HNWIs plan to send their children overseas and this figure goes up to a staggering 90 percent for UHNWIs.

Figure 9.9 shows the popular destinations for overseas studies. The US is the predominant destination for HNWI offspring. The education ministry in China

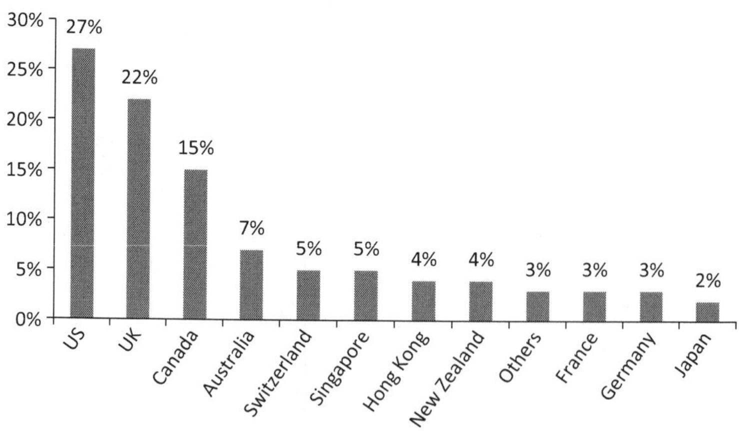

Figure 9.9 Overseas study destinations

Source: Survey on consumer needs of China's HNWIs

has reported that close to 1.5 million Chinese are currently studying overseas and this number has grown more than 20 percent every year since 2009. According to the Institute of International Education, China in 2010 surpassed South Korea and Canada to lead international enrollment in the US. In 2011, the number of Chinese students in the US increased by 23 percent to more than 723,000.

The outflow of HNWIs and their future wealth inheritors is a huge concern for the wealth management industry in the coming decades. If this trend continues, these two factors will put a considerable strain on the wealth management industry as well as the economy as a whole. In the short term they pursue a better life with better education and environment and rights and freedom and this will continue to drive the first-generation HNWIs to move their assets overseas. In the long term, unless there are significant changes in policies and conditions in China, we can expect a massive and possibly crippling outflow of assets when the wealth transfer happens between the current generation of HNWIs and their children. Under these conditions, wealth managers must be prepared to expand their offshore wealth management services in order to avoid losing their clients to the local banks overseas.

9.5. Key success factors and strategies

Improve customer segmentation and target marketing

The expansion of wealth and increased complexity of financial needs of HNWIs in China will pose challenges to the private banking and wealth management industry in the future. More than ever, wealth managers will be required to invest heavily in customer analysis and segmentation. This would be required in order for wealth managers to define their target markets and to develop product and service initiatives.

Some of these initiatives will have to include improved product customization for clients of various profiles. Wealth managers will have to localize their products to accommodate changes in the onshore wealth market in the future. As mentioned early in the chapter, while most HNWIs are located in Tier 1 cities, the population of HNWIs in Tier 2 cities is growing at a fast clip. HNWIs in Tier 2 tend to be less sophisticated and more conservative than Tier 1 clients. Wealth managers can take advantage of this fact by segmenting their marketing, products and services. By providing more conservative products in western provinces and more high-risk product lines in the coastal provinces, wealth managers would be able to capture more business than they would have providing one single generalized product line throughout the country.

Increase share of client wealth by increasing quality of RMs

Currently typical Chinese clients would only put 20 percent of investable assets with any one institution and half of their assets are managed by a wealth manager. In this case, a client with RMB 20 million in assets typically has RMB 80 million of investable assets held in other institutions. This means that for wealth managers, most clients are untapped wells with great potential and, therefore, they must expand their business relationships with their HNWIs in order to capture more of their assets.

In order to increase the share of the wallet, wealth managers must utilize better relationship managers who can provide more personalized services and portfolio management. As mentioned, we are expecting increased demand from both international investors and HNWIs onshore. We predict that many private banks and asset managers shall utilize the Barbell Strategy, which requires the use of both low and high risk products to construct client portfolios. This puts a lot of pressure on RMs because they would need to increase their product knowledge and be comfortable presenting these concepts to onshore HNWIs who might not be as sophisticated as global investors. As the main channel for private banks to educate their clients, relationship managers are a crucial part of the business and training RMs is more important now than ever because of the changing market environments. Private banks should be prepared to make investments in training their RMs as well as reducing the number of clients to enable them to build more meaningful and personal relationships.

Serving tomorrow's clients by understanding them today

Our research has shown that there will be a dramatic shift in the demographics and characteristics of private banking and wealth management clients in the future. With the rise of the middle class along with improved education for the children of current HNWIs, the typical client in the future will not only have a better education but also more sophisticated needs and preferences. Asset managers must invest now to understand these two client segments. Surely, the emerging middle class will produce clients that come from a working background and would have risk tolerance and characteristics that are vastly different from the overseas educated second-generation inheritors. In addition to analyzing the needs of these emerging clients, private banks can also refer to the experience of developed markets. Combining their own analysis with the trends from developed markets, private banks would be more prepared than their competitions to serve the clients of tomorrow. Also, private banks should attempt to capture these future clients today. For example, in order to lock in future HNW clients, private banks can introduce less expensive products and services to high potential middle-class individuals. This could serve as a win-win because it would allow a bank to establish a relationship with these individuals early, while helping the bank to increase its understanding of these clients.

Establish offshore wealth management for overseas Chinese

Currently, HNWIs on average keep 16 percent of their assets offshore, but we expect this number to grow significantly in the future because 60 percent of HNWIs are expecting to increase their offshore investments. This fact, combined with the massive outflow of capital that is expected in the future, means that offshore operations for private banks and asset managers will be a critical part of their businesses.

There are a few approaches that can be used to establish offshore private-banking centers. First, a bank can choose to build its own offshore center under the same brand as is used in China. For example, most recently, in November 2012, Bank of China (Hong Kong) launched its own Private Banking Services in Hong Kong. Using the same brand name, it is hoping to leverage the reputation that Bank of China has in mainland China. With the backing of the parent company, the private bank would be able to coordinate and provide a one-stop service to Chinese clients that either want to establish an offshore account or have immigrated to Hong Kong. Other options to establish offshore private banks would be to acquire an overseas bank, create a joint venture with overseas institutions, or just rely on referrals by partnering with an overseas bank.

Deciding which approach to take would depend on the positioning and the client base of each private bank and asset manager. If a private bank can accurately evaluate its markets overseas and establish functional operations, it can not only help serve current HNWIs having offshore needs, but also limit the leakage to overseas banks when HNW clients and their children emigrate overseas.

9.6. Conclusions

China's private banking sector has experienced tremendous growth primarily driven by China's emergence as a global economic power. Guo Shuqing, Chairman of the China Securities Regulatory Commission (CSRC), believes that "the wealth management industry in China is very promising" and considers it a "sunrise industry". This research has revealed that a combination of favorable economic conditions in Asia, emerging markets and especially China and slowing economic conditions in developed countries provides fertile grounds for the growth of China's private banking and wealth management industry.

However, there are challenges the industry faces such as the outflow of wealth through second-generation inheritors, increased regulations targeted at domestic corruption, as well as a relatively immature market with uneducated investors. In short, China's wealth management industry has a lot of potential but the execution must be precise. The new leadership of the Communist Party will remain the ultimate decision maker in terms of how the industry will develop in the coming years. With each change in policies, the government can bring significant changes in the direction of capital flow, as well as the structure of the market and economy as a whole.

Each day, the markets take new turns that can change investor risk appetite, investment targets and industry sentiment. We are excited to see how China's wealth management industry will develop as we are confident that the demand will drive positive and fierce development.

References

BBC News. China's economic miracle, (2012/10/24) Available at www.bbc.co.uk/news/world-asia-china-20069627. Retrieved 20 December 2013.

Becerra, Jorge, Peter Damisch, Bruce Holley, Monish Kumar, Matthias Naumann, Tjun Tang, and Anna Zakrzewski. 2012, May 31. Global wealth 2012: The battle to regain strength. www.terrapinn.com/2012/americas-family-office-forum/data/bcg-global-wealth-report.pdf. Retrieved 20 December 2013.

China Daily. 2010, December 9. Wealthy Chinese invest in immigration. Available at www.chinadaily.com.cn/china/2010-12/09/content_11677163.htm. Retrieved 20 December 2013.

Data monitor. 2012. Trends to watch in global wealth management www.datamonitor.com/store/Product/2012_trends_to_watch_in_global_wealth_management?productid=CM00213-002. Retrieved 20 December 2013.

Alexis Lai. 2012. Chinese flock to elite US schools. November 26. CNN.com http://edition.cnn.com/2012/11/25/world/asia/china-ivy-league-admission. Retrieved 20 December 2013.

Hurun Report. 2012, March 27. The Chinese Luxury Consumer White Paper 2012, jointly published by the Industrial Bank and Hurun Report. Available at www.hurun.net/usen/NewsShow.aspx?nid=188. Retrieved 20 December 2013.

Hurun Report. 2012, June 4. The Chinese luxury traveler white paper 2012. Available at www.hurun.net/usen/NewsShow.aspx?nid=250. Retrieved 20 December 2013.

Institute of International Education. 2012. Open doors data. Available at www.iie.org/Research-and-Publications/Open-Doors/Data. Retrieved 20 December 2013.

Kelvin S. and Michael F. 2012, August 5. Special Report – China's answer to subprime bets: the "Golden Elephant". *Reuters*. www.reuters.com/article/2012/08/06/us-china-banks-idUSBRE87501T20120806. Retrieved 20 December 2013.

Kao, Ernest. 2012, December 10. China wealth gap continues to widen, survey finds. *South China Morning Post.* www.scmp.com/news/china/article/1102047/china-wealth-gap-continues-widen-survey-finds. Retrieved 20 December 2013.

McKinsey. 2012. The Asset Management Industry: Outcomes are the New Alpha. Available at http://goldsmithandco.com/wp-content/uploads/2013/03/The-asset-management-industry_outcomes.pdf. Retrieved 20 December 2013.

MinSheng and McKinsey. 2012. Report on Private Banking in China 2012. Available at: www.mckinseychina.com/wp-content/uploads/2013/09/Minsheng-McKinsey-China-Private-Banking-Report-summary-of-findings.pdf. Retrieved 20 December 2013.

Page, Jeremy. 2012, February 22. Plan B for China's wealthy: moving to the U.S., Europe. http://online.wsj.com/news/articles/SB1000142405297020380650457718146140131898 8 Retrieved 20 December 2013.

Guo Shuqing. 2012, June 8. Speech in Annual Meeting of China Securities Investment Funds Association, Beijing. Available at www.cs.com.cn/xwzx/zq/201206/t20120629_3389310.html. Retrieved 20 December 2013.

10 Qualified foreign institutional investors (QFII) in China

10.1. Definition and mechanism of QFII

QFIIs are always used in the transition from closed financial markets to those that are fully open to foreign investors. Under the QFII system, foreign institutional investors are allowed to remit foreign capital to QFII countries or regions and then convert it into local currency and invest in the local stock market under regulated accounts. The investment amount and gains can be converted back into foreign currency and remitted out under specific regulations and control, e.g. lock-up period and foreign control, etc.

Besides the capital control, the QFII systems also implement lots of rules and provisions for the foreign investors, such as the capital requirement of the foreign institutional investors, the investment amount, the holdings limit per listed company, etc.

To become an eligible QFII investor in China, the following criteria must be met:

1. Capital requirements: Under China's QFII system, a qualified investor must be either (a) a fund management company, (b) a securities company, (c) an insurance company or (d) a commercial bank. Fund management companies must have been incorporated for at least five years and have at least USD 10 billion in assets under management. The securities companies and insurance companies should have been in business for over 30 years and have not less than USD 1 billion in registered capital and USD 10 billion invested in securities. These requirements ensure the quality of participating institutions and also limit the potential number of applicants.
2. Investment scope and quotas: China's QFII system allows foreign investors to invest in listed A-shares, listed government bonds, listed convertible bonds and listed corporate bonds and other financial instruments approved by the CSRC. The initial amount is USD 1–2 billion in total and around USD 20–250 million for each QFII. The USD 1–2 billion accounts for around 0.2 percent to 0.4 percent of China's total capitalization.
3. Approval procedures: To become a QFII, the applicant should designate a domestic custodian bank to submit the required documents to the China

Securities Regulation Commission (CSRC) and the State Administration of Foreign Exchange (SAFE). Whether the application is accepted or rejected, the examination process, in principle, should not exceed 45 days.

4. Remittance controls: RMB is not a freely convertible currency; China has imposed strict controls on funds flowing through QFIIs. It imposed a three-year lock-up period for investments in closed-end funds; the invested principal is not allowed to be repatriated in the first three years and the period is one year for other foreign investors. Also, frequency of outward remittances should not be more than once a month for investments in closed-end funds while for other foreign investors it should not be more than once every three-month period. In addition, the capital repatriated should not exceed 20 percent of the original investment amount.
5. Shareholding limitation: A QFII cannot own more than 10 percent of a stock while total share holdings by QFIIs in a company cannot exceed 20 percent.
6. Custodial banks: The provisional rules stated that mainland branches of foreign banks, along with Chinese commercial banks, would be allowed to provide custodial services to QFII investors. Moreover, all trading activities should be executed through domestic brokers. Since most foreign institutional investors are normally bound by their internal compliance requirements and can deal only with a few global brokers, we are hopeful that foreign brokers will also be allowed to participate in the QFII scheme as an intermediary between foreign investors and domestic brokers.

10.2. Benefits and barriers of QFII

Benefits for China of QFII

Efficient capital allocation

During 2000, many of the listed companies were under the "protection" of China's government (e.g. Special Treatment – Two consecutive years of losses or Particular Treatment – Three consecutive years of losses). Since the investors expected the government would finally bail out or restructure the loss-making companies, those "poor" companies were greatly attracted to the investors who failed to distinguish the good companies from the poor companies.

After implementation of QFII, the situation was expected to improve; large market-cap with good quality and better foreseeable future companies were expected to be the investment target of the foreign investors.

Enhancement of corporate governance and regulation

Due to the closed stock market of China, the stock market was far behind the overseas exchanges in many areas, such as corporate governance, transactions disclosure and operating effectiveness. It is expected that with foreign institutional investors allowed to participate in the A-share market, it would show the way for the Chinese government, accountants and lawyers to improve the regulations and standards to the international standard.

Improved market stability

Volatility of China's stock market is very significant in terms of standard deviation of the share price mainly because most of the investors are retail investors instead of institutional investors. With foreign institutional investors entering as QFIIs, it is expected that the market would be more stable as foreign investors focus more on long-term and fundamentals-based investment strategies.

Speed up the reform of China's financial markets

Introduction of QFIIs would force the growth of China's broader securities industry as besides the A-share market, foreign investors should be interested in government bonds, corporate bonds and CSRC-approved products also. Future interaction between foreign institutional investors and local brokers / banks would accelerate growth of China's financial markets in general.

Barriers for QFII in China

Corporate governance and disclosures

Corporate governance in China is far behind the mature markets. Although the problems of corporate fraud, insider trading and insufficient disclosures are not unique to China's financial market, regulators and the CSRS still have a long way to go for strengthening existing market practices and implementing strict information disclosure; complete market regulation systems would be a great challenge to China's government.

Regulation limitations

According to the existing regulatory framework, foreign investors are not allowed to register A-share accounts directly with the mainland's securities clearing house CSDCC, which means QFIIs have to register the shares under the name of a domestic bank. In the view of QFIIs, it is too risky that the domestic custodian banks have full control over their accounts. Also, the domestic custodian banks are liable for all default risks of clients.

Foreign institutional investors prefer to deal with different brokers as well as foreign brokers and this constitutes a great barrier for the QFIIs as they are only allowed to deal with domestic brokers.

Insufficient hedging instruments

In China's A-share market, short-selling and margin trading is prohibited. For foreign institutional investors, hedging of their investment positions is necessary.

To manage the risk of investing in China, the government has to provide more channels, such as index futures to meet the needs.

Controls on capital account

China has controls over funds' inflows and outflows and RMB is not a freely convertible currency. The Chinese government is not expected to loosen its policy for foreign investors and this is a great concern for them as they are not able to manage the funds freely. In addition to the lock-up period of one to three years for the investment principal, such controls may be too strict for the foreign investor.

10.3. QFII system between PRC and Taiwan

Some countries had implemented a similar QFII system long ago, such as QFII of Taiwan and FDI (Foreign Direct Investment) of South Korea.

Taiwan's Qualified Foreign Institutional Investors (QFII) mechanism kept it away from financial speculators during the 1997 financial crisis; Taiwan was the least affected among the Asian countries.

China's QFII system is modeled on the basis of the experience of Taiwan. To understand China's QFII system, the evolution of Taiwan's market liberation process is discussed.

The Taiwan Stock Exchange was launched in 1962; the TSE was open only to domestic investors. The first opening to foreign investors came in 1983, with indirect investment: a domestic fund management company raised capital from abroad for investment in Taiwan and the investment fund was listed for trading in New York and London.

In 1991, the government of Taiwan permitted Qualified Foreign Institutional Investors (QFII) – financial institutions with sufficient capitalization, experience and commitment – to invest directly in the Taiwanese market, but only up to a certain quota. Since then, requirements and restrictions on investments have been relaxed. In 1996 foreign individuals were allowed to invest and in 2000, foreign ownership caps were lifted for all but a small number of strategic companies. In 2003, the QFII system was abolished, allowing foreign institutions and individuals simply to register prior to investing in Taiwan.

In China, the B-share market initially segregated foreign investors from domestic ones. In 2003, the China Securities Regulatory Commission announced regulations that diluted the separation between domestic and foreign investors. In addition to opening the B-share market to all investors, China established QFII regulations, following Taiwan's model. Since this initial opening, the cap on aggregate foreign institutional investment has been increased from USD 4 billion to USD 10 billion. The background of implementing the system is similar between PRC and Taiwan.

The comparison between PRC and Taiwan

QFII	*PRC*	*Taiwan* (when introduced in Jan 1991)
Participants	**Fund management institutions, insurance companies, securities companies and commercial banks**	Fund managers, insurance companies and banks
Quota Size	USD 20 - 250 million for each QFII	USD 2.5 billion . USD 5 million for individual investors . USD 50 million for firms
Eligibility	In Experience and capital requirements: Fund management institutions (5 years, funds under mgt > USD 10 billion), insurance companies (30 years, paid-in capital > USD 1 billion, securities assets under mgt in the last fiscal year > USD 10 billion), securities firms (30 years, paid-in capital > USD 1 billion, securities assets under mgt in the last fiscal year > USD 10 billion). Commercial banks must be one of the top 100 in the world, securities assets under mgt in the last fiscal year > USD 10 billion).	. Insurance companies need 10 years' experience and at least USD 500 million in securities under mgt. Commercial banks need to be in the top 500 globally, with at least USD 300 million in assets. Fund management institutions need 5 years of experience and at least USD 500 million in management. Note: These restrictions were implemented for a period after the commencement of the QFII in Jan 1991.
Investment restrictions	All stocks, treasury bonds, convertible bonds and corporate bonds listed on domestic exchanges permitted, except stocks issued by foreign-invested companies	In 1992, only 10% of capital may be invested in short-term time deposits and money market instruments.
Ownership limits	Not more than 20% of each individual company may be held by foreign investors. No foreign investor may hold more than 10% of a company's equity.	Not more than 10% of each individual company may be held by foreign investors. No foreign investor may hold more than 5% of a company's equity.

(*Continued*)

QFII	*PRC*	*Taiwan* (when introduced in Jan 1991)
Holding period	Close-ended funds: Minimum 3 years, after which capital may be repatriated at a maximum pace of 20% of the original quota per month. Open-ended funds: Minimum 1 year; after which capital may be repatriated at a maximum pace of 20% of the original quota per quarter.	Funds should be remitted within 3 months after the quota has been approved. Principal cannot be repatriated until 3 months after being remitted in. Capital gains may only be remitted outward once a year.
Commencement	Dec 2002	Jan 1991
Additional features	Priority: Closed-end funds and funds with good investment track records are given priority in application approval. Regulatory risk: The State Administration of Foreign Exchange is expressly permitted to change the rules of capital repatriation according to external balance of payments	

Source: China Securities Regulatory Commission, Securities and Futures Commission, Ministry of Finance, ROC, Goldman Sachs Global Economics Research

The Taiwanese QFII model is exactly the type of mechanism the early-stage equity markets such as China's need at the moment. The PRC even did not rename it.

Both governments introduced the QFII system to prevent rapid flow of currency in and out because such a rapid flow might seriously threaten the stability of their economies.

China has adopted a QFII system similar to that of Taiwan. In 2003, Taiwanese President Chen Shui-bian surprised investors by announcing abolition of the QFII system by year-end, a full two years ahead of schedule, signifying a milestone in the development of the island's financial markets.

10.4. Timeline for the development of QFII

Date	*Events*
2000	An idea to allow foreign institutional investors to invest in China's A-share stock market was suggested by Mr. Anthony Neoh, chief adviser to CSRC.
18 Jul 2002	Mr. Zhou Xiaochun, chairman of the CSRC, made a valuable comment: "To introduce the Qualified Foreign Institutional Investor (QFII) system in China is an extension of the country's open-door economic policy and another major step in attracting Foreign Direct Investment".

7 Nov 2002	CSRC and the PBoC jointly released the new and unprecedented regulations on opening the China domestic securities market to QFIIs with the investment quota ranging from USD 50 million to USD 300 million.
28 Nov 2002	Temporary Regulation on Domestic Securities Investment by Qualified Foreign Institutional Investors was promulgated by SAFE.
1 Dec 2002	QFII was officially put into effect.
23 May 2003	UBS AG & Nomura Securities Co. Ltd. were approved.
4 Jun 2003	QFII investment quota for UBS AG & Nomura Securities Co. Ltd. were approved: USD 300 million and USD 50 million, respectively.
Dec 2003	12 QFIIs approved with investment quota of USD 1.7 billion.
Dec 2004	26 QFIIs approved with investment quota of USD 3.475 billion.
Dec 2005	33 QFIIs approved with investment quota of USD 5.695 billion.
25 Aug 2006	CSRC publishes the revised version of the QFII Supervisory Guidance.
Dec 2006	51 QFIIs approved with investment quota of USD 9.095 billion.
Dec 2007	51 QFIIs approved with investment quota of USD 10.045 billion.
Dec 2008	74 QFIIs approved with investment quota of USD 13.443 billion.
29 Sept 2009	Regulation on Foreign Exchange Administration of Domestic Securities Investments by Qualified Foreign Institutional Investors (QFII) takes effect.
Dec 2009	93 QFIIs approved with investment quota of USD 16.67 billion.
Jun 2010	Rumors of introduction of mini QFIIs.
Sep 2010	99 QFIIs approved with investment quota of USD 18.97 billion.
Oct 2010	103 QFIIs approved.
Dec 2010	Mr. Norman Chan Tak-lam, Monetary Authority chief executive, stated that CSRC will speed up the study on the launch of mini QFIIs.

Source: China Securities Regulatory Commission, Securities and Futures Commission, Ministry of Finance

Before the launch of QFII

Prior to the launch of QFII, only Chinese domestic investors were allowed to participate in the China A-share market, but with the idea raised by Mr. Anthony Neoh, chief adviser to CSRC in 2000, this became history. Further to the idea and the supportive speech made by Mr. Zhou Xiaochun, chairman of the CSRC in July 2002, the CSRC and PBoC jointly released new and unprecedented regulations on opening China's domestic securities market to QFIIs in which they have investment quotas ranging from USD 50 million to USD 300 million. It surprised the market that the consensus on opening the markets was at the end of 2003 or the beginning of 2004. Nevertheless, the approved QFIIs could enjoy this treasure early and be part of the history of liberating China's securities market.

The progress of QFIIs

The promulgation of the Temporary Regulation on Domestic Securities Investment by QFIIs in November 2002 started a new move in China's stock market. These regulations comprised 7 chapters and 34 sections, with coverage on Custodian, Investment Quota, Foreign Exchange Conversion Management, Monitoring and Management. After three years of development, CSRC published the revised version of the QFII Supervisory Guidance. The QFIIs' minimum assets under management were lowered from USD 10 billion to USD 5 billion. Also, QFII investors were allowed to choose three local brokers, instead of one, for future A-share trading. The diluted requirements helped attract more mid-sized foreign mutual funds and further enhanced the diversity of foreign investors with more long-term capital in the A-share market.

Regulation on Foreign Exchange Administration of Domestic Securities Investments by QFIIs took effect in September 2009. The Regulations increased the limit of investment quotas for QFIIs from USD 800 million to USD 1 billion and reduced the principal lock-up period for selected QFIIs from 1 year to 3 months. QFII institutions were permitted to open fund accounts of different natures and types. Such rules were more flexible in terms of lock-ups and sub-accounts, which serve as a motivation for overseas investors to participate in the A-share market.

Though the Chinese government encouraged participation of foreigners most of the time, there were periods when no QFIIs were approved or the quotas were low, for example in the first quarter of 2004 and the year 2007. This may have been to observe the impact on the A-share market rather than indicative of suspension of the QFII system. It allowed the Chinese authorities time to fine-tune the mechanism and regulation of QFIIs with respect to the overall economy.

10.5. The future and prospects of the QFII system

Channel for Foreign Direct Investment (FDI)

On 11 December 2001, China joined the World Trade Organization (WTO). It was a symbolic moment for China, not only gaining acceptance from the globe but also reflecting the persistent growth of China's economy. FDI would become a very significant growth driver in this role. Further, QFIIs can act as one of the good and efficient channels to better facilitate foreign investment.

In fact, we can see from Figure 10.1 that China's inward FDI kept increasing after WTO and it jumped to roughly 2.2 times of investments after 10 years (China's nominal GDP grew 3.2 times from 2003 to 2010). In December 2007, the State Administration of Foreign Exchange (SAFE) announced expansion of QFII quotas from USD 10 billion to USD 30 billion. We believe that the Chinese government foresaw the seriousness of the "sub-prime issue" starting from Bear Sterns and was better prepared for the risk of economic downturn. In addition, leverage ratios of Chinese banks were far lower than US banks, which provided a safe place to park the overseas capital in 2007. Needless to say, the year-on-year (a.k.a. YoY) percentage change of FDI amount in 2008 was the highest in history. We can also see from the chart that there is a slow or even negative growth in 2003, 2006 and 2009; we interpret it as a "FDI life cycle". The main reasons for the sudden drop should be related to the SARS incident, China's macro-regulation and US financial turmoil in 2003, 2006 and 2009. Year 2012 might be the key timeline for the current cycle.

In the first nine months of 2010, the Chinese government had already approved the establishment of 19,209 foreign companies, 17.5 percent YoY, and the utilized FDI increased 16.6 percent to USD 74.34 billion. Based on this growth rate, over USD 100 billion should be achieved at the end of 2010.

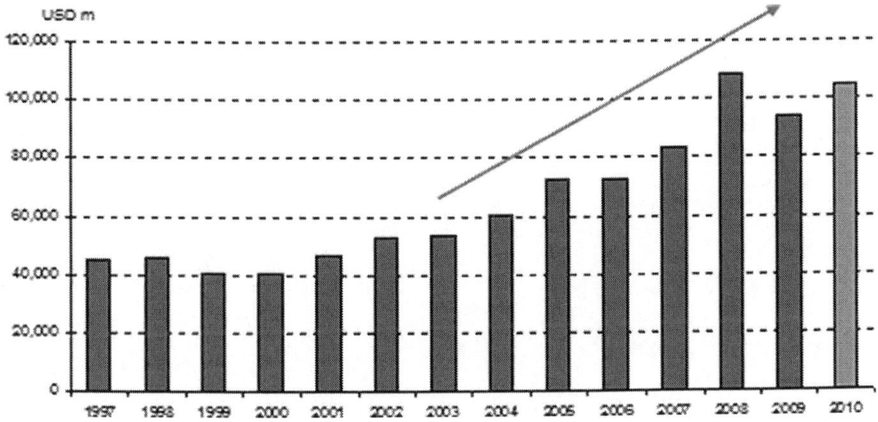

Figure 10.1: China's FDI flow

Source: CEIC

No proof of liquidity drain from Hong Kong–listed China stocks

After adoption of the QFII system, there were many options and comments regarding the ability of QFIIs. Some market participants thought liquidity might drain away from Hong Kong–listed China stocks and hurt the status of Hong Kong as an international financial centre. We think that this kind of concern can be understood and it was a risk to Hong Kong stock market. However, this might have been the case had valuations of H-shares or Red Chips and A-shares been quite close to each other.

P / E ratios for Shenzhen A market, Shanghai A market and Hang Seng Index were 62x, 41x and 16x, respectively, in the beginning of 2003. Most of the QFIIs were hesitant to change from their then existing holdings in Hong Kong–listed China stocks to A-shares due to the high valuations of A-shares. However, new issues in the A-share markets were appetizing. We also figured out that the P / E gap in 2005 between the Shanghai A-share market and the Hong Kong stock market shrank a lot. At the same time, China's government suspended all capital raising in both Shanghai and Shenzhen stock markets for a year (from May 2005 to May 2006). This action drove many large Chinese companies to hoist their IPOs in Hong Kong. China Construction Bank, China Shenhua Energy and Bank of Communications raised USD 9.2 billion, USD 3.3 billion and USD 2.2 billion, respectively, in Hong Kong in 2005. They were ranked among the top five in terms of the amount raised in IPOs globally. After the new IPO policy amendment was released in June 2006, another large IPO by ICBC took place in both the A-share and H-share market at the same time.

From the angle of premium / discount to H-shares of A-shares, we should shed some light on this issue. To narrow down the premium on or discount to H-shares, either lowering the market price of A-shares or raising the market price of H-shares can be used. Many people thought the narrowing premium or discount meant that the valuation between the two markets became closer. The de-rating of the A-share market keeps its valuation closer to H-shares in Hong Kong, which normally have very deep discounts compared to A-shares. We think that this situation is inevitable as some entities are actually the same company in terms of assets, and it will continue in the next few years. However, following a more liberalized A-share market and as the number of QFIIs increases, liquidity drain from the Hong Kong stock market to the China stock market will be an important issue afterward.

Market stability improved a lot

In practice, stock markets in developing countries are generally more volatile than in developed countries. Some market participants think that this is the attractiveness of this market and they are able to make decent profit. China is not the exceptional case. However, after China's WTO entry and after the QFII program started running, many people expected that the stock market would be gradually well regulated in order to facilitate entry of pension funds and insurance companies in the stock market. This implied that the stock market in China would be less volatile. Based on our analysis (Figure 10.2), we found that the stock market stability improves a lot. The standard deviation has dropped significantly for both the Shenzhen and Shanghai markets after 2002. For instance, in the Shanghai market, the standard deviation in the period 1992 to 2002 was 2.85 percent whereas it is 1.47 percent for 2003 to the most recent. We believe QFIIs have contributed a major part of this stability.

The two markets still have much room for improvement in the future, compared with the Hong Kong and US stock markets. This is good news for many potential QFIIs who are fundamentals-focused investors. Most important, they can also help the Chinese government to divest its stakes in state-owned enterprises to improve efficiency and sustain the economic growth.

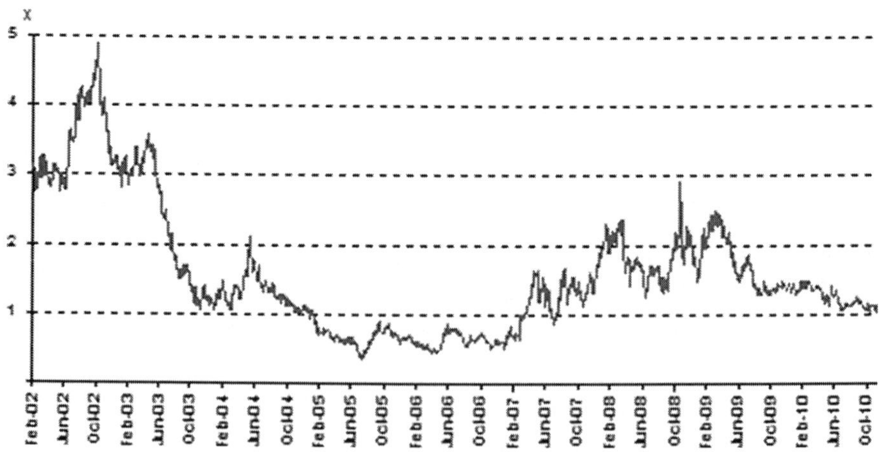

Figure 10.2: A-share over H-share's premium shrinking

Source: Bloomberg

A hedging instrument finally comes

Historically the Chinese government has prohibited shorting activities in the stock market. This has raised great concern about risk management should the QFIIs invest in the A-share market. Hence, many market participants thought that China had to come up with different risk-hedging instruments in order to attract more potential QFIIs.

They expected China to create some kind of index funds or index futures to provide risk hedging facilities in the A-share market. Market consensus was one to three years after the establishment. In 2005, MSCI launched a product called "MSCI China A Index", which was developed specifically for China's domestic investors. We believe that the MSCI index can provide a buffer area for A-shares risk management. However, this MSCI index covered only 25 stocks which might not be a comprehensive approach for full hedging by QFIIs. As a result, many market participants urged a national unified stock index to be compiled by an independent company constituting 200 to 300 companies in different sectors.

In fact, in January 2010, the State Council approved the launch of stock index futures and a margin-trading pilot program, in a move to embark upon further liberalization of financial markets. The long-awaited formal index futures were finally launched in April 2010. The index futures, agreements to buy or sell an index at a given value on an agreed date, are based on the CSI 300 index, which tracks the Shanghai and Shenzhen markets. Such a move would give foreign funds a tool for hedging against downturns in China's volatile stock market, which fell 28 percent from April 2010 to July 2010. The CSRC will unveil regulations for QFIIs to trade index futures.

However, according to some market experts, index futures currently seem to have a life of their own and reveal little about the direction of the underlying stock market. One investor described the futures market as the "biggest casino" for wealthy speculators (Required to have a minimum of RMB 500,000 to open a futures trading account) in China. Rather than being a source of stability, he says, it will only increase volatility in the wider market.

10.6. Role of QFIIs in corporate governance

Corporate governance in China has had a difficult journey since the economy opened up in the late 1970s and made the gradual transition from a centrally planned economy to a market economy. In the 1990s, with the establishment of the Shanghai and the Shenzhen stock exchanges and promulgation of the Companies Law, corporate governance came into vogue. Then, following the Asian Financial Crisis in 1997–1998, corporate governance assumed greater importance. The China Securities Regulatory Commission (CSRC) is the main regulatory body for listed entities and it was set up in 1992. Over the past two decades, it has attempted to institute good corporate governance including transparency, information disclosure, protection of minority shareholders' interests and rules for appointments of independent directors.

The Qualified Foreign Institutional Investor (QFII) scheme was conceived by CSRC and modeled after the QFII scheme adopted by Taiwan in 1991. Improved corporate governance was a major objective. Establishment of the QFII scheme was based on the reasoning that the presence of foreign institutional investors on the register of shareholders would help improve corporate governance in the Chinese companies they invest in. The QFII scheme would influence corporate governance in the following ways:

1. With the advent of foreign institutional investors in the China market, with their more robust due diligence and investment discipline, the QFII Provisional Measures will further encourage greater transparency and improve the compliance and corporate governance process of A-share companies.
2. Participation of global investors in China's domestic securities has introduced professional funds management expertise which provides a new advocate for improving corporate governance.
3. Mainland companies will increasingly benchmark themselves against their international peers; QFIIs will be an important stimulus for improving corporate governance in China.
4. It was presumed by the CSRC that QFII participants, all of whom would be from countries with well-regulated financial systems, would require sound corporate governance in their target companies to justify their long-term investment horizons.

10.7. The survey by the East Asian Institute, National University of Singapore

A survey by the East Asian Institute, National University of Singapore, was carried out from January to June 2006 and November to December 2008. Only QFII participants who had been allocated investment quotas for at least three years prior to 31 December 2007 were considered. The reason for the time frame of the cut-off was that to be fully participative and cognizant of the QFII scheme, a three-year membership was considered necessary. The survey was conducted by verbal interviews which used a standard questionnaire as a basis for open discussion and clarification of their responses on the topic of QFIIs and its impact on corporate governance. Chief Executive Officers (CEOs), General Managers or Heads of Departments of QFIIs were contacted to participate in the survey. The survey questions included the following:

1. How QFIIs select investment targets
2. How QFIIs have impacted corporate governance
3. Direct and indirect impact of QFIIs on corporate governance
4. Areas of influence

Twenty-seven QFII members met the strict criteria and nine institutions or 33 percent of those eligible participated in the survey. More important, most of the

QFII respondents were the pioneers and key players in the QFII scheme. The nine QFII members who responded had total allocations amounting to USD 3.9 billion or 38.3 percent of the total QFII allocations.

The QFII members who participated in the survey were:

- UBS Warburg
- Nomura Securities Co. Ltd.
- Morgan Stanley & Co. International Ltd.
- Citigroup Global Markets Ltd.
- Deutsche Bank Aktiengesellschaft
- HSBC Banking Group
- ING Bank
- JP Morgan
- Credit Suisse First Boston

Results of the survey

How did QFIIs choose companies in which to invest?

- QFII investors concentrate on companies with good management, sound strategies, sustainable earnings and accounting transparency.
- Eight out of nine QFIIs surveyed invest only in the top 100 listed firms because of their greater liquidity and marketability. Research data on these companies are also more readily available.

Evaluation criteria

The list of candidates chosen varies because different QFIIs have different preferences, priorities and research capabilities in different types of companies. The list of companies is subject to further evaluation by the QFII before a decision is made on which stocks to invest in.

- All QFIIs stated that the financial performance of Chinese companies was the most important criteria for choosing which companies to invest in. This includes not only past performance but also future projections.
- Both UBS Warburg and Citigroup require their target Chinese companies to have maximization of shareholder value as one of the stated objectives.
- An evaluation of future financial performance requires voluntary disclosure of additional financial data and financial projections. Thus the Chinese company must be ready and prepared to disclose voluminous financial information to the QFII. If the Chinese companies do not cooperate here, they do not get short-listed. The QFIIs have thus forced Chinese companies to be more transparent with information disclosure being a key part of the process.
- Five out of nine (~56 percent) QFIIs surveyed do place emphasis on the existence of guidelines on good corporate governance and as part of their

evaluation process inquire into measures of corporate governance implemented. However, the rest of the QFII respondents (four) do not pay attention to corporate governance structures in Chinese companies at all.

- Citigroup has an index for measuring corporate governance that it uses to evaluate potential Chinese companies. ING Bank through its joint venture fund, the China Merchant Fund, chooses quality companies to be included in the investment universe and the quality of corporate governance is part of the evaluation criteria.

According to a QFII member, there are three groups practicing different standards of corporate governance amongst China's listed companies.

- The large listed SOEs who are genuinely trying to implement sound corporate governance (and they are making good progress).
- The smaller listed companies who lack transparency and sometimes resort to deception to achieve their corporate goals.
- Resource-rich companies, natural monopolies, big banks and telcos which have dual listings in both China and overseas stock markets. These companies enjoy fairly good standards of corporate governance because of their international exposure and operations.

In addition to meetings between QFIIs and managements of companies, the QFII manager also arranges for meetings between the Chinese clients and foreign fund managers, institutional investors or the insurance company portfolio managers. These meetings are crucial to giving the foreign investors an idea of how Chinese companies operate and what they are like. If a Chinese company passes the financial and corporate governance tests, the QFII may make a decision to invest.

Thus, the conclusion here is that while all QFIIs place priority on financial performance, the majority also pay attention to corporate governance structures in the companies they invest in.

Role of the QFII scheme in promoting corporate governance

The respondents of the survey can be categorized into three categories:

- Those who exercise their rights as shareholders
- Those who provide management support
- Those who do not promote corporate governance

Of the nine respondents, three (~33 percent) actively promoted corporate governance by exercising their rights as shareholders. The other six do not attend shareholder meetings. Reasons range from "inadvertently negatively impact the interests of other Chinese clients" to "it is not our policy to attend AGMs (Annual General meeting) of clients."

Five of the nine respondents (~56 percent) promoted corporate governance through management support, which may take the form of dialogue sessions, seminars and training sessions and secondment of key Chinese staff for overseas training.

Two respondents (~22 percent) do not promote corporate governance at all. They are from large financial institutions holding fairly large QFII quotas and act merely as investment brokers for their foreign institutional clients. They may be the registered shareholders in the Chinese companies but they do not have ultimate beneficial interest in those shares as their ultimate beneficial owners are the foreign pension funds, insurance companies or fund management companies. As brokers they have no direct equitable interest in the Chinese companies and do not monitor these investments. Such a duty would be the responsibility of the foreign institutional investor. The QFII member in such cases merely provides research and custodian facilities.

Board of Directors

It is generally recognized that the Board of Directors has overall charge of corporate governance and that membership confers the ability to participate and effect change. Representation on the board is therefore crucial if a QFII hopes to influence the corporate governance of a company. However, the survey results are negative and indicate that no QFII member has appointed any independent director on boards of the Chinese companies they have invested in.

All QFII participants stated they had no desire to become directly involved in the management of the client companies and that is why they have not sought board positions.

Board of Supervisors

According to China's Company Law, the Board of Supervisors sits above the Board of Directors. In the survey, no QFII had appointed any representative to the Board of Supervisors of any Chinese company. Furthermore none of the QFIIs exerted any influence over the Board of Supervisors directly or indirectly at all.

Specialized committees

In countries with good corporate governance, it would be normal for listed companies to have an audit committee, remuneration committee, investment committee and nomination committee. These committees are responsible for various functions which contribute to sound corporate governance. China's Company Law does not legislate for the setting up of any of the four specialized committees mentioned and the duty is entrusted with the Board of Directors. But as mentioned earlier, all QFII respondents said they had no desire to participate in any direct management role in the companies they had invested in.

Management support

One way for a QFII to make an impact on corporate governance of the companies it invests in, and this is one area that they have contributed to better corporate governance, is through management support. This occurs through regular meetings that the QFII participants have with the Chinese companies where a great variety of topics is discussed. Six out of nine respondents (~67 percent) have frequent meetings with the board or senior management of the Chinese companies they invest in on a quarterly or semi-annual basis. Both UBS Warburg and Citibank have ongoing programs to help improve corporate governance of the Chinese listed companies; the companies even consult them on a regular basis on other matters.

Seminars and training sessions

Five of the nine respondents (~56 percent) contributed to better corporate governance by indirect means through seminars and training sessions. At these seminars, the QFII organizers invite representatives from different organizations, such as fund managers, regulatory bodies like the CSRC, international lawyers and accountants to speak on their international experiences. Providing the training sessions and seminars has been an important contributory role that QFIIs have played in furtherance of good corporate governance. These seminars help instill the culture of corporate governance. The Chinese companies learn about international standards and how corporate managers deal with governance issues in Europe, the US and the UK. They also learn about what constitutes accountability and transparency. But "no budget for corporate governance training" is one of the main reasons why the rest of the respondents do not conduct seminars and training.

The role of QFIIs in corporate governance now and in the future

The survey found that all respondents considered that the QFII scheme had contributed to better corporate governance, although many felt that the impact had been "slow", "in its early stages" and "not significant". One of the respondents felt that the rate of corporate governance progress cannot exceed the rate of progress of the overall economy and another felt that more education and training are needed.

Possible explanations of the slow progress of corporate governance

- The initial expectations were too high.
- The QFII scheme has had a relatively short history.
- The QFII quotas allocated have been quite small compared to the overall market capitalization.
- Not all QFII members take an active role in promoting it. One merely advises his foreign clients "that corporate governance in China being what it is, just add on an additional risk premium for their China investments".

The CSRC had hoped that the introduction of the QFII scheme would lead to better corporate governance. While the results from the survey show that the QFII scheme has improved standards of corporate governance, none of the QFIIs has any desire to take an active management role and hence directly impact corporate governance in Chinese companies. Their influence is at best indirect through other means; however, the management support given by QFIIs is important and where the relationship between the QFII and the Chinese company is close, the corporate governance impact can be effective. The Chinese authorities must eventually realize that only when QFII quotas are enlarged substantially and the QFII rules are loosened considerably will the QFIIs have a greater impact on corporate governance.

References

刘树军. 2003. QFII进入中国指引. 中国金融出版社– ISBN: 9787504931740

谢红霞. 2005. 应对合格境外机构投资者(QFII)的法律规制研究. 人民法院出版社– ISBN: 7802170451

Gillian, Philip B. 2005. Banking regulation in China, Gruson & Reisner's Regulation of Foreign Banks, Volume 2, LexisNexis.

Mo, ParkHung. 2008. Resolving economic dilemmas in China: beyond QDII and QFII. Hong Kong Baptist University. Working paper.

Neftci, S., and Ménager-Xu, M. Y. (Eds.). 2007. China's financial markets: An insider's guide to how the markets work. Elsevier.

Xinhua. 2010, April 29. China's index futures milestone step to develop capital market. *China daily*. www.chinadaily.com.cn/bizchina/2010-04/19/content_9747623.htm. Retrieved 20 December 2013.

Index

An environmentally friendly book printed and bound in England by www.printondemand-worldwide.com

PEFC Certified

This product is from sustainably managed forests and controlled sources

www.pefc.org

PEFC
PEFC/16-33-415

FSC
www.fsc.org

MIX
Paper from responsible sources
FSC® C004959

This book is made entirely of sustainable materials; FSC paper for the cover and PEFC paper for the text pages.

#0195 - 210415 - C0 - 234/156/13 [15] - CB